One Bright Pearl

AN UNHOLY MEMOIR

Volume I

Robert Kaku Gunn

Copyright © 2017 Robert Kaku Gunn
All rights reserved.

ISBN: 0692720588
ISBN 13: 9780692720585

Cover created by Rodney Alan Greenblatt, whimseyload.com

Also by Robert Gunn

Journeys Into Emptiness: Dōgen, Merton and Jung and the Quest for Transformation

One Bright Pearl, Vol II, God is the Source of My Life

The entire universe is one bright pearl. What is there to interpret or understand? "One bright pearl" expresses reality without naming it—it is the name of the universe. It contains the inexhaustible past, existing throughout time and arriving in the present. Presently there is a body and mind; they are the one bright pearl. A stalk of grass, a tree, the mountains and rivers of this world are not only themselves—they are the bright pearl.

We can never escape from the universe, which is nothing but one bright pearl. Even if it seems to you that you have escaped it for a little while you are still in time and all time is covered by the bright pearl.

When the right time comes (the essence of the bright pearl can be grasped); it is suspended in emptiness, hidden in the lining of clothes, found under the chin of dragons, and in the headdresses of kings. The pearl is always inside our clothing (that is, inside of us, our real nature).

How is it possible to doubt that life and death are also the bright pearl? Even if we are perplexed or troubled it is nothing but the bright pearl. There cannot be any action or thought existing separately from the bright pearl. Consequently, even coming and going in the Black Mountain's Cave of Demons is nothing but the one bright pearl.

From "Ikka Myōju," in Shobogenzo,
Dogen Zen-ji, 13th Century Zen Master

Emperor Wu of Liang asked the great master Bodhidharma, "What is the highest meaning of the holy truths?"

Bodhidharma said, "Vast emptiness. Nothing holy."

In deep gratitude, I bow

To Fred Collignon, my friend who helped me believe I had a gift, and who saw my struggling soul amid all my constant doubt.

To Paul Lehmann, my Systematic Theology teacher who taught me to see the theological dynamics of culture and who embodied what he taught.

To Frederic Hudson, who taught me how to write an essay and how to see and enter into issues of the social gospel.

To John B. Elliott, who opened my eyes to Chinese and Japanese calligraphy and the scope of history.

To Richard Cleaves, who gave generously of his time to a very green pastor and troubled colleague.

To Mark Stern who taught me what it was to be psychologically held.

To Jonathan Goldberg, who has steadfastly and gently been a guiding presence in and through my spiritual and psychological meanderings.

To Ann Belford Ulanov whose integrity, presence, challenge and support opened up a new life path.

To John Daido Loori, Roshi, who introduced me to Zen in a very deep and lasting way.

To Roshi Enkyo O'Hara who has welcomed all of me, warmed my heart and continues to extend herself generously as we practice together.

To Yeou-Cheng Ma, fellow warrior against nothingness, superlative midwife of souls, and songstress of many strings.

To the Village Zendo sangha for teaching me the meaning of community on the path.

To all the people of the churches I have served, for loving me, supporting me, being real and sharing their lives with me.

"Hey, Todd, lookit what we got here," the big guy said, coming at me.

"What is it, Sam? Looks like a fairy to me."

I stood still, frozen, staring as they got close. I guessed from their size they were 8th graders. I was in 1st grade and this was my first day of school in 1948. It was recess and I was in the yard in front of the school.

"Yeah, an' a fat one, a little fat fairy."

I turned to walk away.

"Hey, fat fairy, where you goin'?" He grabbed the collar of my new green shirt. "Whoa, fat fairy, ain't you got no manners?" He jerked me around to face him. He was ugly, dirty and big. I looked straight at his brown leather belt with a dulled bronze buckle. "I'm talking to you, fatty." His long hand squeezed my arm, forcing me to look up at him.

"Ow! You're hurting me!" I whined as I tried to wriggle away.

WHACK! The other guy hit my face with his fist. "We gotta teach 'im, Sam. Teach 'im respect."

Again, I tried to pull away, but the older boy's hand was an iron grip. From the corner of my eye, I saw other guys coming over, crowding around.

Thud! Someone hit me from behind. Another fist plastered my face, knocking me down. Someone kicked me and I curled up, covering my face. Another kick to my side. I felt blood run into my hands from my nose. I cried.

"Lookit, Todd, he's a crybaby." Sam knelt down and pulled my head up. "A fuckin' crybaby fat fairy." He slapped me. Another kick to my ribs.

I wanted to run away across the field back home, but I got more hits and kicks and the crowd around me kept growing, standing, staring down at me. I don't know how long it went on, but it kept happening and happening and I asked God to get me outa there and then the bell finally rang and they started going away.

"Thank you, God," I whispered to myself and then someone came over, my size, and he bent down and put his hand on my shoulder, gentle-like.

"Y'all right?" he said in a soft voice.

I looked at him. His brown eyes were kind. He smiled. I'd seen him when I first walked into the classroom that morning in the row next to mine. From feeling grateful to God for the beating being over, I had a strange warm feeling fill me.

"My name's Bobby, like yours," he said.

I stood up and he brushed leaves and dirt off me.

"Don't let'em bother you none," he said. "Everybody new gets it. They'll stop after awhile."

I wiped away my snot and tears and blood with my sleeve. "Oh, boy, mother's not gonna like this," I said.

"C'mon, we gotta go 'fore class starts."

"Thanks," I said, and we trotted back into the school and our classroom just as Miss Wood told us to get out <u>Fun with Dick and Jane</u>.

Around the age of two or three, in the first house I recall in Mounds, Illinois (population, 2000), twelve miles north of Cairo, my mind was indelibly impressed by the image of my cousin Jerry's back beside me in bed one night and the strange but powerful feelings I felt toward him. I wanted to reach out and touch his skin but didn't.

I also have early memories of Paw Paw, my maternal grandfather, who was a preacher on horseback, a circuit rider in the Methodist church in southern Illinois. By the time I could walk, he had turned in his horse for a car and his jodhpurs for a morning coat for Sunday preaching. I first heard him preach when I was four years old. He stood in the pulpit at the center of the Akron Plan sanctuary in Flora, Illinois, towering over his flock. In preaching and singing, his baritone voice, rich and full, rose above all others with power, conviction and clarity. I don't remember what he said, but I was awed by his voice. And I wanted to be like him.

My sexuality and spirituality have always been closely allied in my life, bound together around the poles of ecstasy and shame. That is, I've experienced both ecstasy and shame in both my sexuality and in my spirituality, in addition to experiencing a conflict between them.

Maybe I always felt I had to be on the move, going somewhere else. When I was four I ran away from home. My mother and father were both at work. My babysitter was Mildred. Mildred had honey-colored skin and a gold front tooth. Our house on Delaware Street was only three blocks from the edge of town where the cotton fields began. Somehow I got out of the house when Mildred wasn't looking and walked those blocks to the cotton fields where there was a ramshackle corral and a stable made of rough-hewn split logs with a rusty tin roof. There were two horses and a mule there. One horse was a beautiful chestnut, with a white star on his forehead. The other horse was a dappled gray mare that seemed older. The mule was just stupid-looking—big ears and a nose that didn't match his flanks. I stepped up to the lowest rung of the corral and watched them.

"Here, boy, here," I called out and snapped my little fingers like I'd seen Paw Paw do. The chestnut came over and I held out my hand like I did for dogs to show them I was friendly, and he licked away as if I had sugar. I wanted to ride him, but he was too big to climb onto and there was no saddle.

Pretty soon I heard Mildred hollering out my name. "Bobby? Bobby Gunn?! Where are you?"

"I gotta go, boy," I said to the chestnut and took my hand away and climbed down.

"What're you doin' over here?" She was mad. She swatted me on the bottom and held my hand, tugging me behind her. "Don't you know you ain't got no business over here, boy? You done drove me crazy, lookin' all over for you. What's your momma gonna think?"

I liked Mildred. She could be hard sometimes, but she was mostly nice to me. She had a big bosom and a big smile that sparkled from her gold tooth.

"Am I gonna get in trouble?" I asked.

"Honey chil', that's up to your mother. Running away from home? I dunno. My job is to get you back home and you stay there, you hear?"

My mother had been my disciplinarian for the first years of my life because my dad was in the Army. When he came back, he drove semi-trucks all over the country, so mostly my memory of him is of him not being there. He was, however, present in the first dream I can still recall from when I was five:

My parents, my great grandparents and grandparents on my father's side, were all living in the same house in Mounds. In my dream, I went into my great grandmother's bedroom and saw my father lying on the twin bed that I usually slept in, next to my Grandma Gamble's bed. Suddenly, my father's head separated from his body, and the head began moving down and up one side of his body on the bed. I was terrified.

Before I ever heard of Buddhism, I learned the reality of the first noble truth of the Buddha, that life is suffering, from my brother. Bill was born in 1948, when I was five years old. Premature by five months, he was brought home from the hospital through the front door in a bassinette by my father and mother. Maw Maw, my father's mother, and her mother, Grandma Gamble, and I gathered around the tiny baby. Though they spoke baby words of welcome, I recall the feeling of the moment as tense, hesitant, with as much concern for my mother as for the baby. Perhaps the precariousness of his life lent an unusual seriousness to his arrival, an ambivalent alloy of joy and sadness.

Bill had been put into an incubator as soon as he had been delivered. Shortly after that, he had developed pneumonia that cut off an adequate supply of blood and oxygen to his brain. My mother said he turned "black as a stovepipe," and Dr. Elkins, the family doctor, gave up, saying there was nothing more to be done. My father, by some stroke of intuitive genius, gave my brother mouth to mouth resuscitation. As a result, Bill survived, but with part of his brain paralyzed by the period of oxygen deprivation. The impact was not fully known at first. I remember a vague sense, when I tried to play with him lying on the floor, that I should treat him with special care.

Before I started school, I learned to change my new brother Bill's diapers, even when they were really stinky, and how to be careful not to stick him or me with the pins. I learned how to hold him, and support his head so it didn't flop around. I spoon fed him in the high chair and rocked him to sleep. I learned how to anticipate his moves to keep him from falling over or dropping his drink. Yet, I don't recall ever getting mad at Bill.

I somehow knew by the way my parents treated him that his limitations required us to see everything from that point of view, of what he could and could not do, and not to expect more. I had to realize that any impatience or frustration I might feel was about <u>me</u>, not about him, and I had to learn to cope with my frustration at what he couldn't do, and what, therefore, was left for me or my mother or father to do, such as getting him dressed, putting him on the toilet, or giving him a bath. I was therefore trained at an early age to be long on empathy and short on aggression.

With his hands, Bill could grasp things, but his movements were spastic. Though he was high in what we now call emotional intelligence, his functional, thinking intelligence was very limited, and he never learned to read or write beyond his own name.

In the summer of 1949, the year after my brother was born, my father got a job as a switchman on the Illinois Central Railroad in Bluford, 100 miles north of his parents in Mounds. We moved into a small house with white slate siding and a small porch. The house was one T-shaped room with a closed bathroom. The rent was $20 a month. We pumped water by hand at the kitchen sink from the well in the front yard. We made water hot by heating it on the stove for baths and washing up. Phone calls were received from our neighbor on the left who had a big house.

The small schoolhouse where I first encountered the bullies during recess on my first day there, was about half a mile across the field in front of our place. I walked to school by myself each morning, wearing bib overalls, which I hated, even though my father wore them on the railroad. Most of the kids in my school wore the kind of jeans that required a belt. There were two two-seater outhouses, one for the girls and one for the boys. It was cold there in wintertime.

Mr. Meyer was the teacher who taught the older kids. He walked with his left forearm held horizontal, his hand dangling down at the wrist and I imitated him one day at home.

"What are you doing?" My mother's tone of voice made it clear that whatever I was doing was wrong.

"Mr. Meyer does it," I stammered.

"I don't care who does it," she replied. "You don't do that."

I had no words for what was at stake in this exchange. Yet intuitively, at age six, I knew. He was a sissy and I should not be. I should imitate more manly men, and restrain any impulses to move in ways that were girly.

Even before we got to Bluford, we always had a dog. In those days, dogs never came into the house. The first one I remember when I was about three, was Jitter, a red Irish Setter Spaniel, and after Jitter we got a Chow that didn't last long because she bit someone. When we got to Bluford, I had Ol' Bill, a black one-eyed 'coon dog that used to belong to Paw Paw. Ol' Bill was my best friend before I ever read the dog stories of Alfred Payson Terhune. He was my consolation when the world wasn't fair and when I was all alone. When he died, I got a mixed-breed puppy that was tan on his back with a white patch on his chest and before I could decide whether to call him Squirt or Brownie, my father backed up over him with the car and killed him. Not on purpose, of course. Another time my father backed out over my tricycle, also not on purpose, of course.

In each case, my father was driving our blue Plymouth. Then a friend of the family, Wack Casper, who delivered Schlitz beer, came and took the car because my father couldn't keep up the payments. I was glad as I watched that blue Plymouth being taken away.

Later that year, when my brother Bill had surgery to cut the tendons of his legs so they would not contract involuntarily, he was taken to St. Mary's Crippled Children's Hospital. The hospital was in Springfield, 150 miles from Bluford, so it took us three hours to get there. Because I was six and not fourteen, I had to wait in the car by myself while my parents visited Bill between noon and 4 p.m.

I remember sitting alone in the new red Nash Rambler we had by then, restless, waiting for them to return. I would keep looking at my Mickey Mouse watch to see how much longer they would be there. In the winter, it got cold in the car. When warmer weather came, they would take him outside and I would meet them on the outside of the chain-link fence and I could see Bill and talk to him in his wheel chair through the fence. He and I would reach out to touch fingers through the fence and I just wanted to walk through the fence and give him a hug.

I remember biting into a big, red tomato, ripe from the vine, and staining my white T-shirt. And I remember kissing Peggy, a girl in my class, in the prickly weeds of the sunny summer day. Another day that summer I remember being secretly interested when Larry Brown wrestled me to the ground, pinned my arms and tried to get me to suck his thing, but it was dirty, so I didn't want to. Before summer's end, I remember "playing nasty" with David, another classmate, in the girls' cream-colored outhouse of the closed school. He wanted me to put mine in his big butt, but I couldn't understand why anyone would do that, and I didn't know how anyway, so I didn't.

Mother taught me to memorize the Lord's Prayer that same year. Up until then, the only prayer I knew was "Now I lay me down to sleep. I pray the Lord my soul to keep. If I should die before I wake, I pray the Lord my soul to take." That prayer helped calm me down.

I remember Mother was asked to sing at her step-sister's wedding in Flora where Paw Paw was the preacher. To me, she had the voice of an angel, and I memorized all the words and sang along with her sometimes.

My father also had a good voice and there were times when we were riding in the car together that the two of them would sing songs. Mother was a soprano and Daddy was a tenor, and they harmonized beautifully as I leaned on the front seat from the back.

One afternoon, when my Mother had gone somewhere, I came home from school about my usual time of 3:30 to an empty house. My father was supposed to get off work at 4, so I just waited for him. I kept the radio going and kept looking out the window. There was a clock on the mantle of the fireplace that would chime on the hour, and I remember when it chimed 5.

It was winter and it was dark by then, and I began to get kind of scared. I turned all the lights on in the front room and turned up the radio. The clock chimed 6 and I needed to go to the bathroom, but I was afraid because what if somebody came in the house while I was in the bathroom, or maybe they were already there because I didn't turn the lights on in the bathroom. And I tried to focus my attention on the radio, but it was a lot of news and talking about grownup stuff, but at least it was company. I tried rocking the platform rocker fast but that didn't seem to help.

At 19 minutes before 8, I saw headlights of a car drive into the driveway. I prayed it was Daddy. Footsteps on the porch....were they his? He opened the door, and I ran to him and hugged him before he could even put his lunch pail and lantern down.

"I'm so sorry, son. I couldn't help it. I had to work late." As he hugged me, he said, "Hungry?"

All the men in my family were hunters, and sometimes I would go with them. I went possum hunting with Paw Paw, goose hunting with my father and Pop (his father), squirrel and rabbit hunting with Uncle Harold, (my father's brother-in-law), and fox hunting with Uncle Joyce, my mother's brother. I remember going out into the woods at night hunting possum with Paw Paw and

Ol' Bill. Ol' Bill treed a possum and Paw Paw shot it with his .32 pistol. I don't remember what we did with the possum. And I don't know why a dog who treed possums was called a 'coon dog.

Uncle Joyce had about ten beagles that he used for fox hunting. He took me with him one night. We got into his old Ford and all the dogs piled in back.

"Where's the gun?" I asked.

"We don't need one," he answered. He said he'd explain when we got there. We reached a huge field of mowed hay. There was a half-moon. The sky was clear, filled with stars. As soon as we stopped the car, the dogs started barking, all excited. He handed me a blanket.

"Take this," he said as he got the dogs out on their leashes. Next we walked onto the field a ways, then he asked me to spread the blanket. When he let the dogs go, he said, "Go, boys, get 'im." And they were off, howling, baying, as they ran.

After we lay down on the blanket, surveying the stars, I asked him, "Is this fox hunting?"

"This is it, son," he said.

"How do we catch a fox?"

"We don't. The dogs do, they chase him. We just listen. We listen to them run. We hear the differences as they run, the change in their howl when they get on the scent. The dogs'll find one, chase him a bit. He always gets away. They go chase him again. We just lie here listening and looking at the stars and the moon."

Uncle Joyce was an alcoholic who kept a bottle of whiskey under his car seat. He died, in the end, of cirrhosis of the liver. My mother said Paw Paw the preacher used to beat him with a leather shaving strap. But it seemed to me Uncle Joyce knew something most others didn't—at least about being a man.

My father gave me a Red Ryder BB gun for my 6th birthday. I would take my gun and my dog and scour the cornfields, woods and pond out behind the house. I found a dead baby rabbit one day and brought it home. I was getting ready to nail it to the fence.

My mother came out and said, "Bobby, what're you doing!?"

"I'm setting it up for target practice."

"No, you're not," she said, walking toward me, wiping her hands on her apron. "That's not how a man learns how to hunt. It's just a baby, and besides, it's dead already. You don't treat animals that way."

I felt ashamed. My would-be tough guy aggression suddenly melted into sadness and remorse over this lump of fur in my hands, as I wondered yet again how a boy becomes a man and just what was a man anyway?

My father smoked Lucky Strike cigarettes. I remember they were 25 cents a pack, because sometimes he would ask me to go buy them for him. I never tried cigarettes until high school, but I did try one of his cigars once when I was four years old--- William Penns—only 5 cents. When he found out, he took several of them in hand, told me to go into the bathroom with him and had me smoke them. He was trying to cure me by making me sick, but I didn't get sick.

I remember him getting dressed to go to the train yard. He wore white long johns, big boots, and a red and white-checkered flannel shirt. I remember him sitting at the table in his undershirt, the kind that showed his bare shoulders, and thinking how big his arm muscles were. His chest, too, looked nice, a bit of hair in the middle. His lantern would be standing on the table, the one he used to signal whether a track was ready. My mother would put a sandwich into his black tin lunch box with a thermos of coffee.

He took me to the railroad yard one time to show me how he switched tracks for different cars to be placed for the loading of coal, and showed me the long lists of the numbers of the box cars that would tell him which to unbuckle to be placed on which tracks. He took me up in the locomotive engine and showed me how they stoked the fire with coal.

After seeing the trains, the railroad yard, and how he threw switches and hopped on boxcars, I took comfort whenever I would wake up in the middle of the night and hear the sound of boxcars going over the tracks, the KBAM! of cars forced to link into each other, and the whoosha......whoosha....WHOOSHA....WHOOSHA... WHOOSHA... WHOOSHA...WHOOSHA of a locomotive picking up steam and speed, because now those sounds told me where he was and what he was doing.

My father tried to teach me to swim in the local reservoir, but I was too afraid. Mother was standing in the water with us and I remember wanting to go to her rather than him. The water was dark and you couldn't see anything and it tasted awful. He put his hand under my stomach to support me and tried to get me to kick and move my arms up, over and down. But every time he let go in the slightest, I would just sink and swallow water and sputter, "Mother!" I didn't know how to relax and he didn't know how to teach me. But I wondered, why couldn't I do what he told me?

On the other hand, my father also took me to the railroad locker room once, where I had my first shower. At home, we only had the claw-footed bathtub. In the shower, he showed me how to pull back the skin on my penis to wash it, and said that was important to do. It was the first time I recall ever seeing him completely naked, and though I had no words for it at the time, when I later felt shame about my body, thinking back to that time with him in the railroad locker room made me feel better about it.

My father taught me how to mow the lawn with a push mower, how to divide the yard into either strips or squares. One day after I finished, I threw the dead grass into our well. For a couple of weeks, we had to tie a rag around the pump in the kitchen to strain out the grass. But Daddy didn't really get upset and I don't recall him ever being mad at me for anything.

The only time he ever spanked me was when I was four and had crayoned all over the parlor wall of his parents' house. Maw Maw, his mother, was upset and made him spank me with my pants down. All of us were living in their house at the time and Pop and my mother stood by as Maw Maw instructed Daddy to spank me. She must have suggested the lowering of my pants, because they never used to do that. I remember very clearly, however, that Daddy was not mad at me and might even have liked the fun I had, and I felt that he was only doing it to please his mother.

One night while we were still in Bluford, I found myself in a local Nazarene Church, down the road a bit from the schoolhouse. I don't recall how I got there. I went there on my own. At some point in their service an invitation was given for people to do something, and I stood up in front of the entire group of strangers and sang "Jesus loves me." Everyone liked it. I remember my parents being puzzled how I got there and why. I didn't know.

That same year, I walked in on my mother as she got out of the bathtub once. She was drying herself with a towel and she pulled it close to her, covering herself and hollered at me, "Robert Walker Gunn! Get outta here! You don't barge in when a door's shut!".

I had never heard that tone of voice from her before. She was mad at me, but there was something more. It was fear…she didn't want me to see her body. But I'd wanted to.

Later, I felt I had done something really bad. I felt ashamed for wanting to see her that way. From that, I not only learned to knock before entering a closed door, but that somehow the body was something fearful, to be ashamed of and kept hidden.

The worst switching I ever got from my mother was one day when I took the long way home, walking Frankie Guitar to his house, and returning along newly poured tar. It wasn't real pavement, but tar and cinders covering the dirt road. Try as I might to avoid it, tar spattered all over my shoes and my new jeans, and Mother was furious.

"Robert Walker! Look at what you've done! Your brand new jeans! And your shoes! I'll never get all the tar off them!" She went on. "Don't you have a brain in your head? And why did you come that way anyway?"

"Because I was walking Frankie to his house."

"You didn't have permission to do that! You know I expect you home by 3:30, and look at it now—it's almost an hour late! And your brand new jeans! Take 'em off, and your shoes and put them on the back porch."

I pulled my shoes off and began taking off my pants. I took them to the back porch and left them there. I walked back in and looked at the clock. 4:25.

"You look at me when I'm talking to you! I have been worried sick wondering what happened to you!"

"Yes, ma'am. I'm sorry." My whole body felt like collapsing. No energy. But no place to rest. Nothing to do but stand there and take it.

"Well, you should be!" Her voice was still loud

"But, I didn't think I was doing anything wrong…"

"That's the problem: you didn't think! You just did what you felt like, forgetting about rules, forgetting about the tar on the road and not thinking at all how I might feel, sitting here waiting for you!"

Nothing I could say counted. I felt so bad…like, I was bad. I wanted to sink into the floor. The clock chimed 5 p.m. I thought she would stop, but she didn't. I wasn't quite naked, but I felt like I was.

"I guess I'm going to have to give you a reminder to be home on time!"

"No, ma'am, I'll remember."

"Don't talk back to me Robert Walker! I don't know what got into you!….."

"Then just switch me and get it over with!" I cried out in tears.

"Oh, I will, mind you; I will. When I'm good and ready! When I think you've gotten it into your thick head that you just can't go off and do what Mr. High and Mighty wants to do." Finally, she told me to go get the switch, which was kept on the back porch. It was a 3 foot long slender branch of a tree. The knots had been cut off so it was mostly smooth. It was flexible and supple. I was still in my Jockey shorts. I brought it back in and gave it to her.

"Come here," she said. I went to her and she grabbed my left shoulder and started whacking me on my rear. I flinched in pain as she hit my thighs. I put my hand back on my butt to protect me, but she moved them away. I have no recollection how many times she struck me.

Most days when I came home from school, my mother would make me peanut butter and jelly sandwiches on white *Holsum* bread. She always stirred the jelly and peanut butter together. One day when I came home and walked in, I saw she was crying.

"What's wrong?" I asked.

She hollered at me, "Get out! Just get out and leave me alone!"

I was stunned. I dropped my books, ran out the screen door to the back of the house, Ol' Bill, my dog, following. I felt I was falling out of my world. I ran through the field of dried yellow cornstalks, sobbing at leaving a world behind, unsure of what world I was entering. I ran till I was out of breath, then stomped and stumbled over clods of grey dirt and broken cornstalks until I came to the muddy pond at the edge of the woods.

Finally, I sat down on the old grey tree, long dead, shorn of its bark, that lay extended into the pond. Ol' Bill came up and nuzzled against me, trying to comfort me. A turtle sat at the end of the log, staring at us. I hugged and petted Ol' Bill. Looking into his eyes was always weird: one eye was brown and clear and you knew he saw you through it; the other eye was clouded over like death with blue and white film. "At least I have you," I said to Ol' Bill, then, as if understanding everything, he licked away the tears from my face.

It was perhaps on that day, as Ol' Bill licked my face and I thought of my life between age four and six, that I made a decision. I had felt a huge emptiness inside as I moved through the cornfield and into the woods, the cumulative effect of not belonging and being thrown out. Without putting it into words, I vowed never to let this happen again. Better to be alone with animals and trees and the open sky than to rely on a place you think you belong and get thrown out.

It was only much later, while I was in college and knew my parents were having trouble in their marriage, that my mother told me what her short temper and tears had been about: my father was having an affair with another woman (as he was when this was revealed), and my mother was very alone.

I remember my father's sister, Aunt Billy, who taught third grade in Mounds, talking with my mother about our moving back to Mounds at the end of that summer and soon after, we did. At that point, we had lived in five different houses, had had at least five different cars, I had attended three different schools and had had four of my dogs die or go away.

Bill was then two, and doctors discovered his heart had a leaky valve, so he was taken to St. Louis, Missouri, eighty miles north, for open heart surgery. In 1950 that was a new procedure and considered very risky.

At the school I attended in Mounds, I used to "play rocket" with my pencil. One day, during class, when Brenda, who sat in front of me wearing a yellow flower print dress, bent over, I crashed my rocket into her rear end. It didn't really go in, but she ran crying to our teacher, Mrs. Williams.

"Bobby!" Mrs. Williams called out for me. I went up to her and she grabbed my hand, pulled me out of the classroom into an adjacent empty room and started lecturing me. She was good friends with my Aunt Billy, so Mrs. Williams called in my aunt and explained what I had done because she wanted Aunt Billy to approve of her spanking me. Aunt Billy went along with it. I thought it was silly and wondered, "What's the big deal?". But I showed the proper remorse and accepted the whacks of the broad flat wooden paddle, which didn't really hurt that much. Maybe I wanted to appear like a tough boy and not cry after that spanking or maybe Mrs. Williams took it easy on my, but either way, I knew deep down I was not a "tough" boy.

One afternoon my cousin Jerry had several of us in his backyard and brought out two pairs of boxing gloves. I had never used boxing gloves, even though Saturday nights my father and I often watched boxing on TV. Jerry and I put on the gloves and we started jabbing at each other. He landed a couple of hard blows to my face and I started to cry. He and the other boys laughed at me. I ran home crying. When I told the story over supper, my father laughed at me also. I wanted to crawl under the table, I felt so humiliated.

In the end, though, my father taught me how to box. He got some boxing gloves and spent several afternoons outside, showing me how to hold my hands to protect my face and stomach. He showed me how to stand and move my feet and stay in motion so as not to be an easy target. The next time Jerry brought out the gloves, I sparred with him again and held my own. I felt good and we began to play together more, and his mother, Claudia, would offer us lemonade on hot days.

As I thought about how Jerry's mother was always upbeat, I began to realize that my mother's mood was usually unhappy. One day I came home and my mother seemed very down and suddenly I blurted out, "I wish Claudia was my mother! She's more fun!" Mother burst into tears and ran into her bedroom. I ran after her, saying "I'm sorry. I"m sorry."

Another time when I was eight or nine, I was playing cowboys and Indians with friends and I took my shirt off. In the movies, cowboys kept their shirts on but Indians never had any. I liked the Indians. Grandma Gamble came out of the house and told me in an unusually harsh voice, "Put your shirt back on. You shouldn't be out playing without a shirt." I didn't know why I shouldn't, but the shame I felt triggered by her tone was clear. Already not feeling good about being "pudgy", my shame of my body grew.

In the middle of third grade, we moved back north to Mt. Vernon. We were in a small apartment first, then the upstairs of a duplex on High Street. My parents became friends with the Andersons downstairs. They had a daughter my age, named Connie. She and I used to talk a lot. We played "doctor" but we never took our clothes off.

One of my other classmates, Earl, lived across the street and sometimes I would go there to play basketball. Earl got together with another boy one afternoon and started bullying me, pushing me around. We were underneath a weeping willow tree, and Earl shoved me down to the ground and threatened to pull off one of the branches to whip me. I got scared and ran home crying to my mother, expecting sympathy. Instead, she marched me back out to where I left Earl, and made me stand up to him. At that point, I was more scared of my mother than I was of Earl, so I somehow muddled through the requisite moves I imagined a boy standing up for himself should make—drawing my shoulders back, puffing up my chest—though none of it felt natural to me. Yet, somehow, I'm still not entirely clear why, but I never had any more problem with Earl after that.

The next year, we moved to a house on South Cherry Street in Mt. Vernon where I started fourth grade. Paw Paw had been living with us on High Street and this house had a small cottage in the back where he could live beside us but not in the same house. There was a lot of discussion between my parents about him; it seemed to me nobody wanted him. He would live with one of my uncles and then the other one, and then come to us. Looking back, I realize that though he lived with us in three different houses, I have no memory of his sitting down to dinner with us in any of them. I felt sorry for Paw Paw and wondered if that's what happened to all old people—that you end up alone, and never quite at home anywhere.

That same year we were living on South Cherry Street with Paw Paw out back, my mother was pregnant, but there was tension around it that I didn't understand and no one explained at the time. What I did remember from another time when my mother was pregnant was being awakened in the middle of the night in Bluford and riding in the old Chevy back to Mounds and getting out of the car in the dark. I remembered how my parents spoke in a tone of restrained tension with gaps of ominous silence that night, and how the feeling was apprehension. Years later, I learned she'd had a miscarriage that night, but as a boy, it all just confused and scared me. Now that my mother was pregnant again, everyone was very wary with fear about this pregnancy. Grandma Gamble moved in with us while Mother was still pregnant, to help with cooking and laundry. It turned out the delivery went smoothly, and my new sister Jeanne was born terrifically healthy.

While worrying and waiting for Jeanne's birth, Grandma Gamble gave me a membership in a Junior Book Club. I didn't understand why the house felt tense, but Grandma helped by giving me *The Little Lame Prince*, by Dinah Maria Mulock Craik. That book told the story of a boy whose legs were paralyzed by a childhood trauma, who was given a travelling cloak by his fairy godmother, which he used to go on adventures in which he learned compassion. Although it was my brother whose legs were crippled, I identified with the Little Prince. In retrospect, Grandma Gamble was my fairy godmother. She is the one I remember reading to me from my earliest years in her red velvet platform rocking chair.

We moved back to Mounds from the end of my fourth grade to the end of seventh grade. First we were in a house on McKinley Street, which was small with two bedrooms and a screened-in front porch. I saved money from mowing lawns and bought a new maroon and gray Schwinn bicycle. Our house was next door to a classmate, Barry. He was a sissy, very effeminate, but I kind of liked him and one night stayed over at his house. We took off our pajamas and felt each other's bodies with our little stiff penises and I remember having this feeling of fullness like something wanted to get out, and it felt good.

But soon after my interesting sleepover at Barry's house, we moved again. In the next four years, we lived in three more different homes.

Paw Paw was put into the Methodist Old Folks home and died there.

I was never part of any discussion about our frequent moves before 1956. Looking back, sometimes they seemed related to whether Paw Paw was going to live with us, but more often they seemed related to my father's frequent job changes and money problems.

"Did you go to college?" I asked my father once.

"I started college at Carbondale (Southern Illinois University), but I dropped out before the year was up because of an argument I had with Pop and Maw Maw."

"What was that?"

"They wanted me to be a doctor and I wanted to be a lawyer. So I quit." I didn't question his reasoning at that time.

I saw pictures of my father when he was in high school. He was dressed in a very fine white suit, and drove an MGT convertible. A fancy dude. Then I found an old report card of his. His grades were some C's, many D's and some F's. I was shocked. I complained to my mother, "How come you get on my case when I make a B, but he never ever made more than a C?" She was quite irritated that I had seen the card and retorted, as she pulled the card out of my hand, "Because you can and you should!"

My father was, in fact, a very likeable and handsome man. He dressed well. He was slim and I thought he was handsome. He had a winning smile and walked with a jaunt. As I grew into adolescence, I realized he could strike up a conversation with most anyone...a talent he inherited from his father, Pop, who owned and ran a drugstore in Mounds and was the real breadwinner of the family.

Pop had gray and black hair that was combed straight back, no part. He always wore a suit and tie, and a gray or brown fedora. In a deeply segregated town, Pop held the respect of people of both races because he delivered prescriptions to everyone, never thinking twice about going into "colored town," night or day, though I recall classmates talking about how scary it would be to go there.

On the morning of September 13, 1953, a month before my tenth birthday, in the First Methodist Church in Mounds, Illinois where Paw Paw used to preach and my parents were married, I had what is commonly referred to in Methodist circles as a conversion experience.

It was at the end of a week-long revival which I had attended every night. That Sunday morning as the service ended with a call for those who wanted to accept Jesus into their hearts to come down to the altar, I struggled to sing as a lump in my throat got bigger and bigger. The preacher called out the invitation to come down and give our lives to Christ. "Almost persuaded," we sang, "now to believe—almost persuaded, Christ to receive. Seems now some soul to say, 'Go, Sinner, Go thy way…some more convenient day…on thee I'll call.'"

Guilt and shame overwhelmed me. I was being called to leave my sin behind, to let go and come to Jesus. "Come home," we sang on, "come home…. ye who are weary, come home….earnestly, tenderly, Jesus is calling, calling, O Sinner, come home."

People kept singing though I could not. My voice choked as I struggled against the impulse to surrender to the call. Finally, as they sang, "Just as I am, without one plea, but that thy blood was shed for me," I could hold back no longer. I ran down, sobbing, feeling the release of letting go, the release of giving in and falling into the love of Jesus. I ran down to kneel at the altar rail where others—all grownups but me—were also kneeling and crying and praying and giving their hearts to Jesus. The preacher bent over and put his hand on my shoulder, welcoming me with compassion and understanding. I felt I was at the very throne of God, welcomed, unworthy sinner though I was, into the fullness of His mercy. I was home.

For me, the experience was utterly profound, transforming and real. At that moment, I knew who I was because I knew who God was. Jesus was calling me, calling me to himself, and to God, calling me home. Who I was, was this wretched sinner, hopelessly lost except for that call to come home where I was accepted, received, welcomed with open arms "just as I am." The boy who had never stayed in one house for more than a year, found his unconditional home with God, Whom he would never have to leave again, Who promised never to leave him.

From the time of my conversion, as long as we were in Mounds, I became religious. I went to prayer meeting every Wednesday night and testified about what the Lord had done for me each week. I went to Sunday School, Morning Worship and Methodist Youth Fellowship every Sunday. Not yet having changed voice, I sang soprano and received many compliments. I banged out sermons on the typewriter Maw Maw and Pop gave me for Christmas in '53, to preach to the youth group and, more rarely, to the adults. I took my Bible to school and read it during recess while others played softball. I took it in my knapsack with a canteen of water and went on long hikes along streams and hills to find a place of solitude to read. By the time I was twelve, I had read the entire Bible cover to cover twice.

My conversion and my subsequent Bible studies gave me a place in the world such as I had never had before. Whereas before, I felt very lost, like a stranger wherever we moved and whichever school I attended, I now felt part of God's family, adopted, as Paul says in I Corinthians. This gave me purpose and direction. My business was God's business, just as Jesus told his parents when they left him behind in the temple in Jerusalem at age twelve. When they found him, he said, "Didn't you know I must be about my father's business?"

At first, I carried a pocket "Red Letter Edition" of the New Testament onto the playground and read it while others played ball or climbed the jungle gym. But as my faith grew and I read more of the suffering and tribulations of people in the early church, I felt a growing inner strength in facing bullies and hecklers that I never had before. I took refuge in the promises of scripture: "If God is for us, who can be against us?"; "Perfect love casts out fear."; "Do not be afraid of those who would harm the body, but rather be afraid of those who have the power to destroy the soul."

I also realized that people who engage in hurting others like bullies did me, did so because of their own insecurity and I felt myself growing out of my insecurity and into a new courage. I stopped being afraid of them. I stopped trying to avoid them, and instead, engaged them in friendly conversation, or quoted scripture to them – which always stopped the conversation.

My new religious zeal was not greeted with complete enthusiasm from my parents. "We want to talk to you, son," my father said to me one night. He and my mother sat together on the sofa, and I sat across from them. This had never happened before. I don't remember whether it was the same night or on different nights, but they told me two things.

"We're concerned about you, Bobby, about how much time you spend in church and such," he continued. "You know, being religious doesn't necessarily make you a good person."

"You can be real active in the church and still be a hypocrite, you know?" my mother said. "Paw Paw and Maw Maw are kind of like that. Paw Paw may have been a preacher, but I can tell you he was mean to my brothers growing up. And now he sits around, expecting to be taken care of."

"We're not saying religion is bad, Bobby. It's just not the only thing in life. You need to be more rounded." my father said. So they encouraged me to spend more time socializing, playing softball or basketball. I later learned that my principal at school had talked to them about my reading the Bible during recess, and suggested I should take part in sports more.

However valid their concerns were, this conversation with my parents introduced a cleavage in my mind: on the one hand it enabled a healthy skepticism about religion; but on the other, it stole a certain kind of joy from my whole-hearted idealism in a way that made me reluctant to give myself without reserve ever again. I became suddenly self-conscious about my religious life. How do I be real? How do I not be a hypocrite? The church seemed to teach how to be religious: go to church, read the Bible, pray, be kind. If you did these things, you'd be considered a good Christian. But evidently there was some other thing which, if you didn't get it or didn't do it, you'd be a hypocrite, and it would completely undo all the good you had tried to do and be. Some sliver of doubt now slid into my mind that was not about whether God was real, but whether I was. How in the world was I supposed to answer that?

Sometime after that, I began putting on puppet shows for the school, not just in my backyard. I asked our librarian, Mrs. Hartman, to order me a book on puppets. Of the plays I wrote, the only title I remember was the play I called "The Squander Bird." The Squander Bird would come onstage screeching out, "Squander! Squander!" and entice other puppet people to spend all the money they had until they went broke and had to be rescued by a do-gooder like Howdy-Doody. I, of course, identified with Howdy Doody.

I don't know how I even knew the word "squander" back then, but maybe I realized that that was a driving impulse of my father, based on the Plymouth that got returned. In any event, Mr. Finley, our principal in Mounds, was so impressed by my performances, he drove me to the neighboring school in Mound City to perform for classes there. I entered the local 4H Talent Show, and won first place, then moved on to the Southern Illinois Regionals; but it was hard for people in an auditorium of several hundred to see my homemade cardboard puppet theatre, not to mention to hear my pre-adolescent soprano voice coming from behind the screen.

In this way I underwent a social transformation from an isolated scared kid to a person who entered into others' world, and with the help of a few puppets, became outgoing and friendly. But underlying it all was the conviction I still retained from my conversion, that I was unconditionally loved by God, and so was everyone else, most of whom didn't realize it.

Shortly after my conversion experience, I asked to take piano lessons. Pop and Maw Maw lived about four blocks away and had a dark mahogany Knabe Console on which Maw Maw practiced her music as pianist for the church. I began taking lessons from Mrs. Bodie for a dollar a week on Maw Maw's piano, where I tried to practice regularly.

It was the era of Liberace. On the small black and white television that Pop and Maw Maw had, I would try to watch him every week. His playing was brilliant and dazzling to my eyes; I was awed at his ability to move his fingers so rapidly over the keys, whether it was playing Chopin or Tchaikovsky. With his crystal candelabra sitting on whichever Baldwin concert grand he was playing, he always chose Romantic classics and smiled into the camera as his fingers flew gracefully, seemingly thoughtlessly, up and down the piano.

Whenever Liberace was on, my father would walk out of the room. If anyone mentioned him to my father, he would make snide remarks or grimace. The implication was clear to me: Liberace was a fairy, and that made everything he did useless. The link between music and my sexual orientation became indelibly fixed: only queers play piano. I didn't stop playing, but I felt the shadow of shame cast a pall over my enthusiasm.

At the same time, however, as I became more adept, I played certain songs over and over again. I remember singing and playing "Sometimes I feel like a motherless child," and felt that was deeply consoling whenever I was feeling down, but I wondered why it moved me so much, since I had a mother. Methodists have always been known for their singing. The founder of Methodism, John Wesley, was usually joined by his brother, Charles, who wrote many hymns. I learned to play them on the piano and memorized them more easily than other pieces. One day as I finished playing, I realized Pop had been listening to me hunched over in his chair in the next room.

"That's real nice, Bobby," he said as I walked up to him. I leaned next to him and put my arm over his shoulder. He said, "I'd give that Lincoln out there in the driveway if I could play like that."

"You could still learn, Pop! Mrs. Bodie could teach you!"

"No, son, I'll be content just to hear you play like you just did. Don't ever stop playing. Stick with it."

Coming from Pop, the oldest man of the family, that meant more to me than anything my mother or Maw Maw could have said. It could not erase the imprint of my father's view; but at least it gave me some support where there had been disdain.

Pop's remark revealed a side of him that also came out in his love of flowers. He always had bushes of roses or azaleas growing at the side and front of his house. He would water them faithfully. This side of him could also be seen evenings before dark when he would sit at the chrome and red formica kitchen table looking out at the bird bath in the back yard, watching the birds splash and spatter the water all over from the oppressive humidity of southern Illinois summers. Pop was evidence to me that you could be a man and still have a softer side.

On another occasion, I remember my parents sitting me down to talk about sex. They did not seem to realize that their earlier concern about my not playing ball or socializing was connected to this second issue. I did not naturally want to play softball and basketball; I preferred to read a book, whether it was the Bible or something else. I was teased and called sissy and queer for not playing ball, or for trying and not doing it well. The playground was another shame-filled place because I was always the last one picked if teams were chosen.

I was just beginning to think, from the shadow corners of my mind, that maybe the labels of "sissy" and "queer" were earned honestly, though I pushed it hard out of my mind. In third grade I had strange feelings for a classmate across the street named Larry. I simply wanted to be near him, to do things together, but I had no idea, especially as a new kid on the block, how to arrange to be together, nor would I have termed my feelings as sexual.

Also I remember another third grader named Terry, and though my feelings were not the same for him as for Larry, I remember he had a large brass belt buckle. In 6th grade, about the time of my parents' "talk," I knew I had a crush on Johnny Connell, my blond, blue-eyed classmate. I stayed over at his family farm one night and we sat on the little veranda outside his second story bedroom looking at the perfectly clear sky and full moon.

"Isn't this wonderful?" he said as we stared at the moon.

"Yeah," I said.

"If only we had some girls with us," he said.

"Yeah," I said, rather than "no, actually, I'm happy to be here with you and would love to hold you and hug you."

I had also begun to notice certain boys in the locker room when we changed after basketball practice. I especially remember seeing our center, Tommy O'Sullivan, naked- six feet tall, blonde, blue-eyes and a killer smile.

I was nearly twelve by then, and my parents said they knew I would be thinking about sexual things before long.

"We want you to know that it's normal to have sexual feelings," my father said as he handed me a few pamphlets and asked if I had any questions.

"We just want you to know you can talk about any of these issues with us," he added. I shrugged and remained silent.

For 1955, in our little town, they were being very progressive, and I believed them that if I wanted to ask a question, they would try to answer honestly. I remember desperately wanting to ask them if there was such a thing as the word that begins with f, and did they really do it, but I was too afraid to ask, because I knew it was a "bad word." I had bought a book called <u>Sex and the Teenager</u> at church camp the summer before, and read that it took one pint of blood to make one drop of some kind of white fluid that came from a boy's penis. I didn't yet know about that either, but I dedicated myself never to lose my blood that way. At least that was my intention.

Of course, I had another question I wanted to ask, but it was even scarier than the f word. I had begun to realize that I had feelings for boys that were different from those I had for girls, and the words I heard others use for those feelings I never wanted to be applied to me, even though that's what bullies had called me. So I didn't ask. In retrospect, in the small town we lived in, it was probably a good thing I didn't. In 1955, no one in the country would have been able to help me, because neither psychology nor religion had developed beyond a would-be benevolent pity at best for people with a complex sexuality.

Despite religion's inability to help me with my uncertain thoughts about my emerging sexuality, faith had still come at the right time. Between ten and twelve, I came face to face with mortality. When we were living in the Hodge house, Grandma Gamble had cancer. I had been kept from seeing her as she got worse, but finally I said I wanted to see her before she died. She was in the bed at Pop and Maw Maw's and her face was gaunt, her thin skin barely covering the cheekbones and jawbones. She was unconscious, breathing through her wide open mouth, flecks of white lining her tongue and lips, smelling awful. If it was not for her obvious breathing, she had every appearance of being already dead.

When I got the call from my mother a few days later that she had passed on, I stopped by our Dairy Kone, got an ice cream cone and then went to Pop and Maw Maw's house. I remember feeling embarrassed to be eating ice cream while everyone was standing around speaking in hushed tones. I was sitting in Pop's big blue chair, eating the cone, wishing I hadn't brought it, wanting to hurry up and finish it and suddenly had a strange feeling, a feeling of being somewhere else even though visually everything and everyone was familiar. But it all had become dream-like, as if it weren't really real, as if I wasn't really where I was. But my eyes told me I was in Pop and Maw Maw's house. I could feel the cold ice cream as I licked it from running down the yellow cone. I could feel the texture of the chair with its white embroidered doily on the chair's arm. It was my first conscious experience of what I later learned was derealization, a form of psychological splitting.

I remember going to the gravesite, Grandma Gamble's casket sitting beside the green fake grass ground cover, a huge pit opened up at the side. She would lie buried beside Grandpa Gamble. Then I noticed a smaller gravestone next to theirs. It had a picture on it of a boy on a tricycle. The name was Robert Gamble.

"Who's that?" I asked my mother, pointing to the picture.

"That's Grandma Gamble's son, Robert," she answered.

I subtracted the dates. "He was twelve years old?"

"Yes." She put her arm around me. "You were named for him. You're his namesake."

I looked up at her. She was crying. I was twelve. "Am I gonna die, too?" I wanted to ask, but didn't.

A few months after Grandma Gamble died, Paw Paw died. He had gone into "an old folks' home" for retired Methodist ministers. He was buried in Eddyville, "where I was born," Mother said. I remember sitting between Mother and Daddy in the middle of the seat of the turquoise and white 1956 Bel Air Chevrolet, Dad's "demonstrator" of the year, as we drove north. It was a cold winter day, and the Chevy's heater blew directly on me and it felt good.

Once again, I stood next to Mother and Daddy in front of a casket covered in funeral flowers, sitting beside a huge hole in the ground, a gray gravestone at the head where my mother's mother's name, Nettie Reid, was engraved. After the funeral, we went to see people from his side of the family I'd never met before: Paw Paw's uncle, Grandpa Bennett, who had a handle-bar moustache, wore bib overalls and a red checkered flannel shirt, and chewed tobacco that he spat into a spittoon beside his old rocking chair. And I remember meeting Uncle Ted, Grandpa Bennett's son, who was a hunchback and shorter than me.

A few months after that, in the spring, the phone rang early on a Saturday morning. It was from Aunt Lillian, my mother's brother Lowell's wife, telling us that my cousin, Billy Rue Reid, about a year older than me, had died suddenly of a rare strain of polio. He had gone to the hospital with a headache and was diagnosed with polio and died within three days. He was 13; I was 12.

I'd often spent weeks together during summers with Billy Rue. We played baseball, took hikes into the woods, played with his green parakeet, and compared penis sizes.

I remember seeing him in his casket, and I remember wanting to cry to get rid of the lump in my throat, but there was no release. I remember wanting his baseball glove, but feeling like I shouldn't ask for it, so I didn't even mention it to my parents.

Within the space of less than three years, seeing the dead faces in caskets of those I loved, and those who had loved me, had became familiar. In a twist of coincidence, the very house I had lived in when I was 4 to nearly 6, was converted to the Crain Funeral Home. The very same room whose walls I had crayoned on, the room where my cousins and I used to tell ghost stories, had been turned into the parlor in which the funerals for Grandma Gunn, Grandpa and Grandma Gamble and Paw Paw had all been held.

My faith told me they all went to heaven. But inside me, the deaths of so many family members, combined with constant moves from place to place, not to mention the loss of my dogs, gouged a huge gap between the love that I had known from them all and its loss. The realization that I was named after someone who died at my age, followed by my cousin's shockingly sudden death when he was one year older than me, did something to me.

Without knowing it at the time, I began to numb out, to disconnect from my closest feelings --which no one had really asked about. I threw all my feelings into religion and my Christian faith. The power of death to steal away those close to me made heaven all the more important and real, and it made all attachments tenuous. In retrospect, I became more deeply divided inside and crammed away my painful feelings from my own awareness.

In this regard, I think I began to follow Maw Maw's temperament. She was very even-keeled (also a Libra), but tight-lipped and not emotionally expressive. It was at some point during the same three year period, when I was between ten and twelve, my mother told me Maw Maw had a brother named Bill who had been placed into what they called in those days, an "asylum for the insane," north of Mounds about 30 miles. As Maw Maw never talked about her brother and no one ever visited him since I had been born, it was abstract news to me, an introduction to another type of death that no one spoke of at all, or only in hushed tones.

Although many Christians may find consolation from loss in the belief in an after-life, my mind and heart split in the face of so much death and loss when I was still a boy. Joy and hope shifted entirely over to the future, the return of Christ to usher in the holy city, and the things of this life only had meaning by reference to the life to come.

My pain was buried and both expressed and hidden in hymns: "Shall we gather at the river," "Softly and tenderly Jesus is calling," "Rock of Ages, cleft for me, let me hide myself in thee," "When the roll is called up yonder," "In the sweet bye and bye." I knew myself as a stranger on earth, God's child who temporarily was living in a strange land while awaiting transport to eternity. Liveliness was only found in the thoughts and anticipation of heaven and God.

Onto the Christian notion that my real life was on hold here on earth while I anticipated the advent of an even fuller reality in the advent of the kingdom of God, my feelings and my basic belief about reality became split. I was experiencing impermanence as a chronic emptiness inside from so many goodbyes so soon after just beginning to learn to say hello. Then to the list of those whom I'd lost through death, I added all my known friends as I left them behind in Illinois and moved with my family to Florida just before my thirteenth birthday.

We moved to Jensen Beach, Florida, a town of about 6,000 in 1956 (12,000 wintertime), on the Indian River, the other side of which was Hutchinson Island and the Atlantic Ocean. The Indian River flowed north up the Intracoastal Waterway to New Smyrna Beach and flowed in the south into the St. Lucie Inlet, at the tip of Sewall's Point, where it was met by the St. Lucie River from the west. In that area of Jensen, Rio and Stuart, you could drive for many miles without losing sight of water, reflecting and refracting sunrises and sunsets. While we waited for our new house to be built, we lived on Sewall's Point, which required taking a bus for six miles into Stuart for school.

As important for me as the loss of friends was the loss of a church community and a relationship with a pastor who knew me and with whom I felt comfortable. For months I wrote letters to my friends in Illinois, and tried to keep in touch. Gradually, the letters dwindled as I became more settled into my new school. I turned 13 shortly after we moved and soon experienced the physical eruptions of adolescence. I finally discovered what the white stuff was I'd read about in the book on Christian boys and sex back in Illinois.

While my parents, grandparents and aunt and uncle worked long hours at Sun-N-Surf, the restaurant/drug store/Dairy Kone we'd built, I became the family babysitter for my brother (7), my sister (3) and our cousin Mike (4), the adopted son of my aunt and uncle. Bursting with hormones I'd never experienced before, I spent my days after school babysitting, until our parents came home, often late into the evening. Living so far from the center of school activities, I felt all the more isolated as a newcomer.

The worst part of the situation was when Mother came home from work. If I hadn't managed to clean the house and get everything shipshape before she arrived, she would break into several minutes of complaining. She would frown and glare at me.

"I work all day and you can't even pick up the house? Look at that! All those dishes. Now you expect me to do dishes AND make supper for all of you!? I could really use some help around here! What exactly have you been doing all afternoon?"

In an odd counterbalance to my life at home and the loss of a church to attend several times a week, each morning at school we had a Bible reading, a prayer ending with the Lord's Prayer, and the Pledge of Allegiance to the flag. I volunteered frequently to lead the Bible reading and prayer. I accepted these rituals and enjoyed them without question at the time.

After a few months on Sewall's Point, the house we were building still wasn't finished, so we took one of Buck Henry's tiny cottages, a block away from Sun-N-Surf. When the house was finished, it sat on the hill above the center of town, the beginning of Skyline Drive. From Dad's place at the kitchen table, he could look out the low-built jalousie picture window, and have his first cup of coffee watching the sun come up over Hutchison Island.

Wanting us to capitalize on our newly found waterland, my father bought a 20' inboard boat from Mr. Youngblood, an old salt who seemed to know everything about wind, tides, currents and fish, and was happy to pass on his wisdom. She was called "Lucy II" and she was beautiful: white hull, dark hardwood trim, nicely stained, waxed and polished. From Bailey's Boatyard where we kept it, we went deep sea fishing, water skiing and cruising. We would carry Bill onto it and place him into a chair that one of us had to anchor with one hand while we held onto Bill with the other.

The boat epitomized the meaning of the move to Florida. It was part of the dream that made people leave their jobs up north and come to the Sunshine State, just as we had done: leave the homeland and risk it all for the good life. Within the year, we had to sell the boat. The new family business was not doing so well and Bill needed more and more care. For all the change in geography, as we moved three different times within the small town of Jensen, it seemed a continuation of the frequent house changes in Illinois, just as the loss of the boat seemed like the loss of the Plymouth. And right after we moved to the new house, my collie, Cindy, died. "Dogs born up north don't do well in Florida heat," locals told us. "Their heart gives out."

I became the main person to help Bill get into bed each night from his wheelchair. Once in bed, I would remove his braces, we would talk a bit and then he would say his prayers. One night after prayers, he looked at me with a particular seriousness and said,

"Bob, do you think I'll ever be able to walk?"

He had been through many weeks of a regimen of trying to walk between a set of parallel bars my father had built, in most of which he ended up crying from the pain. We had finally stopped the exercise, and with it, surrendered hope of his ever walking on his own.

"As much as we wish you could, Bill, I don't think so." I hated being the one to tell him.

It was shortly after my conversation with Bill about his not walking that my parents decided that he would perhaps get better care learning skills in coping at the Sunland Training Center in Orlando.

"It'll be better for him, Viv," my dad said as my sister and I joined them around the kitchen table one night.

My mother was crying. My sister was crying.

"But how can we do that to him?" my mother wiped her eyes and blew her nose. "Won't he feel we've abandoned him?" In front of her on the kitchen table was a glossy brochure from the Sunland Training Center in Orlando.

"We'll go visit him every Sunday," Dad said. "It'll be hard, but the doctors told us he'd actually enjoy his own life more because he'll be with others with similar handicaps." He got up with his coffee cup, pointed to Mother's. She shook her head and he filled his cup and sat back down.

"I can help with the driving," I offered. I had just turned 13 and, though I didn't have a driver's license yet, Dad had taught me how to drive and often let me take the car.

"I just can't think of life here without him," Jeanne said. Tears kept rolling down her face. "How can we do this to him? It just won't be the same."

"Jeanne, the doctors say they can train him how to take care of himself better, how to dress himself and get around. He'll feel more pride in what he can do," my mother said.

"Judge Crary says he has seen many people go through this," my father added. "He says in the long run, it's better for everyone concerned."

"And we'll be able to bring him home on holidays, or vacation."

"Yeah, like who ever gets a vacation," I added. "We never go any where."

"Enough of that, Bobby," my mother said.

"Well, it's true. We sold Lucy II. We take Bill to Orlando. We may go see him, but we'll never take a vacation," I said. "That's what Yankees do when they come down here, but we're not Yankees any more."

"We have to be thankful for what we have," she said.

"Hopefully Sun-N-Surf will do better this winter," my father added.

For months, one or both of my parents would drive to visit him three hours each way, every Sunday. Then he was transferred to Ft. Myers, which added another hour each way, and the visits began to lessen in frequency. If neither of them could go, I would go. Later he was moved to Wood House, a halfway house specifically for people with cerebral palsy in Ft. Lauderdale, which was only an hour and a half away. We made sure to bring him home on the major holidays, often for the week, and for weeks in the summer. We noticed that the other children at Wood House were rarely visited by their families. They were essentially abandoned to state care.

At the end of one of Bill's weeks home with us, Mother was sewing name tags on all of Bill's clothes before taking him back.

"Mother, for all the work you do sewing those on, when they pack his suitcase to come home, there's always clothes that don't belong to him, and some things we send down with him we never see again. I don't know if the name tags do much," I said.

She looked up at me with a set mouth and defiant brown eyes and said, "Whether he keeps all his clothes or not, doesn't matter. This makes him know that we care and he's not forgotten." She picked up the needle and pointed at me. "And it lets everyone down there know that Billy Gunn has a family that cares!"

Sometimes I was really proud of my mother.

However strange on the inside I felt as I began 8th grade in Stuart, on the outside, I'd lost my fat, trimmed down, and started paying attention to how I dressed. Still, despite these external changes, I was shocked to find that, rather than being the object of ridicule or bullying, somehow I was actually popular.

It was an odd introduction to the way the world works sometimes, focusing on and rewarding the external view, the superficial; still, I was glad to no longer be bullied. In the 8th grade at the time, you knew you were "in" by whether classmates passed notes to you or about you to others. To "like" someone or "go with" someone didn't necessarily mean you dated, though you might. It meant sitting together at a basketball or football game, or between classes or at lunch, and maybe, if you were that confident, holding hands. I had a lot of notes passed around to me and about me. "Do you like so-and-so?" "Who do you like?" In fact, when it came time to vote for a Freshman class president in 9th grade, I lost by one vote to Grant Luckhart, because I voted for him.

By the summer of 1958, my brother Bill was living at the Sunland Training Center in Orlando, Jeanne and Mike spent days with Aunt Billy who'd resumed teaching 3rd grade and had her summers free, which gave me more freedom, too.

"Purple People Eater," "Witch Doctor," and Fats Domino's "I want to walk you home," topped the pop charts, and Billy Roberts and I rode our bicycles from Jensen across the causeway to the beaches of Hutchison Island nearly every day. He brought a radio so we could listen to those songs while the surf rolled in. We got deeply tanned. Leaving our bikes at the main entrance to the beach, we would walk north about a half mile or so, beyond cars and parking places, where it was deserted, undeveloped and out of sight. There we would try to compensate for the remaining white spots on our midriff by taking off our trunks and exposing our still pale skin to the sun. Of course we would get erections and jerk off. I wanted to do more, but didn't really know what "more" might mean. Then we'd jump into the sparkling turquoise water and wash off and feel the tide pull and push, then float and let it carry us, wash over us and take us into shore. Near 4 o'clock or so, we'd put our trunks back on, go back for our bikes and head home.

Whereas I'd known a spiritual ecstasy in my religious experience in Illinois, in Florida I was discovering a more sensual form of it when swimming naked with fellow Boy Scouts in the river under moonlight, then getting together in tents afterward. As we engaged in mutual masturbation, we said we were pretending to be with a girl, but I knew that was not in my imagination. I was right where I wanted to be. It always seemed to me that those experiences meant more to me than the other guys, so, heavy with guilt and shame, I tried to put them out of my mind.

By the age of fourteen, such experiences with boys created a deep inner conflict. I went to the library and read everything I could find on homosexuality. There were no books on the subject; only entries in encyclopedias. One article said homosexuality was a stage that adolescent boys go through and usually grow out of. Despite such writings suggesting I was merely going through a stage, the polarity between my sexuality and spirituality became a chasm which I couldn't imagine being bridged, especially by God.

My sexual self became filled with shame and so I stored it away; my persona, which was all that was good, acceptable and rewarded in the world, contained my spirituality. Thus, there was no room in my mind for sex, except as a cause of remorse, confession and self-hate. I became adept at dividing my thoughts, feelings and words between what was spontaneous and shameful (and, therefore, to be suppressed), and what was acceptable in society. In this way, I felt like I was killing my self slowly on the inside, while successfully conforming on the outside.

In high school, I dated several girls, but for some reason, the ones I was most attracted to seemed to be the furthest away from me, romantically speaking: Lynn Mauldin, Homecoming Queen and my vice president on the Student Council; Cathy Conley, Claudia Smith, whom I took to the Junior Prom; Cookie Smith (not related) whom I took to the Senior Prom; Martha Crowder, and Susan Son, probably my best female friend, who lived just down the street from me. I would talk on the phone a lot with these girls, especially Susan. She was smart both academically and emotionally.

At a certain point in dating each of them, I tried to advance the physical contact beyond kissing, however, each time I did, I was rebuffed, not, they said, because they didn't like me, but because they didn't like me "in that way." They wanted to be "friends." In the end, each of them said I was "handsome," "nice" and "good," but could not explain why I was not sexy to them. Perhaps these girls sensed, but could not articulate, what I feared most about myself.

I had resumed piano lessons after we moved to Florida, studying with Terry Austin, a graduate of the Cleveland Conservatory of Music in Ohio who played the organ at the Methodist church in Stuart. Within a year, I expressed interest in learning the pipe organ because I loved Bach. For nearly a year I took both organ and piano lessons from him, until he suggested I totally concentrate on organ. I immediately started playing the organ for our local church in Jensen, the Community Church. They had a two manual Hammond organ with only two octaves for pedals.

Meanwhile, my parents started letting me drive the Simca, a small French car with 4-speed on the steering column. By letting me drive myself, Mother could stay home after work while Dad, who had started selling cars again after the failure of the Sun-n-Surf restaurant, drove a "demo" Chevrolet. Dad had taught me how to drive, especially how to start the car from a stopped position on a hill in first gear. Unlike swimming, when it came to driving, he was a good teacher; he gave clear instructions and never lost patience with me. The fact that I had only a learner's permit and was fourteen was less important, in my parents' eyes (and mine!) than whether I could drive well, safely and responsibly.

It was a time in a small town where everybody knew everybody, including the sheriff, and a good deal of latitude was given as long as you didn't cause problems. To my mind, drag-racing was something that could fit within the guidelines of what was responsible and safe. Although the little Simca was no match for most American cars, one night a classmate, David Brinkley, challenged me to race him with his Renault Dauphine and my Simca on the cut-off road between US1 and Jensen. David was a big guy, who filled the driver's seat of his little Renault to overflowing. I beat him hands down.

"You cheated! You cut your wheels into me and I couldn't get off the starting line till you were already ahead of me!" he complained.

"Yeah, yeah! Excuses!" I replied.

Another evening, Grant Luckhart had his parents' '55 Chevy station wagon, and I had my father's new 1960 Chevy Impala. Cookie Smith was with me, and Mary Jo Fenton was with Grant. We'd been to a movie in West Palm Beach and were returning north on US1. We sidled up to each other, one in each lane, and started racing. We got up to 110 mph and suddenly I saw red flashing lights in the rear view mirror. We were pulled over by a Florida Highway Patrolman, who made Grant and I both get out of our cars and stand in the headlights of the cruiser to show him our driver's licenses. He gave us a lecture, then asked me, "You Henry Gunn's son?"

"Yessir," I replied, my heart sinking.

"Works for Bill Greene Chevrolet?"

"Yessir."

"I'm gonna give you boys a warning. But if this ever happens again, it'll be the worse for you."

"Yessir, thank you sir," Grant and I said together.

The next morning I didn't say anything to my dad. The second morning, he called me into the bathroom while he was shaving. "Have anything to tell me, son?" He pulled his double-edge Gillette razor over his foamy face, rinsed it in the water in the sink.

"Nope, nothing I can think of."

"Well, Jerry Wheeler stopped by the sales office and told me he'd given you a warning night before last."

"Oh, you mean the Florida Highway Patrolman?"

"Ummhmmm."

"Well, yes, he did," I answered sheepishly.

"He said you and Grant were both doing over 85."

"Well, I guess so. Guess we weren't paying much attention," I lied.

He jerked the razor away from his face and looked at me, like I'd said something stupid, which I had.

"No driving my demonstrator for the next month," he said. "That's my work car. Anything happens to it, I'm responsible and I have to have it to make money." He rinsed his razor in the water again.

"Yessir. Sorry."

After working awhile at Winn Dixie, I saved enough to buy a new table and chair set for the kitchen and a new lamp for the Florida room. I was ashamed of the table we had, because it was very rusty, and the old lamp had a stained shade. I had it all delivered in time for my parents' anniversary. I thought it would make my mother happy.

Coming home from work, as soon as she walked in the door, pointed to the table and said, "Happy Anniversary, Mom!" Jeanne and I stood beside the new table: beige formica top, brass trim around the edges. "Look, Mom, no rust."

She glared at it, touching it slightly. Then she looked over at me. "We didn't need this, Bobby!" she exploded.

"I thought you'd like it." I was shocked.

"There was nothing wrong with the old one. What do you think we are, poor or something?"

"Well, not that poor…just that I wanted us to have some nice things, like Tommy Jones and Susan Son."

"We weren't poor and the table we had wasn't that bad!" She glared at me.

"Just keeping up with the Joneses, right Bob?!" Jeanne said with a big grin and a chuckle.

"Thanks, Sis," I said with a frown.

My mother sat down at the table, put her head in her hands, crying. I went over to her and put my arm around her.

"Mom, I'm sorry. I didn't mean to offend you."

She picked up her head, wiped her tears, blew her nose and looked out the window. "With all we've been through, I think we've done pretty well. Of course, I have to work all the time, but there's no shame in that."

"No, Mom, of course not. You're great!....I'm sorry. I'm sorry."

"I just never had any idea how you felt….that we're poor…."

When I was sixteen and legally licensed to drive, I got my first car, a light blue 1951 Chevrolet stick shift-on-the-column sedan. It was my sophomore year in high school and I drove that car all over Florida to attend various meetings at Key Clubs around the state as a Lieutenant Governor. Dad also bought me my first suit, a solid light grey, and Florsheim shoes from Anthony's in West Palm Beach. Over a year later, I found a collection notice from the shop for the unpaid bill.

I enjoyed Key Club, the service organization for high schools founded by Kiwanis. It gave me the opportunity to speak in public, to travel and meet other students from around the state, and to work with adult Kiwanians who were leaders in actual life: lawyers, judges, doctors, dentists. I was beginning to reach beyond the borders of my small town. Although I started out very intimidated, I made friends and got more comfortable.

All the Key Club lieutenant governors and state officers met at Bill Nelson's ranch outside of Melbourne one weekend. Bill was a tremendously likeable, down-to-earth guy who had been the lieutenant governor the year before. He had presence, poise, smarts and personality. One of the topics of the weekend was how to position him to win the election for Key Club International president when we gathered in Toronto in the spring. I earned the distinction of having his Palomino roll over on me after rearing up on its hind legs. Evidently it was very sensitive to the bit, and I had pulled too hard. Fortunately, I got up and walked away unscathed, just shaken. Bill not only won the election to the international presidency of Key Club; later he became a U.S. Senator from Florida.

It was during my trips driving around Florida for Key Club that I noticed a shift in my relationship with my mother. Our talks became more frequent and I noticed every time I came home, she was especially glad to see me. She would want to know when I'd return so she could make fried chicken. She would come out to the car as I swung into the circular driveway, and we would hug and she would kiss me on the lips. I began to sense her leaning on me emotionally in the stories she would tell. I wasn't sure how I felt about it. On the one hand, it was an acknowledgement that I was growing up and was ready to know about adult things; on the other hand, why was she talking to me rather than to Dad?

In my junior year, I decided to run for Key Club governor of the state. I had no real idea about how to run a political campaign, but John Goldner, a classmate, committed to helping me. I drove all over the state, making speeches about the future of Key Club and why they should vote for me. The finale of the race was the annual convention, which was held at the Hollywood Beach Hotel. I had a very large sign made, saying "Gunn For Governor!" and hung it across one wall in the convention hall. I gave what I felt was a good closing campaign speech. John and I sat in our room with some other friends as we awaited the results. I lost and was heartbroken.

As we took down my sign, John quipped, "Here's to 'Almost Governor Gunn!'"

"Thanks, campaign manager!" I replied.

In Florida, my religious life never rose to the intensity I knew in Illinois. None of the churches I tried seemed to have the zeal I experienced up north. Although I enjoyed playing the organ at the Community Church in Jensen

Beach, which insured I would attend church regularly, none of the ministers I met could keep up with the intellectual (never mind emotional and sexual) challenges I was facing. I do, however, remember Rev. Foster. He was a boring preacher, but he genuinely cared about us teenagers. He introduced us to the game, "spin the bottle." In one of our youth meetings, he told the story of a man who took in a baby tiger cub and fed it as it got bigger until one day it turned on him and mauled him to death. He asked what we thought the point was, and no one seemed to know so I said, "be careful what you feed and encourage, because it can turn on you." It's my first memory of the use of metaphor to make a moral point.

Around this time, I was invited to the house of one of my teachers whom I respected, Mrs. Sims, where I was introduced to numerous pamphlets published by the John Birch Society. The thinking of the group was outlined to me and I responded rather non-commitally. I had never before heard of the John Birch Society, but I knew something felt a bit off about it. Only later, when I understood politics more, did I wonder how Mrs. Sims, who had gone to Columbia Teachers' College, could wind up in the John Birch Society. Perhaps it was a reaction to the liberalism she found there. In Stuart, Florida at the time, Columbia was assumed to be a "commie pinko" school. It was in Mrs. Sims' house that I discovered something about people and religion and beliefs.... sometimes people can get very prickly over it all.

After that, I carried my parents' skepticism farther than they probably intended. Thinking of becoming either a minister or a doctor, I read inspiring novels of the time about the lives of doctors and priests, such as *The Edge of* Sadness, by Edwin O'Connor, *The Citadel* by A.J. Cronin. It was not just the change in churches or geography; I, too, was changing as I began to think critically about Christianity. While still seeking the God who was rapidly disappearing from view, I wrote a favorable book review for our school paper of Bertrand Russell's *Why I Am Not A Christian*.

With other friends in my class, I often went camping in Jonathan Dickenson State Park, twenty miles south of Stuart. After my piece on Bertrand Russell's book, I recall a long argument one night around the campfire with a classmate, Grant Luckhardt, on the nature of God, truth and the universe. We talked into the wee hours, while our other mates went to sleep, having gotten bored by our intellectual concerns.

While I wasn't sure what was pushing Grant's strong feelings, I was just starting to get my first hints that maybe I was trying to make sense of religion in the face of things that weren't fair. If there was an all-loving, all-powerful God, how would he permit my brother's condition? Yet, if there was no god, did that mean my conversion experience in Illinois was unreal?

Despite my confusion about religion and God, I had become extremely popular: a member of almost every club and organization, 10th grade class president, Key Club Lieutenant Governor, Boys State Supreme Court Justice, Student Council president. I was trying very hard to live up to society's expectations....more than that, I had my eyes set on living a notch or two above where I felt my family was. I wanted to be somebody.

Harl Son, Susan's father, had told me, when I said I thought I wanted to be either a doctor or a minister, "Well, Bobby, if you're going to be a preacher, you'd better learn something about sin, so you know what you're preaching about." I figured that meant drinking, along with knowing where to put gas in a lawnmower.

Judge Crary, with whom I'd flown to Tallahassee for Boys' State, advised me to "Work hard, and play hard." That, also, I figured, meant drinking and partying. In the back of my mind, drinking was a sign of being down to earth and real. It was the way to insure that you weren't a hypocrite. It certainly seemed to be what it took to be a man.

Without really thinking about it, Ricky Smith, Grant Luckhart, Tommy Jones, Howie Begle, David Slauter, John Goldner and I constituted the leadership elite of the school. One of the ways we expressed our higher sense of social status was by our choices of what to drink and smoke: we drank Lowenbrau, not Schlitz; Chivas Regal, not Jim Beam. And we smoked Upmann cigars rather than White Owls. Ricky, who became our Senior Class president, had a family place a few miles outside of town that no one lived in, called the Revestment. It was used just for family entertainment. It had tables and sofas enough to accommodate our group. One of us would get wine, beer or liquor with a false ID, then we'd play poker and swim naked in the pool into the wee hours. Our parents knew we were there and doubtless knew that we were drinking, yet they left us alone, probably content that we weren't out driving after drinking.

One night after a lot of drinking, playing cards then horsing around in the pool, when everyone else had gone to bed on one or another of the sofas, David Slauter and I shared a sofa together. We had hard-ons from the pool, but had dried and put our jockey shorts on. We just cuddled and went to sleep.

On Sundays, I would get up early and arrive at the church just in time for the pre-service choir practice. In wintertime, when the influx of northerners forced us to have two services, I would usually get very sleepy during the sermons' second hearing. If I nodded off, my mother would poke me from behind to wake me up. The capacity to drink all night and show up at church on Sunday seemed a good formula for being a man and not being a hypocrite at the same time.

Music became the container for my religious life. At sixteen I gave my own recital, playing Bach's *Toccata and Fugue in D minor*, the *St. Anne's Prelude and Fugue*, Mendelssohn's Organ Sonata No. 6, Widor's *Toccata* and Mulet's *Carillon Sortie*. Soon I was evening organist for a church in West Palm Beach, and had one night of fame on Palm Beach television playing the *Toccata and Fugue in D minor* on an Allen organ. My teacher wanted me to go to his alma mater, Indiana University, to study organ.

I loved to play the organ, but I knew that the questions of God, faith, and the purpose of life were stronger, deeper drives within me than my love of music. Furthermore, when it came to choosing a potential career, for my father, for me to have chosen a career in music would have been to declare myself as "one of them"—a fairy. That prospect terrified me.

Nevertheless, from the very first year I started playing piano back in Illinois, I had been immediately drawn to J.S. Bach's *Minuet in G*. That short piece, simple as it was, contained the elemental structure of Bach's genius. When I discovered Bach on the organ, the whole world of music expanded for me. I was enthralled by Bach's fugues. As I studied his organ music, I came across the recordings of Albert Schweitzer and ordered his two-volume work on Bach. Then I realized that I had a philosophical companion in Schweitzer as well, and read his *Philosophy of Civilization* and his *Out of My Life and Thought*. He was a living example of someone who was a serious musician, theologian, philosopher and doctor. It was possible to actually live out every one of my dreams! I had found another hero. I, too, could be an organist, theologian, philosopher and doctor!

It was 1960, and in both Illinois and Florida, males who were seriously involved in music were assumed to be "homos" until proved otherwise. So my super-activity in high school, including working 14-20 hours a week at the local Winn Dixie as a bagboy, were part of my diversion technique, trying to prove to everyone I was just a regular guy, meaning, not-queer.

On one of the rare evenings when my dad was home in time for supper, when we finished, as he got up from the table, instead of going in to watch TV, he asked in a low voice for me to join him in the living room. Mom cleared the table and started washing dishes. He sat down in his recliner, pulled out a cigarette and I sat on our sofa across from him.

He lit his cigarette, took a long puff on it, let it out. Clearly, something was up.

Continuing in his near-whisper, he asked, "Have you ever been—uh—er—propositioned by Gus the barber?—you know, sexually?"

My father never stammered. He might hesitate while he was thinking, but he was clearly uncomfortable broaching this subject.

In fact, Gus had invited me on a fishing trip in his boat, along with a friend of mine, Billy Roberts. Billy was the real reason I accepted Gus's invitation; Billy and I had enjoyed so many afternoons on the beach and I was turned on by him. But when Billy cancelled, I went ahead, being too polite to make it obvious that I didn't want to be with Gus by himself. I don't know if I had even consciously considered that Gus might try something sexual. He was in my mind an old man --at least 40-- chubby and balding; I had no attraction to him whatsoever. After fishing for awhile with no luck, we landed for a picnic lunch on a small beach near the inlet.

It started with the blanket, strewn out for the iced tea and sandwiches. Then he packed the leftover items back in the carrier and suggested we lie down for a bit of a nap. Then slowly I realized he had shifted close behind me and pulled me into him. He rubbed against me. I was terrified. I froze. Where could I run on this deserted patch of an island at the south end of the St. Lucie inlet with its treacherous currents? Without penetrating me, he came on my back. I remember getting back in the boat under the very hot sun. I avoided looking at him. He anchored and suggested fishing again.

"No," I said, still avoiding his eyes, looking out for other boats. They were far away.

"Want some orange juice?" he asked, pulling out a carton from the cooler. I felt like throwing up. I just shook my head. The boat rocked back and forth with the rolling waves from the inlet.

"I'm not feeling good," I finally said. "Can we go home?"

"Sure," he said, and pulled in his line and weighed anchor.

I lied to my father and said no, Gus had never come on to me (although he had come on me, I carefully thought to myself). I did not want to suffer Dad's disappointment or kindle his outrage. He said he asked because Jimmy Bolling, a classmate of mine, had complained that Gus made sexual advances to him, and several men had joined Mr. Bolling and had "escorted Gus out of town." Based on other stories I had been told, I am sure Gus's escort was bloody. My inner door slammed tighter than ever.

Some months later, one sunny Sunday afternoon when I was sixteen and my parents were gone, I invited David over to the house, where we moved from the living room to my bedroom.

Like one who gets lost and doesn't remember how he got there, I don't remember how we managed to get from the living room to the bedroom. At some point, we began wrestling, which was odd, since neither of us ever had before. And soon, perhaps blaming the heat of the Florida afternoon, we removed our shirts. Mostly, I remember the laughter, the struggle, the falling on top of and all over each other on the bed, the glorious magic of skin on skin, jeans on jeans, skin on jeans and hardness attesting to passion. But I also recall that when David tried to kiss me. I turned my head. A kiss would have suggested this was real, not just a manifestation of a fantasy.

Then there was a knock at the front door. Barefoot, shirtless and panting, David and I both went to the door. It was Reid, another friend of mine. I invited him in, but I could tell by the way he looked at us that somehow he sensed something had been going on, and he said no, quickly, and left.

After that, David and I went back to the bedroom, where we lay back down, but the energy had changed with Reid's appearance. It seemed we'd stopped before enough would mean too much, before satisfaction would lead to dissatisfaction, before we would have been forced to open our eyes. Suddenly David stood up, put on his shirt, then we left the bedroom and walked to the front door.

"I think we have a problem," David said.

"What problem?" I asked.

David didn't answer, just opened the door and left. Then, as I stood by the door and watched him walking away, I realized that I felt two things simultaneously. On the one hand, I really liked David. I was attracted to him and also enjoyed his company. How could there be anything wrong in that? So there was no problem. On the other hand, I felt really ashamed when Reid happened by and saw us, and so I wanted to erase it all, make it go away. So there was a problem.

The experience of shame was not new to me. My family was what I would call lower middle class. Not poor, but always having difficulty making ends meet. As soon as I started working after school, my parents urged me to save some of what I earned. They had no savings, and I followed their example rather than their advice. Except for John Goldner, I was the only one of my friends who worked. Despite my disastrous experience when I bought the new table and chair for the kitchen, I still wished our home looked nicer.

I remember distinctly, as I began thinking of college and my future, that my own aspirations really boiled down to the notion that I wanted to be somebody.

The problem, however, with wanting to be "somebody" was the implicit assumption that I was not "somebody" already. Wanting to be "somebody" springs from the pain of believing you're not; by contrast, a healthier attitude would be simply to want to be the best one can be. The first comes from deprivation and feeling "not good enough." The second comes from a trust in oneself and in the process of one's own unfolding. But how could I trust myself since my spontaneous desires were declared sinful by my church and sick by my society, despite the fact that what I had experienced in my conversion was a complete unconditional acceptance of who I was by God.

The sources of anti-gay prejudice in the Bible are clear: they come from a literal and ahistorical reading of a few specific texts in the Hebrew and Christian Bibles (Leviticus 18:22; 20:13; Romans 1:26; I Corinthians 6:9-10; I Timothy 1:9-10). In my growing up years, along with most Christians, I understood these verses as literal condemnations of all same sex relations. There was no other perspective available that I knew of. Contemporary Biblical scholarship, and anthropological and ethical analysis has demonstrated that whatever the circumstances were from which such comments were drawn, they reflected the values of the cultures of their respective periods and the extremely limited understanding of human behavior available over 2-5 millenia ago.

In 1960, the church, whose mandate is the saving of souls, was united with society in condemning mine. If God is the one you turn to when everyone else lets you down, what do you do when you're told that, on this issue, not even God is there for you? What kind of spirituality can you have when your core self is buried in shame? The very tools by which I'd learned to live in the world and survive in such a situation, such as denial or repression, were barriers, I feared, to the experience of grace, because my heart, from which all feelings flow, was already condemned for its longings.

I remember high school graduation—I was one of the class speakers. Caps and gowns and diplomas scattered in front of me, I was perhaps one of the most popular and liked members of my class, and as great as I felt as I gave my speech on the importance of taking the hard, not the easy, path in life, based on a poem by Edgar Guest, I felt terribly empty inside. I couldn't wait to get through the celebrations with the class to head to my friend, Ricky's family place, the Revestment, and get royally drunk.

I suppose at the end of high school, I was like a juggler, spinning three things in constant movement in the air. Only instead of juggling balls, I was juggling spirituality, sexuality, and my longing "to be somebody." These forces were present in my college applications. In my college essay I said I wanted a liberal arts education in order to find the meaning and purpose of life. That was the spiritual ball in the air. My application to Ivy League schools was to keep my urge "to be somebody" moving and aloft. As for where or how I would find clarity and peace with my sexuality, I didn't have a clue, but kept that in the air as well, at least in my thoughts.

I applied to Harvard because it was, reputably, #1. I applied to Columbia because it was in the Ivy League as well as in New York. I applied to Florida State as my safety school.

However, before hearing from any colleges, I went with other Floridian Key Club members to Toronto for the International Key Club Convention. En route, we stayed for three days at the Hotel Martinique on 32nd and Broadway in New York City. I happened to read in the *New York Times* that Virgil Fox was giving an organ recital at Riverside Church. I had not heard of Riverside before, but I had certainly heard of Virgil Fox. I went to the concert and was transported into the heavenly realms to hear and see him playing (with the large mirror reflecting back to us his feet moving over the pedals as well as the four manuals). I went up to him afterward and introduced myself, and he was very ingratiating to me, noting that he had previously been organist at Bethesda-by-the-Sea in Palm Beach only forty miles from my high school. I was thoroughly dazzled. New York was indeed the Emerald City for me and, more than I realized, everything was set in motion for me to follow the Yellow Brick Road.

I was turned down by Harvard and waited desperately to hear from Columbia. I asked my father, "Dad, if I get into Columbia, do you think we can manage it?" He put his book down, looked at me, thought for a second, and replied, "I don't really see how we can, unless you get the Stokes scholarship." The Stokes was the largest local scholarship given, an award of $500/year. Columbia's tuition was $2500.

Columbia accepted me the next week.

"Dad, I got accepted to Columbia. Can I go?"

He smiled and said, "I guess we'll just have to find a way."

That's exactly what I wanted to hear: we'll find a way. Actually I had already decided I was going, no matter what he said. I had accepted my acceptance before I knew whether I would get the Stokes. When I did get it, the $500 from Columbia and $500 for cafeteria work scholarship, plus the $500 Stokes scholarship still left $1000, just for tuition. I figured I could earn $500 from my job over the summer, and another $500 by other work in school. I knew my parents had no savings and were always in debt.

So that summer, in addition to working as a bagboy at the local Winn Dixie, I joined my father in delivering newspapers. He woke me at 1:30 in the morning then we'd drive to Stuart to get the papers, roll or stuff them, depending on weather, and toss them onto people's yards.

In June, shortly after my acceptance letter from Columbia, I was invited with my parents to meet another freshman-to-be, Richard Goldman, at the home of the alumnus who had personally interviewed us, Dr. Andre in West Palm Beach.

I washed and polished the new 1960 beige four door Impala that Dad drove as a demonstrator. It was a typical hot spring day. I wore my suit. Dad wore brown slacks and a beige sport coat. My mother carried gloves. As soon as we arrived, we noticed that our host, as well as Richard's father, Dr. Goldman, were dressed in casual sport shirt and slacks.

Dr. Andre suggested we take off our jackets and ties and relax as we followed him to the pool in the back of the house. We removed our jackets and ties, but to relax was impossible. I don't think my parents had ever socialized with doctors before. To my grandparents, doctors were the people whose prescriptions they filled at their drug store. To my father, a doctor was what his parents wanted him to be, which he never became. I shrank inside when Dr. Goldman asked him, "And what do you do, Mr. Gunn?" and my father answered, "I sell Chevrolets."

I felt very ashamed and very "hillbilly" or "country," as my mother might have said, but without skipping a beat, Dr. Andre asked my father a few more questions about selling cars as if it were the most important thing one could do in the world. He then asked if I had brought my bathing suit and I said no. The thought of appearing in a bathing suit amid these people whom I saw as so superior to me was anathema—as impossible as it was for my parents and myself to relax.

The mystique of class as a personal experience continues to puzzle me. I don't recall that my parents talked about that event, nor did I bring up anything of what I felt. I felt shame; I felt "less than." I know my mother was terribly intimidated by people with money or education or both. And yet she is the one who told me stories of her mother having taught her to treat everyone as an equal (specifically as it pertained to race or poverty). I have no memory of the rest of the conversation that afternoon. Dr. Andre and his wife were consummate hosts and knew how to carry a conversation easily when my parents or I dropped the ball. I am sure of this: that whether we said anything or not, my parents and I were very relieved to get back in our car to return to Jensen Beach.

On one level, meeting strangers in a strange context from another part of society raises the question of what to talk about, as well as how to speak. But that should be a neutral, even an interesting question. How does it become an experience of shame with feelings of inferiority?

Part of the answer, I thought, might be language. Perhaps what I hoped words would give me was not only the power to heal my brother, but to save my self from the shame of not knowing what to say in a strange situation.

One summer Sunday in 1961, we had a guest preacher at the Community Church where I still played the organ before I left for Columbia. The guest preacher was Frederic Hudson who was working on his doctorate in a combined program at Union Theological Seminary and Columbia University. He was 30, tall, skinny, and clean-shaven, with pale blue eyes that appeared always to be noticing and feeding his mind. If his eyes hadn't been kind, they would have been intimidating. He spoke from a perspective on the Bible I had never heard before. His sermon portrayed human beings as human and valid in their own right, not just as creatures of God. He made references to society that were critical and at the same time, related to the Bible. After services, when I introduced myself and told him I was headed to Columbia College in the fall, he invited me to meet his wife, Kate, and their three children, Jeff, John and Lisa, who were 8, 6 and 4 at the time. I remember going with them that week and bringing my sister Jeanne, who was 8, to Lion Country Safari. Before they left, Frederic invited me to visit them when I got to New York.

During the same summer, I also got a job as a part-time busboy at the Outrigger Restaurant on Sewall's Point, just south of Jensen Beach. Owned by Ralph Evinrude of Evinrude motors for boats, and Frances Langford, the movie star from the 40's (previously married to Jon Hall), the restaurant looked over the Indian River and specialized in an Americanized version of Oriental food, a novel idea at the time. The cooks were Chinese, from Hong Kong via Cuba, and had come over to the U.S. after Castro came to power in 1959.

One night, I asked these cooks questions about their experiences and the older two were evasive, obviously not wanting to get into the topic, but the third cook, the young and handsome one, Joe, was more open to me and we bantered back and forth as we worked. He was probably only a couple of years older than me, but in the politics of the kitchen, I knew he was very well respected by the other cooks. I felt very close to him and one day when I came to work a bit early I found him in the back staring out across the river. He was already wearing his white work pants and short sleeved shirt, that set off his golden skin. As I said hello and drew closer to him, he put his arm around me and I could see tears in his eyes.

"What's wrong," I asked. I felt my whole body wanting to move into his.

He looked at me with very open brown eyes, trembling thick lips, then out again at the river. "Sometimes I get very homesick," he said, and pulled me closer with his arm.

"For Hong Kong or Cuba?" I asked.

"Hong Kong," he said.

"It must be very hard," I said.

We just stood there, a moment frozen in time. I didn't know what more to say. I didn't know if I had already said the wrong thing. All I knew was that I didn't want this to end.

"Well," he said, wiping his eyes, "we'd better get to work, right?" He took his arm from my shoulder.

Every day after that, I tried to think of something to say to engage him, to connect with him. I dreamed of going places with him--somewhere, anywhere.

On one of my nights off from the Outrigger, I got together with my friend, Grant, to go drinking. Grant had a Porsche 911. He loved race car driving and frequently went to Sebring. His hero in the auto racing world was Sterling Moss.

I picked him up in Stuart and we headed back to Jensen Beach in my father's current demonstrator, a 1960 white Corvair. I wanted to show Grant that the Corvair could corner as well as his Porsche. So as we came into what we called "Dead Man's Curve" (about a 90 degree curve), I was doing about 50 in what was supposed to be a 25 mph zone. As I made for the turn, the rear end started to fishtail and I countered it by turning into it. Suddenly a car appeared from the other lane, however, headed right into us, so I gunned it back into my own lane. The fishtail spun us completely around and the car completely rolled over in an instant and we landed right side up. The front window was shattered. The roof nearly touched my head.

"Are you okay?" I asked, my whole body shaking.

"Yeah, are you?" Grant answered. I was so relieved that he was alive and evidently not hurt.

"Yeah, I think so. But my shoulder really hurts."

He was able to open his door and crawled out.

I managed to get out, but the pain in my shoulder was really sharp. Looking at the car lying there—even in the dark it looked like we should have been killed: the roof was squashed; the whole body was creased; glass was everywhere.

The people from the other car were rushing over to us asking us how we were. They were teenagers also, barely older than Grant and me. Amid reassurances and questions, they took us to the Stuart Hotel coffee shop, where I called my Dad who took us to the hospital. Grant really was okay; I tore ligaments in my shoulder and my arm was put in a sling. Six weeks, the doctor said. Dad dropped Grant off and drove us home.

By the time we got there, our local Deputy Sheriff, Morgan Sprott, was there waiting. He was about 5'11", my dad's age. He had a pot belly and had on his green and grey uniform, and his belt, complete with handcuffs and gun. He made our kitchen look small. Mom had already poured him coffee. The Sprotts and my parents were social friends. I babysat their children sometimes.

We sat around the kitchen table while I told my story.

"Bobby, were you boys drinking?" he asked.

"No sir," I replied. I didn't say we were on our way to the liquor store. I also left out the part about trying to show Grant that the Corvair could equal the Porsche's cornering ability; obviously, it couldn't.

Morgan just said, "You know, Bobby, those Corvairs are just not made for cornering. The rear end engine throws the balance off completely."

"Yessir. I sure know that now," I said, sheepishly.

He wrote up the accident report but didn't give me a ticket. "You just watch yourself, okay? Don't do this again."

"Yessir, I won't," I said.

With torn ligaments in my shoulder and my shoulder in a sling, I was in no shape to lift the heavy trays of dishes at the Outrigger. My busboy career was over. So much for making money for college, I thought.

But, beyond the practical concern for not making any more money at the Outrigger, I was troubled that I would have no more excuse to see Joe. And that was something about which my dad would definitely not be so understanding.

I went in the next day and told the maitre d'i, Paul Stuart, what had happened. My arm in a sling was convincing. I looked for Joe, but he hadn't come to work yet.

At the end of the week, when I came to pick up my last paycheck, I made sure to time it when Joe would be there. I told him what had happened.

To this day I remember the sparkle of his eyes and his big smile with perfect shiny white teeth. Perfectly winsome. "But you're okay, right? You're gonna be okay?"

"Yeah, it's just going to take some time."

"And then it's off to New York for you, right?"

"Yeah, near the end of August."

"So give me your phone number and address," he said.

"Sure," I said. I explained that the only phone would be a hall phone shared by everyone on the same floor, but I gave it to him.

"I'll be coming to New York in the Fall," he said, "and I will take you to a real Chinese restaurant."

I couldn't wait. I even cried as I left the restaurant, frustrated that I didn't know how to say more, how to connect more, how to tell him how I really felt about him. In 1961 I had no idea how same-sex romance might be developed and sustained in real life, nor did I realize I was in love more deeply and truly than ever before and I was moving 1200 miles away.

When my parents and my sister Jeanne put me on the train for my first trip to college, my mother cried and I had a lump in my throat. Still, I was happy to be putting some distance between us. Our closeness was sometimes too much.

Dick Joyner came up as it was time to board and I introduced him to my family. Dick had taken over as organist/choir director of the Methodist Church in Stuart when Terry Austin left. He was riding the train with me to New York where he was entering the Master of Sacred Music program at Union Theological Seminary, across Broadway from Columbia.

After we took our seats and the train pulled out of the station, I went into the lavatory and completely broke into tears. I thought of Mother, Dad and Jeanne standing there. And I thought of my brother Bill who I wouldn't see now for months and cried some more. Would Mom see him as often without me to help drive? How would Jeanne do in school? I dried my tears, pulled myself together and returned to the seat next to Dick.

When we pulled out of Ft. Pierce, Dick nonchalantly pulled out a paperback and showed it to me. It was *The Sixth Man*. The front cover declared under the large title, "One of Every Six Men in America is Homosexual." He asked if I had seen it, and I said "no." I had in fact seen it at the magazine and smoke shop in Stuart, but had been too afraid to buy it.

I played coy with him because I had already sensed he was interested in me in "that way" but I did not return the feelings. He was not my type. He was too effeminate. Besides, he was older by four years! He had been my teacher and I wasn't ready to be peers—I wasn't ready to leave the protective status of student and naïve innocent.

I wasn't ready, in sum, to "come out" to him --though I had no words for that yet. I'm sure he sensed that I was "a member of the tribe", though I was not obvious, meaning, I was not effeminate. I had lost weight, played sports, honed some muscle with yard work and track, hadn't been called "sissy" for five years. Maybe it was something I could grow out of, like the books in the school library said, I told myself, although the nagging voice in my head told me this wasn't true.

While I was happy to be going to Columbia, now representing my confidence and ambition, I nevertheless retained the sting of not having been accepted to Harvard. Harvard represented my shadow side, the part of me that never felt good enough, smart enough, or rich enough. Therefore, I took it personally when, in Freshman Orientation, we were told, "Welcome, Harvard rejects!"

During Freshman Orientation Week, a group of guys from the Columbia Glee Club, called "Notes and Keys," performed and invited us to join the Club. At that time, the College, like all the Ivies, was all male. I had enjoyed singing since childhood, and had often been asked to sing solos in churches, but had never been part of a choir. The Notes and Keys seemed to have fun, were funny and very good, so I decided to give it a try. I remember my audition with Oats Harvey, the director, and Jerry Weale, the assistant director, at the piano. I kept singing "My Bonny Lies Over the Ocean" at increasingly higher pitches until they decided I could not only carry a tune, but was a first tenor.

The entire Glee Club went to Camp Columbia in Connecticut for a few days to learn the basic repertoire and new songs. In between rehearsals, we swam in a lake and played softball. The freshmen rehearsed separately for the first two days and I volunteered to be the piano accompanist under Jerry Weale. Barry Wood, already an alumnus of the college, studying to be a doctor, alternately played piano and directed Notes and Keys.

Saturday afternoon of the weekend, Barry invited me join him and Jerry for a drink before dinner. "How sophisticated!" I thought to myself, pleased to be invited to an inner circle of the Glee Club's leading pianists/directors. They had amply demonstrated they were both very smart and very gifted musicians.

Before we finished our second round of scotches, Barry somehow led the conversation around to homosexuality without using the word. It was not an implied invitation or suggestion; it was simply "there" as a fact in the room and for the first time ever, I had a slight hint of a breeze of the freedom to talk matter-of-factly about what was buried so deep in shame within me.

I felt excited at such freedom, but also nervous. "Where was this leading?" I wondered. Both of them were somewhat pudgy—a lot pudgy to my mind!—and therefore not physically attractive to me. In addition, Barry wore "Coke bottle glasses" so his eyes looked small and distant when you looked at him.

It was already apparent to me that they were "that way," though I could not tell you how I knew, for neither of them was particularly effeminate. I had no name for this kind of intuitive knowing, and I certainly never talked about it with anyone. The word "gay" to describe someone who was homosexual had not yet come into parlance, nor, therefore, had its antonym, straight. Until the word "gay" was chosen by homosexual and drag queen activists after Stonewall, people of a distinctly "other" sexuality were given labels, such as "fag" and "queer," that conveyed shame more than they described an objective sexuality.

There was no time for more cocktail invitations from Barry and Jerry that weekend, and nothing for me to worry about. Whenever either of them conducted or played, complete focus was on the music and our singing. I had never sung under such dynamic and exciting leadership.

It was also at Camp Columbia that I met Fred Collignon and, as clearly as I knew that Jerry and Barry were "that way," I knew that Fred was not. Fred was a strong and resonant baritone, also on the pudgy side, so I also wasn't physically attracted to him, but he had an interest in religion, so when we returned to New York from camp, I invited him to join me in eating a "hero" from the deli across Broadway, after one of our rehearsals.

We hit it off immediately, talked for hours, sharing our histories. He was from Baltimore, grew up in the Church of God- Anderson, Indiana-brand, loved singing gospel, said he had also had a conversion experience but decided his true calling was not in ministry but in politics and economics. One of the most important things he said that night was that he had been accepted to Harvard but chose Columbia because of its course in Contemporary Civilization. I felt subtly redeemed by the fact that someone who'd been accepted at Harvard would choose Columbia instead; perhaps there was destiny in my Harvard rejection, I thought to myself. Fred wanted to manifest Max Weber's definition of the Protestant Ethic and bring a Christian perspective to the American political economy. He had already read people I had barely heard of, such as Reinhold Niebuhr and Paul Tillich, and could give a clear, concise synopsis of what they said in ordinary conversation. Fred had a point of view, and a way of connecting the dots, that was unique and greater than any sources he ever quoted, regardless of whether he was talking about theology, politics, economics or history. It was a capacity to integrate large, complex concepts and apply them to ordinary life. For example, when we had our talks that were very deep and personal, he named this a form of prayer. And I immediately got it: we were sharing with an openness of heart and mind that is of the essence of prayer. In spite of the amazing trust I felt with Fred, however, I was still not ready to talk with him about my sexuality. What was I looking for, I wondered—men who were open about the world of my secret longings, like Barry and Jerry, or men who I could connect to intellectually and spiritually, like Fred? And then there remained the physical component—could a combo of these attributes be found in a trim and fit body? But the very thought of actively looking for such a man was enough to make me dizzy. New York was a long way from Florida, but I still needed to get my bearings.

After joining the Glee Club, I began pledging at Sigma Chi fraternity. Robert Goldman, from West Palm Beach, signed up also. Among the various fraternities, Sigma Chi had a reputation for people who took their studies seriously, were involved in school activities, sports and government, but who wanted to have a good time socially—my father's concept of the well-rounded individual.

The reputation was generally well deserved; there were many fine men there, but I still wondered whether to join. I wrote my father to ask his advice. He urged me to join to balance out my academic life. I pledged, but had such ambivalence that I didn't immediately become a full member. I would go to parties and girls would come over from other schools and I would feel not so much shy as disinterested.

I was still working my persona, and had some vague idea that being a Sigma Chi would keep me normal, but my true fraternity was the Glee Club.

I lived that first year in 401 Hartley Hall, a room with bunk beds, a sink and a window looking out onto the Columbia quad. My roommate, Steve Bravy, was a senior; our being together was some quirk of bureaucratic fate, since roommates were usually of the same class year. He had been born in Israel, but moved as a child with his parents to Queens. Steve was one of the brightest people I had ever met and extremely well read beyond his own primary interest, which was mathematics. He was also very kind and considerate.

He was equally dedicated to being both an atheist and a Jew. Like many Jews I was beginning to meet, he could not believe in a God after the holocaust. The reality of the holocaust for him was as vivid and contemporary as my conversion experience was for me. Through many discussions with him, and other stories I heard, and photographs of people at Auschwitz and Dachau I saw, I was beginning to feel the depth and breadth of anti-Semitism and the horror of the holocaust. I was also learning about this from another member of the Glee Club, Bill Wertheim. I learned about the Vatican's collusion with Hitler, and the United States' reluctance to respond to reports of mass executions. I had no answer for Steve or Bill about how God could allow the extermination of six million Jews. It was parallel to my own internal argument with God regarding my brother Bill, but carried now to the level of the entire human race.

At the same time, in Contemporary Civilization, I was becoming acquainted with the writings of all the major philosophers, political, economic and moral thinkers of western culture, and it was becoming clear that the traditional arguments for God were to a large degree tautological: valid only if one assumes a need for a beginning, for a being that preceded finite beings.

My entire conception of the universe as I had assumed back in Florida, was beginning to seem increasingly arbitrary, or perhaps filled with assumptions that were an escape from reality more than an entry into it. I began to doubt the faith I had first learned in southern Illinois and just begun to wrestle with in Florida in high school. But in high school I'd only scratched the surface. In New York, I began to see that the assumed necessity for a Prime Mover was tautological: it was no more self-evident that there had to be a creator in the beginning than that there was none. Also, my roommate's views moved me: how, indeed, could there be a God who allowed 6 million people to be murdered?

In addition, as I learned more about the history of the United States, my image of America began to crumble as I faced the underbelly of American patriotism, the history of white power, the subjection of people of color, including women and the exploitation of those without power by those with power.

In just a few months away from home, on my own for the first time in my life, in New York, I was beginning to open my eyes and see that much of what I had assumed was normal --that everyone believed in some kind of God, or that all boys were only attracted to girls, or that America was always right and we should "love it or leave it," was questionable. On the deepest level of my self, I was starting to find a link between my questioning my faith, ideas about patriotism, and my internal struggles about my sexuality. All was linked by a limited notion of normalcy that still was sold and bought in the South, but wasn't entirely bought here in the North.

I got a call one evening from someone I had never heard of named Charlie Pass. He was a student at Union Theological Seminary across Broadway from Columbia and was working in the chaplain's office. He was trying to meet Freshmen who'd checked "Christian" on their registration form, and he wanted to tell me about the programs they had at Earl Hall, Columbia's religion center. He was a very friendly fellow, with something of a rough edge. He led a group studying Tillich's *Dynamics of Faith*, and wanted to know if I'd join them.

I knew that Tillich, a German pastor and theologian, had been so profoundly horrified by the evil of the Third Reich and the holocaust in his own country that he was driven to construct an entirely new theology, but my knowledge of his work was limited. After my phone call from Charlie, I joined his group where I learned that Tilich's theology was based on understanding God as the "ground of being," rather than an object just the other side of infinity. His views, which redefined the meaning of faith, spoke to me directly and deeply. For Tillich, faith was not about a belief so much as a state of mind, a matter of being "ultimately concerned."

My spiritual wrestling continued after most arguments for and against God as we read philosophers and theologians in Contemporary Civilization had been exhausted. I felt that intellectually, the existence of God could be argued indefinitely both for and against; but that argument never reached what I experienced inside as restlessness and turmoil. I resonated with the experience Tillich described as the "the shaking of the foundations." I completely identified with the state of mind he talked about as being ultimately concerned. Whatever one's ultimate concern was, was faith. Religion was the organization of people around that ultimate concern.

By these definitions, the meaning of both religion and faith could even be broadened to encompass what had previously been considered utterly secular. As Charlie put it in one of the group discussions, "The American Dream, for example, could be construed as a religion, complete with upward mobility as an ultimate concern, and the rituals of work and socialization as liturgies. Looked at this way, a society and the church itself could be scrutinized for how fully their ultimate concerns were truly ultimate. Only God could satisfy the criteria for ultimacy. Furthermore, for Tillich, faith was distinguished from knowledge by the fact that it could not be proved, and that doubt was thus an inherent aspect of faith. This idea, that doubt was an essential aspect of faith, was music to my ears.

Apart from thoroughly enjoying Charlie's group and all I learned there about Tillich's views, the funniest thing I remember about Charlie was that in our first phone conversation he had used the word "shit." I was very interested in anybody who could use the words God and shit in the same paragraph without a blink or an apology. It suggested the possibility of overcoming the hypocrisy my parents were worried about and the fundamentalist dualism that was tearing me in two.

As I struggled in silence over the conflict between my unacceptable desires and my spiritual yearnings, I engaged the mind/ body problem in philosophy in hopes of a resolution. Much Christian theology and Biblical interpretation disdained the body in order to elevate and develop the spiritual. Monks sometimes flagellated themselves and according to the historian Eusebius, third century theologian Origen castrated himself, the better to follow Jesus' instruction: "if thine eye offend thee, pluck it out, lest thy whole body be thrown into hell." I didn't think castration would solve my problem.. This dichotomy between the carnal and the spiritual in religion was paralleled in philosophy by the mind/ body problem.

As I continued my studies at Columbia, I returned to reading Plato, who my friend, Grant Luckhardt (the one who shared the Corvair crash with me in Florida) first introduced me to. In going back to Plato, I found the entire mind/ body issue derived from Plato's view that the body was transient and subject to decay, whereas the mind produced ideas and forms that could be eternal.

Meanwhile, I was also studying behavioral psychology, which tried to reduce all animal and human behavior to multiple levels of conditioned response. There was no such thing as mind or soul; there was only the physiological body and brain, which was conditioned to behave as it does by external positive or negative stimuli. It was a direct attack on the notion of the human soul. According to this view, thoughts and feelings had no objective reality. But if that were so,

I wondered, why are my feelings and desires so compelling, driving me beyond my conscious intentions into shame, guilt and self-hate?

Like many sensitive freshmen of a curious bent, I wanted to face the truth about what it meant to be human, to be real. I had an additional personal agenda, which was my determination not to be a hypocrite like my grandfather. In my mind, which did not exist apart from my brain, according to behaviorism, I searched for the source of all I had known and experienced of and about God and sexuality. I wondered if my attraction to people of my own gender was simply a matter of my historical conditioning, and could I be de- or re-conditioned?

I read Gilbert Ryle's *Concept of Mind* with enthusiasm because he rejected the dualism of both Platonic and Cartesian thought and said that dualism only arises when one separates the functions of the body and mind as distinct. They should not be separated, he urged, and developed an understanding of higher levels of consciousness not reducible to behaviorism's stimulus-response paradigm. What this meant for me was that feelings were still real, thoughts were real, and that there were higher and more complex categories and systems of human consciousness that were not reducible to the body, but not separate from it. I felt it somewhat confirmed my sexuality by this: I was insisting that my body receive consideration in my effort at integrating and resolving my inner conflict.

Another helper in my quest to be at peace in my own skin, complete with my theological doubts and sexuality issues, appeared that first year in my teacher, Mr. Stern. This professor, who was quite effeminate, suggested that Socrates' interest in young men was more carnal than the Jowett translation indicated. The translators of Plato had in essence de-sexualized him and turned him into an ethereal teacher of the ethereal realm of Ideas and Forms. In essence, Jowett had, wittingly or not, turned Plato into a reflection of Christian thought complete with Victorian ideas. Mr. Stern was the only teacher I had who invited our class to his apartment for a beer. It was a refreshing gesture in an academic atmosphere that seemed to leave no room for the personal, not even the body. When, at the end of the semester, we accepted Mr. Stern's invitation, I found myself asking the questions that had never quite fit into our class discussion: was homosexuality really acceptable in ancient Greece? If Socrates was really gay, why did he marry? Did he and Alcibiades ever really get it on? The initial silence with which my questions were met made we wish I'd never asked, but then I suddenly realized that no, the silence is because they, too, cared about the answers. I am not alone. All semester I felt I was, and now I didn't.

That still didn't give me the courage to talk to the young man with the deep brown eyes and blue jeans I'd had my eye on all semester. I went back to the dorm and, Steve not being there, I decided to relieve my frustration by myself. Just as I was getting close, a voice at the door said, "Can I come in?" and before I could answer, Steve's friend Carl opened the door, saw what I was doing and shouted out, "You know you should really lock the door if you don't want anyone coming in!" and slammed it shut. I was overcome with shame, totally lost interest in my fantasy and wanted to scream.

The inner conflict I felt drove me to my knees. Getting on my knees to pray had always carried a seriousness that went beyond any words I could say. It had always meant asking for help, most especially when I didn't know what kind of help I needed. I remember getting down on my knees in my dorm room, door now carefully locked, elbows on my bunk bed, hands clasped together, head bowed.

"Lord, make me a man," I prayed. I didn't quite know what I meant by that: it wasn't that I thought I was a woman or effeminate, nor was it a petition to turn my sexual feelings into total heterosexuality. In fact, I never asked God to make me entirely straight. Without articulating it even to myself, it seemed that my attraction to people of my own gender was an intrinsic part of me that I could no more get rid of than I could stop liking peanut butter and jelly. I think I was asking for the power to be whoever I was with integrity, with courage and without shame.

One night I went out for dinner with Jay Clark, a friend from high school who was going to New York University. After dinner we went to Times Square for a movie. At some point I realized that the stranger who had just sat down on my right (Jay was on my left) was fondling me underneath a raincoat he had subtly shifted over my lap. I was shocked; didn't know what to do or say, but didn't really want him to stop. I looked at him out of the corner of my eye. He was a young Filipino. The movie came to an end soon after and I left abruptly with Jay.

Another weekend Grant came up from St. John's in Annapolis and met Jay and me. We decided to get some vodka even though none of was yet eighteen, the legal drinking age in New York at the time. I remember walking into a small liquor store in Grand Central Station and getting a pint of Smirnoff's. Still nervous from the purchase, I tried to subtly slip the paper bag of the pint into the inner pocket of my raincoat. Nonchalantly, I placed it where the fold seemed to be, only to have it slide right through onto the marble floor of Grand Central Station, crashing into hundreds of vodka-soaked pieces. We continued walking without skipping a beat or looking back until we got out of the main terminal, at which point we totally broke into laughter and an argument over whose crazy idea it was in the first place.

One day in early November, to my joy and surprise, Joe Miu called and invited me to dinner in Chinatown. I dressed up and met him in a Chinese restaurant. "This is real Chinese food," he said with relish. I don't remember what else was said. I had no idea how to bridge the gap between our cultures nor did he. But the biggest gap was that we could not talk about what we felt for each other, could not even acknowledge that we had "special feelings."

In December I received a small Christmas card from him, signed, "Love, Joe". In my own narrow-mindedness and denial, I could not take in the possibility that he meant what he said. I wrote it off as a Chinese cultural thing, a sign that he did not know that we only use the word "love" to indicate a very special, close, perhaps romantic relationship. I could not acknowledge that that was exactly what it was: his expression of his close feelings for me. It's not that he was confused about our culture, but that because of my culture I was in denial about his feelings and mine as well. When I went home for Christmas, I stopped by the Outrigger, only to be told that he was no longer there. They said he had moved to New York. Back in New York, I looked Joseph Miu up in the phonebook. Over twenty Joseph Miu's. One was in bold: **Joseph Miu Restaurant**. I called in fear and trembling and asked for Joseph Miu. A voice came on I did not recognize. I asked if there was a Joseph Miu there who had worked in Jensen Beach. The man said no. I didn't know what else to do to find him.

Frequently I went to the Cathedral of St. John the Divine for the service of Holy Eucharist. I loved the chanting responses, the kneeling and standing.

I found a deep consolation in the Episcopal liturgy and the Book of Common Prayer. It had a power through song and symbols that still reached me amid my growing doubts. Had I been freer from my own fundamentalist past or less bound by class consciousness, I probably would have joined the Episcopal Church.

Nevertheless, the contradictions of faith seemed epitomized for me by the presence of the multi-million dollar unfinished Cathedral overlooking the rat-infested tenements of Harlem, which I learned about from Frederic Hudson who lived there. How could people give so much to build a big temple while right in front of their faces was a poverty and a suffering that that money could have been given to ameliorate? I began to see the Church not just as the holder of questionable theologies, but as capable of great complicity in evil. However, in those years I could not recognize conflict between my view of the lavish cathedral next to Harlem and my own longings to be affluent and famous.

Meanwhile, I bought my first Brooks Brothers suit, a light tan summer weight for $140, adding in, of course, a couple of white (the only color offered) button down shirts and rep ties. I also went to Peterson's Pipe and Tobacco shop right across 42nd Street from Grand Central, where I was treated with the same aristocratic assumption by the staff as I had been at Brooks, and returned regularly to get my supply of Peterson's No. 7 pipe tobacco, as well as to survey the exquisite and expensive pipes that were offered. Such purchases absorbed more than I allocated for "entertainment" or "clothing", and had I not been working in the school cafeteria, I would doubtless have gone hungry more often. Barely a year out of the family house, without realizing it, I was already repeating a pattern I had learned from my father—of spending more than I had.

Frederic and Kate Hudson, with their children, Jeff, JohnJohn and Lisa, lived in a high-rise subsidized housing project on Amsterdam and 123rd Street. They were one of the few white families there. Frederic became a real mentor for me: he urged me to call myself Bob rather than Bobby, and to call my mother Mom and my father Dad, rather than Mother and Daddy. Also, I sometimes babysat Frederic's children, told them bedtime stories and generally found an oasis in their apartment, a family when I'd left my own family behind.

One evening, Frederic showed me Bonhoeffer's *The Cost of Discipleship*. Bonhoeffer had been a Christian pastor in a German Concentration Camp during World War II. Frederic turned to the poem on the first page and gave it to me to read. Certain of his lines struck home hard :

Who Am I?
Am I...all that which other men tell of?
Or am I only what I myself know of myself?
Restless and longing and sick, like a bird in a cage...
Powerlessly trembling for friends at an infinite distance,
Weary and empty at praying, at thinking, at making,
Faint, and ready to say farewell to it all?
Who am I? This or the other?
Am I one person today and tomorrow another?
Am I both at once? A hypocrite before others,
And before myself a contemptibly woebegone weakling?
Or is something within me still like a beaten army,
Fleeing in disorder from victory already achieved?
Who am I? They mock me, these lonely questions of mine.
Whoever I am, Thou knowest, O God, I am Thine!

I couldn't keep back the tears. I, too, felt a severe conflict between what others knew of me and what I knew of myself; I, too, trembled for friends at an infinite distance with my sexual longings; I, too, felt "empty at praying," "faint and ready to say farewell to it all." I, too, saw my turmoil in the context of my relationship to God, but without the consolation that Bonhoeffer seemed to find, because God was as much a question as my own identity.

There was something else important for me about this story of a Christian pastor in the concentration camps. Not all Christians had been silent. Some had been there simply because they had done the right thing: they'd said "Nein!" to evil. I was hearing more from my Jewish friends and seeing more from photos of the camps, and to know that at least one Christian had been there, had suffered alongside the Jews, the homosexuals and the handicapped offered an empowering identification I was not yet ready to voice. I identified with the Jews because I was a homosexual.

Late one night before a final exam in Contemporary Civilization at the end of freshman year, I returned my Glee Club friend, Fred's, class notes to him. Inside them I had left a note quoting Psalm 14, "The fool has said in his heart, 'there is no God.'" To which I added, "Then he cried." Fred read the dismay on my face before he read the note. "What's wrong?" he asked. "Nothing," I said, and burst into tears. The truth was, I'd been depressed. What began as homesickness turned into a lethargy that made me want to sleep a lot. I had trouble concentrating. I would spend too much time alone, read awhile, then sleep, read some more, then sleep. I felt overwhelmed by the study load, mostly because I had never developed discipline. I smoked my pipes day and night and obsessed over cleaning them; anything to avoid the tension around my inner conflicts that hounded me.

After I stopped crying, Fred suggested we go for a walk and we talked into the wee hours about life and death and God and the universe-- everything except sex. His compassion and caring helped, nevertheless, because even then I didn't acknowledge how deeply linked the vitality of God and the vitality of my own libido were.

What I didn't tell Fred that night was that I felt like killing myself. I even knew how I would do it: I would jump off the George Washington Bridge. But every time I thought about doing it, my mother came to my mind, and, knowing how much I knew she loved me and that I didn't want to hurt her prevented me from making that lonely last walk to the bridge.

I tried to limit my phone calls to my mother, which were done from a pay phone where I had to "reverse the charges." Often I would be crying when I talked to her, and then she would start crying as well. Homesickness is common enough for many during college, but for people of a religious bent, there is an added estrangement as one encounters entire new modes of thinking and thinking about one's faith.

Faith is a world-view, a *weltanschauung*, every bit as important as family, indeed it _is_ family--the home of one's mind. In that sense, I had first left home spiritually when we moved from Illinois to Florida, and the move to Columbia was an intensification of that loss. What had been home to me spiritually in Illinois could never be home again. I could never again believe the literal truth of the Bible, nor assume that any problem could be resolved through optimism or mental belief. There was no going back to that way of understanding. There was, in essence, no home to go back to.

What made my experience so gut-wrenching was that, even if everything the Bible said turned out to be myth, I could not deny the utterly profound conviction I sustained from my conversion experience that I had been met by the unconditional, unshakeable, eternal love of God and that nothing in the empirical world could take that away. So it was not that, "Oh, I see there is no such thing as God, so I'll forget about him/it…" It was more like, okay, so the Bible is full of holes, contradictions, myths and illusions; how, then, do I account for this remaining conviction that I am both a sinner and loved unconditionally, forgiven unconditionally, by God? How could I to put together my powerful personal truth, that my spontaneous erotic interests were more for people of my own gender, with the Christian tradition which condemned such desires as abominations?

If Christianity, as I had been taught it, were true, then the gospel of God's unconditional love was false, because I would be rejected for my homosexuality, in which case I would be forever lost, and life would not be worth living. If, on the other hand, Christianity was not true, then my conversion conviction of God's unconditional love was an illusion, in which case, again, I would be forever lost, and life would not be worth living.

"If you'd spend as much time studying as you do cleaning your pipes, you'd get all A's," Steve remarked one night. He also suggested I see someone at the Columbia Counseling Service, as he had been doing twice a week for three years. I didn't think my depression was that bad (actually, I thought Steve was far more neurotic than I was, *ergo*, I refused to ask for help and suffered on).

I escaped into books—books that were not part of the curriculum. Sartre and Camus put words to the abyss I felt inside. Kierkegaard became my dearest friend, both in his biography and his Journals. Paul Tillich, with his assertion that doubt was of the essence of faith, kept my quest going amid the aridity of linguistic analysis and behavioral psychology. I went to his lectures at Low

Library, and although his German accent was thick and the vocabulary of his metaphysics new to me, I was inspired and given hope by the example of this man whose faith had survived the holocaust and World War II.

I had arrived at Columbia at the end of a golden age of intellectual giants. To hear Moses Hadas read Plato in Greek was to feel transported back to 5th century Athens and the very presence of Socrates. To hear Abraham Heschel speak of the holiness of time was to feel transported into the very heart of God. John Herman Randall was still chair of the philosophy department; Ernst Nagel was still teaching philosophy of science and education after John Dewey. Virgil Fox was still organist at Riverside Church. Reinhold Niebuhr was no longer teaching, but appeared aperiodically to speak out against the Vietnam War. John Knox, Roger Shinn, Cyril Richardson, John Bennett and Paul Lehmann were in their last years of teaching at Union. Leonard Bernstein was still at the helm of the New York Philharmonic and the Metropolitan Opera was still just south of Times Square.

But perhaps my roommate, Steve, was right—I should've pursued counseling in the mist of my depression and I did spend an absurd amount of time with my collection of pipes.

To help with the cost of my fondness for my Peterson pipes, late in the first semester of my freshman year, through Barry, I got a job directing a choir and playing organ at St. Paul's Methodist Church in Inwood, Long Island for $50 a week.

Every Wednesday, I would take the Long Island Railroad out for choir rehearsal, return to school and go out again on Sunday mornings for worship services. The pastor, Dick Monkman, and his wife Margaret, welcomed me into their home for dinner after the service on what became a regular basis. Like the Hudsons, the Monkmans took me into their home and family. I also often babysat their kids, Richard, Jonathan and Elizabeth.

Dick had studied theology at Drew University and at Edinburgh, Scotland. He was tall, handsome, rather soft spoken, and a man of deep compassion. He also had a strong faith commitment and an intellect that left no room for nonsense and pretension. I brought my liberal views to him and he did not flinch. Although one night he called me an intellectual, which I thought was a compliment, until I realized he was pointing to something more important than ideas—the human person.

As my Freshman year drew to a close, although my mother wanted me to come home to Florida for the summer, I got a summer job that paid well ($500 for the summer) at Long Island Lighting Company. I spent the summer reading meters with men for whom this was their life career. They were either Irish or Italian, and they bantered back and forth about baseball and told jokes about women, and they teased me about my Ivy League education.

Meanwhile, I had one of the most disturbing dreams ever that summer. I was reading Erich Fromm's *Art of Loving*, which I felt clarified something about my relationship to my own mother. Fromm's thesis was quite simple: real love means caring for the other person in their own right and for who they are and who they want to be, not for who you want them to be. I felt my mother loved me for her own reasons that had nothing to do with the real me. I think the book prompted the dream: I was stabbing my mother in the chest. It was so vivid and real, I woke with a start, gasping for breath, having to check my vision to be sure where I was. I was terrified by this image and thought, "Do I really hate my mother?" Violence was rare in my dreams; never had I dreamed of killing someone, least of all, my mother. It did, nonetheless, symbolize my deep need to establish my life apart from her. That much, at least, I could recognize.

Whereas Freshman year had been overwhelming in the readings for Contemporary Civilization and Literature Humanities, Sophomore year became challenging and exciting by the course in "rat psych", an introduction to psychology that involved conducting our own research on rats and operant conditioning. I was not ready to accept that we were just a higher version of rats, totally conditioned by unending sequences of stimulation/response; but I found it utterly enthralling in the questions it raised for human freedom, for education and consciousness. But without having read much of either Jung or Freud, I felt the lack of what might be called a soul or a self in behavioral theory to be a severe and telling limitation.

That same year I was taking organ lessons with Searle Wright at St. Paul's Chapel, Elementary Harmony with Joseph Newman, and a course in philosophy taught by Sidney Morgenbesser, one of the most engaging teachers I encountered. His class was at 8 a.m., and if you went to sleep in his class, as I did, he would call you out and ask if he were boring you.

At first, nearly failing French, my interest in the French Existentialists saved me and sparked a new interest in the language, so I could read Sartre and Camus in the original. Camus put the existential position succinctly: "I refuse to live in a world where innocent children suffer and die." Sartre's description of life as a closed room (*Huis Clos*) from which no one can escape, felt like a true description of the human condition, which he proposed be faced in a combination of hopelessness and courage: "l'homme se fait"/man makes himself. Facing the nothingness of our existence, rather than imagining a God that does not exist, was mature courage; anything less was *mauvaise foi*, bad faith.

In sophomore year, I felt pressure to declare my major, but I was as confused about picking a major as I was about my growing issues with God and sexuality. Uncertainty seemed to abound for me on all fronts, while clarity and concrete direction resisted me.

At first, I was told I should major in English, so I took a course in 17th century English poets. It was a terrific course that opened up for me the tremendous power of poetry, and I loved reading Donne, Vaughan, Herrick, Crashaw and Marvell. The critique of the poems, however, fell quite flat to my mind and I decided poetry, and by extension, English literature, was not my métier, even though I had been told it would be a fine major for Law school, yet another direction suggested to me.

I also thought seriously about majoring in chemistry and going into medicine. I loved philosophy, but everyone said, "what can you do with a philosophy major except teach," and I didn't think I wanted to teach philosophy. So, I discounted philosophy as a possibility, despite the fact that I was accumulating more credits in that field than in any other. Not to mention that it was also the only field in which I made straight A's.

It may seem obvious that someone who wants to discover the meaning and purpose of life would major in philosophy, but I still was riddled with doubts as to what came most naturally to me. Finally, I enrolled as pre-med, though I struggled to get passing grades in chemistry.

I also had considered majoring in music. My private tutorial with Searle Wright on the four manual Aeolian Skinner organ at Columbia's St. Paul's chapel was thrilling; but I was too absorbed in my sexual and religious conflicts to practice well. In Florida, Terry Austin had urged me to go to his Conservatory in Indiana, but I knew I wanted a full liberal arts education. Although music remained vital to me, as I studied music and practiced, I felt constantly drawn back to the basic questions of life: what is it all about? is there a God or not? why is there suffering? does anything ultimately <u>matter</u>? These questions drove me back to philosophy and religion.

Frederic Hudson had introduced me to the East Harlem Protestant Parish (EHPP), a project started by Union Seminary grads several years before by Bill Webber, Archie Hargreaves and Don Benedict. They chose to live in East Harlem, identify with the problems of the neighborhood, become politically and socially active, and live the gospel among the poor by being poor themselves. I got involved in conducting a survey for them and for several weeks knocked on doors and asked for information that would then be used to give rationale for needed political and educational change.

One of the people who had worked there was William Stringfellow. His book, *My People is the Enemy*, expressed both the anguish of the people of Harlem, and the anguish of white people trying to take responsibility for their own history of racism.

There I met Bonnie Waite, a white student who had come to Harlem also through Frederic Hudson, and had taken a year off from University of Wisconsin to volunteer for EHPP. She was bright and I was impressed at her guts in actually living in East Harlem. I dated her for awhile, but wasn't really attracted to her; I just liked her. So when she started making sexual moves, I turned off. As had happened often before, I wanted to want her but didn't.

The experience with EHPP, however, left a lasting impression on my mind, and was the logical solution to the conflict I felt about churches with a lot of money that spent it on themselves, rather than giving it to the poor. If ministers gave their lives to live with the poor, then their actions would match their words. In that sense, East Harlem Protestant Parish was a symbol for me of what faith in action could look like, and in that sense, it was a powerful symbol of hope for the Christian promise.

Despite such positive experiences as working with the East Harlem Protestant Parish, throughout my sophomore year, I was still routinely anxious, depressed, and no closer to coming to terms with my own sexuality or my confusion with God. In the midst of such feelings, certain friends stood out in stark contrast to my own self image.

Steve Johnston, another baritone in the Glee Club, was quite an independent person, always tuning into things and people off the beaten path. He introduced me to the Fulton Fish Market downtown near the Seaport. We got up about 1:30 a.m. and took the subway, arriving in time to watch the various vendors receive and set up their fish that would be sold to restauranteurs and other markets within the hour. The area covered a full city block with fish and other sea creatures of every kind, shape and size imaginable, many still alive and squirming.

I grew close to Steve that year—he was handsome, charismatic, had a rich, deep voice and was always full of different ideas. One night, Steve announced he was going to take time off from school to hitchhike around Europe. He was not wealthy; he simply knew how to live on very little. He asked if I wanted to go with him. The prospect terrified me. I very much wanted to go, but I did not trust myself to manage so much newness. In addition, I was afraid to take time off from school, wondering whether, if I left, I might not be able to come back. Would I lose my scholarship? What about my jobs playing organ and selling souvenirs? On a deeper level, I was afraid that if I left, I might lose my motivation to finish. It was another case of me holding back from what a big part of me really wanted. Two roads diverged in the woods and Steve took the one less travelled by, while I stood frozen at the fork.

After Steve left for Europe, my life in the Glee Club took on more intensity as we planned a tour out west. Although I was born in Illinois and went to high school in Florida, I had never traveled west of the Mississippi since I was a year old. There is a picture of me on my father's shoulders with the Rockies in the background. It was 1944, and he was in the Army before the war ended. So one of the high points of sophomore year for me was our Glee Club National Tour. We traveled by bus or train to colleges and universities in Cleveland, Detroit,

Denver and Manhattan, Kansas. We were treated extremely well everywhere we went. Kansas State (KSU) greeted us with a full band at the train, and made much of our being from "the other Manhattan." By that time I was accompanist for the Club.

The tour consolidated and reinforced the comraderie I had already experienced with the Club. It is not clear to me to what extent my always feeling like an outsider was a product of my unacknowledged sexual attraction to men, or to the experiences of constant relocation in my life up to high school, where I never stayed in one school for more than a year. The Glee Club tour helped me feel a regular part of a group that I really enjoyed.

The delight in both singing and hearing and feeling the sound made by 80 voices is uniquely bonding, transcending differences in personalities and grievances in the creation of a living sound. Of course the college songs themselves attest to this experience. One of this genre, *Gaudeamus Igitur,* goes back to the 13th century:

> Let us rejoice therefore
> While we are young.
> After a pleasant youth
> After a troubling old age
> The earth will have us.
> Our life is brief
> Soon it will end.
> Death comes quickly
> Snatches us cruelly
> No one shall be spared

We ended our tour with our annual Spring Concert at the new Lincoln Center. We sang in what is now known as Avery Fisher Hall. It was exhilarating to be singing in this brand new concert hall, and for me to be playing the piano made me feel proud.

In the summer of 1963, I worked again for LILCO, this time at the power plant in Far Rockaway. I lived with the Monkmans for the summer, continuing to play the organ and direct the choir, and sometimes babysit the kids. The highlight of my work at the power plant was the ride I got each morning on a Honda motorcycle with Frank Rizzo. He was strikingly handsome, with deep set brown eyes, slicked back black hair and a slender body whose waist I was happy to hold onto. However, ever living in restraint, I knew Frank was as straight as they come and so I gave no indication of my feelings for him.

Beyond frustrations on the back of Frank's Honda, the summer was difficult for me because I had no friends my own age or with similar views. I was reading Kierkegaard while most of my fellow workers read the *New York Post*. By contrast, the newspaper I would read during lunch was the *New York Times*. I usually avoided arguing because I knew no one was really open to changing their minds. However, when Medgar Evers, the civil rights lawyer and activist, was assassinated on June 12, 1963, everybody had a very strong opinion about the growing concern with civil rights issues. Tempers flared, and I felt like I was back in Florida, with most of my co-workers expressing a prejudice every bit as powerful as southerners.

By the end of August, when Martin Luther King, Jr. gave his "I have a dream" speech at the March on Washington, the lines were drawn, and there was little to be said. The estrangement I felt among most of my fellow LILCO workers on the civil rights issue only deepened the loneliness I felt.

At the end of the summer, going home to Florida before returning to Columbia, I got into increasingly heated arguments with my parents, family and other adults. I had never realized before how deeply racism was entrenched at home. My parents had taught me non-discrimination, but the civil rights marches and demonstrations evoked anger and fear from them, not understanding. They could not understand the importance of demonstrations and sit-ins. It was all too much chaos and was threatening. This increased the gap I felt between them and me and thereby my own sense of alienation.

After the high of Martin Luther King, Jr.'s speech in Washington, it was all the more horrifying to read in mid-September of the four girls killed in the bombing of the 16th Street Baptist Church in Birmingham, Alabama. Denise McNair was 11; Cynthia Wesley, Addie Mae Collins and Carole Robertson were

14. The Civil Rights Movement was heating up and that was stirring reactions among those who persisted in trying to keep things as they had been.

Back in New York, Fred Collignon and I were roomates in Hartley Hall. I was glad to be away from the views I'd encountered at LILCO and then again back in Florida, but there was an uncertainty in the air, a cloud hovering over America as we all wondered what would happen next and what we should do. More and more frequently, people appeared at the Sun Dial in the middle of the Columbia campus to organize and recruit students to get involved in voter registration drives in the south, where the percentage of Black people registered to vote was way under 50%.

Amid constant discussion about methods and tactics of social change in my junior year, I began what was probably my best course at Columbia, John Herman Randall's History of Philosophy. It was a *tour de force* history of all the major thinkers in western philosophy, similar to the course on Contemporary Civilization, but with greater focus, analysis and elucidation. Randall's two-volume version of the course ran over 1200 pages in small print. His lectures were brilliant, but arduously and boringly delivered. We had to write a ten-fifteen page paper every week on the readings. I was, it appeared, in my element. I got all A's. Fred Collignon, after reading some of them, identified my particular gift as being able to make quite complex ideas appear clear and accessible (I thought he was the master of such an ability).

It was a time of bewilderment, only the more complicated by my own ongoing personal sense of bewilderment with both the world outside of me and the world inside of me.

I took a Directed Private Study with Professor John Taylor and focused on Linguistic Analysis and Logical Positivism. I wanted to explore the connections between the behavioral psychology I had found elegant but wanting, and what seemed to me to be the philosophical and epistemological corollary of linguistic analysis. I remember visiting Taylor in his office. He smoked a pipe and had a large hound lying at his feet. His manner was calm, curious and supportive.

What a life! I thought to myself. A good pipe, an affectionate dog at one's feet, and time to find a bridge between psychology and philosophy. But in that time, it was not so easy to keep the outside world at bay.

On November 22, 1963, I was in my room studying when I heard shouting in the hallway that President Kennedy had been shot. We ran to the tiny dormitory lounge television hoping against hope that he would survive. Time compresses so much in memory: the wait until his death was confirmed; the sight of LBJ getting sworn in on Air Force One; the arrest of Lee Harvey Oswald and then the murder of Oswald by Jack Ruby on television.

I felt a hollow pit in my stomach. It was impossible to concentrate on our studies with all the tension, conflict, and theories—did Oswald act alone or was it a conspiracy of many? Many people talked about the end of Camelot- certainly many of us idealized JFK and Jackie, and mourned the premature loss of the possibilities for inspired greatness in government, however flawed it may already have been in reality.

After JFK's assassination, I found myself thinking of mortality more, and this also somehow led to my thinking of sex more.

The arguments against the soul and against God that I found in logical positivism were attractive to my intellect, but my heart felt abandoned. I added A.J. Ayer, Gilbert Ryle, and Ludwig Wittgenstein to the standard two-year intensive History of Philosophy course. I was struck by the fact that at a certain point in all the Platonic dialogues, when Socrates' searing questions reached an apogee of the limits of human knowing about ultimate reality, Plato leapt to poetic imagery and away from the rigorous logic of language.

With one exception, I talked about my attraction to men with no one. I "disguised" my journal entries of the topic with the letters "hs," never stopping to think that the "h" could equally signify hetero- as well as homo-sexuality, much less questioning how much the code protected my secret from any stranger who might read (upon my death, was my fantasy) what was there. My shame, fear, guilt and torment grew in proportion to my own burgeoning preoccupation.

I dated several women, none of whom interested me. I thought perhaps if more had been available, I would have been less haunted. But I was repelled by the sexual jokes and banter I heard from other men. At the same time, I was still burdened in my mind by how the existence of God seemed tied in with my sexuality. It seemed that if I could get rid of one, I could have the other. But I was unable to abandon either God or my sexual attraction to men.

As far as my studies went, reflecting my own conflicts between a disembodied faith and bodily desires that society still declared sick and sinful, I shifted my philosophical focus to the mind/body problem in epistemology, the relation of language to reality. Without acknowledging the direct personal origin of my interest, the "mind/body problem" was a container in philosophical form for integrating my inner conflict regarding my sexuality, in which my body had yearnings to which my mind said no. An external concept housed my internal conflict.

The exception with whom talk was possible about "hs" was Barry Wood. After our initial meeting at Camp Columbia, our paths crossed when he would direct the Notes and Keys, of which I had become a member. At one point he invited me to come up to Bard Hall at P&S (College of Physicians and Surgeons where he was a student) so he could show me around, play some piano duets, spend the night and attend a class the next morning. He was the first person I ever had sex with who talked about what was happening and how I felt and how he felt. Every other encounter had ended in a blank wall of silence, a sexual-disappearing act. When I returned to my dormitory the next day and Fred asked where I had been, it was hard to make a case that my staying to play the piano with Barry required staying overnight, since P & S was only about five subway stops away. So I did my own disappearing act and made excuses that I wasn't available when Barry called to suggest we get together. The conversation was stilted by my feeling too ashamed to own up to the relationship. I imagined that Barry thought I simply wasn't interested in him. Physically, my attraction was limited; I loved being around him; but I couldn't imagine an acceptable reason to let anyone know it. We drifted apart.

Looking toward graduation, the summer after I finished my Junior year, I didn't like the internal world that was opening up to me with Barry, so I chose to escape to the larger external world that I thought I might see with the Peace Corps. Perhaps lingering from the decision not to go with Steve Johnston to Europe, I felt a need to travel, to see more of the world, especially a part of it that was not essentially Western and European. I applied and was accepted into the Peace Corps for training in the summer of 1964, between my junior and senior years, to go to French West Africa after graduation from.

The training was held at Dartmouth College. It was a crash course in the politics and economics of the United States in the world. Conceived by Sargent Shriver and promoted by president Kennedy, my training also involved an immersion in French language and culture, particularly as it would be found in French West Africa.

Over the course of three months, we not only learned to speak everyday French from native French men and women, we studied the history of French West African countries from pre-Colonial to post-Colonial rule.

"I left America to go help the people of Côte d'Ivoire," one young woman who had spent two years there said to us, "only to discover the poverty of my own middle class America privilege, and the riches and beauty of Africa. How naïve and misguided I had been to think I had something to teach! Slowly, I learned to learn, instead." This experience of going, expecting to give, and learning to receive instead was a theme repeated in different ways by each of the returning volunteers.

We read English or French translations of native writers, such as Chinua Achebe; Babtunde Olatunji and his band brought us the music from Nigeria; young people from Nigeria, the Ivory Coast, Camaroon, and Guinea spoke directly from their own experience of life in their respective countries, including those who'd lived through the rise and fall of Lumumba in the Congo. For those three months, we absorbed an intensive and extensive socio-political analysis of the impact of these countries' colonial domination, complete with the differences made by British versus French modes of both domination and withdrawal. We began to see that the history of colonialism made it impossible for wealthy countries like the U.S. to be helpful without undermining indigenous authority and autonomy, without reinforcing the very paternalism whose effects we were aiming to allay. In our idealism, we discovered seeds of our own paternalism and privilege, and that the only way that could be broken through was in the intimacy of specific relationships that might be forged while there.

Based on what we were taught and what we read, it seemed clear to me that the real problem was the United States itself, and its proclivity to use a country's raw materials and to manipulate the country's politics in order to protect our vested interests. "We have met the enemy and they is us," as the Peanuts cartoon said.

Thus it was that when president Lyndon Johnson pushed forward the Gulf of Tonkin Resolution before congress in August, alleging that on two separate occasions North Vietnamese boats had attacked United States vessels, all of us in the Peace Corps training program questioned the veracity of the attacks and believed that this was, as indeed it turned out, Johnson's pretext for expanding our involvement in South Vietnam. We felt we saw unfolding right before our eyes exactly the kind of manipulation of public (mis)information in our own country that would justify expanding military intervention. Why go to a foreign country allegedly to help them, when our own domestic foreign policy was creating more problems than it was solving? This was the question I brought back from Peace Corps training to my senior year as I still struggled to think through what to do after graduation.

In senior year, Fred and I moved out of Hartley Hall and into a two bedroom apartment with Chris Morren, a bass in the Glee Club, and Joe Beckman. They had been living there for some time already, and each of them had a bedroom. Fred and I shared the large living room with two twin beds.

With Fred and I sharing the living room, privacy was an issue, most especially if there was to be a date. Chris and Joe offered to "sleep out" in the living room if Fred or I wanted to use their room. The thing was, it required planning. A tie on the door knob meant Do Not Disturb.

I was dating Fred's best friend from high school in Baltimore, Janet Duval. Janet was smart and pretty, and worked at the Interchurch Center at 475 Riverside Drive for Global Missions. I liked her very much. We dated for several months. As had happened before with Bonnie, when we reached a certain point of physical intimacy where it was obvious what the next step should have been, I backed away. It seemed to me that I liked both Janet and Bonnie from my head, but below my waist there was no impulse to go further. This became all the more disconcerting with Janet when I met her brother Roy and whammo!—below the waist was working fine, even though he was 14, seven years my junior.

I didn't say anything about my feelings for him, and certainly didn't do anything with someone so young. But my sexual response to him told me clearly what I was not feeling for his sister. Breaking up is always hard and painful, all the more when there was nothing she did wrong, nothing to get angry about. I was happy to learn later that Janet was happily married. Fred of course was puzzled why she and I broke up, but I'd no language to explain it to him. Despite our close friendship, there was no vocabulary, no words I dared utter for fear that any words might somehow reveal the truth.

That Senior year, in philosophy, I took a course on "Action" with Arthur Danto. I had no real idea what the topic meant, but Danto was held in high regard as a teacher, so I thought I would try him out. Insofar as the course focused on motivation, my psych 101 course helped prepare me for it. But Danto was investigating the nature of action in terms for which I was not prepared, which picked up important aspects of Taoism as Buddhism entered China. He was investigating the contrast between Western assumptions of action and the Eastern understanding of *wu wei,* acting without acting, or non-action.

I also took a course with Ernst Nagel in the philosophy of science. He was highly regarded also for his contributions to logical positivism. I loved the clarity and rigor of his thinking, and remember him standing in front of the class, short (my size) with graying hair and a grey suit, white shirt and green tie, thinking before speaking, speaking sometimes slowly, sometimes rapidly, but with a gentleness that conveyed a high regard for us students as well as a complete dedication to the enterprise of care-filled thought that constitutes the best of philosophy.

I had not, of course, resolved the question of life's meaning and purpose after four years of philosophy at Columbia. Nor had I in any way come to terms with my attraction to men. The closer the time came for me to prepare for going to the Ivory Coast, the more terrified I became that I might get there and someone might find out I was gay. My assumption was that I would then be recalled and sent home in shame and rejection.

As graduation neared, I applied to seminaries. My interest was genuine, but I knew I felt safer trying to understand my sexuality in America than in a foreign country. Yale turned me down (another Harvard rejection!). Colgate Rochester Divinity School not only accepted me with full scholarship, but the president came to town to have lunch with me to coax me to go there.

Union Theological Seminary, across the street from Columbia, accepted me, but asked that my parents fill out a financial aid application. I rejected the acceptance, saying my parents had nothing to do with my seminary studies, so I wouldn't be able to come. I did not feel they supported my going, and I wanted this to be my choice. The Financial Aid officer, Bob Broadwell, called me, and asked me to come over to Union to talk about the matter. He managed to convince me that, even though my parents couldn't help financially, all they would need to do is fill out the form. I was greatly moved by this act of caring on his part. It was such a contrast to what I experienced with the Columbia bureaucracy that it warmed my heart and I did as he suggested.

I had developed the habit, over the four years, of turning in papers at the very last minute. The History of Philosophy course was the only one where I had not kept up to the last minute rule; nevertheless, as the deadline for graduation approached, I did manage to finish my last two papers for the course and was thus cleared to receive my diploma.

My parents, Jeanne and Maw Maw drove up to New York for the first time, for my graduation in 1965, the second year of the World's Fair. In separate conversations, the Dean said, "Congratulations, Gunn. We weren't sure you would make it," and my father said, "Congratulations, son. I didn't think you'd make it." I was still too polite to say what I felt to either of them, but my pride felt a bit slippery. It was not a happy time in other ways: at a restaurant, Dad told the waiter on the sly to put whiskey into his coffee cup, for fear that his mother, Maw Maw, would see it as a cocktail and criticize him. It became clear that he and Mom were not getting along well.

Probably in large part because I felt my parents' relationship falling apart, I returned to Florida for the summer between college and seminary. I had some vague notion of influencing my father to stay with my mother, but by the time I got there, although legal proceedings had not started, he had already moved out. I spent many hours listening to my mother's recitation of the history of my father's affairs. She said he was impotent and still tied emotionally to his mother. I spent some time with my father also, hearing his side of the story. He said she had always been very inhibited sexually as well as socially. My mind, of course, tried to imagine how both things could be true and yet they were unable to see each other's side. In retrospect, they both told me too much. Yet I had this need to know and to understand even while their marriage and my world came unraveled.

In September of 1965, nearly four years to the day from the time I visited Dick Joyner in his new room in Hastings Hall at Union, I moved into the floor beneath what had been his. The first thing I noticed was that, in contrast to Columbia, everyone was friendly. People said "hi" passing in the halls. Even the registrar was friendly and took time to help. Strangers got into conversations with each other on lines. Secondly, the young men were much better looking on the whole than Columbia students; they seemed healthier, skin a livelier tone, smiles with better teeth. They dressed better.

The night before classes began, there was a knock on the door. It was John Knox, Professor of Practical Theology. He had a list of new students, whom he was welcoming to the seminary. He wanted me to know that if I had any questions or needed anything, I could ask him. We shook hands and I thanked him and he left. In all my four years at Columbia, no instructor, much less a full professor, had ever visited anyone I knew in their dormitory.

My roommate was John Robinson. He was Black, stood about 6'1", and came from Washington, D.C. He was the only roommate I ever had who wore pajamas; his were of the dull, faded plaid kind I had not seen since childhood. He was Baptist and seemed to have just begun to realize the Bible was not literally true. He had about him a certain Christian niceness that I had also had when I first arrived at Columbia: the kind that seemed never to get angry, always to be understanding, and that shied away from conflict, whether personal or political.

The social issues of the day were plastered over walls and elevators of Union, with meetings held in the Pit (a kind of coffee house) or in dorm rooms. One group focused on the role of Citibank in the maintenance of apartheid in South Africa. Another group took an intern year to live and work on voter registration in Albany, Georgia. We marched down 5th Avenue against apartheid one month, against the War in Vietnam another month.

Alone among his Black classmates, John was not a part of such organizing. He saw his primary purpose as academic and religious, preparing him for parish ministry. It seemed to me that he was intimidated by his Black brothers' organizing. Since he sometimes had trouble with the academic requirements as well as not fitting in with the activist crowd, I sometimes wondered if he would survive the year.

When he saw me reading Claude Brown's *Manchild in the Promised Land*, he said, "What're you reading that for? Have you done your Old Testament assignment yet?" Two weeks later, as I was reading *The Autobiography of Malcom X,* he said, "Bob, he's a Muslim. You're a Christian. Why are you reading that stuff?" As I read James Baldwin's *Another Country*, he said "Baldwin left America for France, why're you reading him? Besides, he's an atheist—and a queer, from what I hear!" When he saw me reading Baldwin's *Giovanni's Room*, he didn't say anything and I hoped he wouldn't. Even more explicit than *Another Country* had been, *Giovanni's Room* was a gay novel, not a novel critiquing America, and I could not imagine having that conversation with John.

I felt ahead of him in social awareness. The deeper truth was, John represented a shadow side of myself: he came, as I did, from a lower middle class background, had been raised with middle class values to be somewhat upwardly mobile, to get a better education than his parents, to mind his manners, be morally upright, and above all, not to cause trouble. In 1965, though I joined in demonstrations and marches, inside I was still this scared white boy trying to be "with it" in a world that was coming apart at the seams, revealing the violent substratum of racism, poverty and war. No doubt, if I'd had an activist black man as a roommate, I would have felt intimidated myself.

Whatever it was-- my roommate, the friendly students and amazing professors, or the attractive young men-- by the end of the first week of classes, I knew I was home at Union. Samuel Terrien taught Old Testament. Standing at about 6'2" in his solid navy suit and silver silk tie, he assumed the authority and power of Moses. W.D. Davies taught New Testament and seemed always to dress what I called British frumpish, complete with a slightly tattered old British tweed jacket. He made a point of setting us straight about how we should always dress properly when going to church. Roger Shinn taught Ethics, and Paul Lehmann taught Systematic Theology and Ethics.

Lehmann became another hero for me: he seemed to embody the values he taught. When a student committee began investigating the salaries of our non-union staff, Lehmann joined the committee. In class, appearing each morning impeccably dressed in a three-piece suit, replete with watch fob, he was always reaching for words to express the theological meaning of the past while bridging it to the very much alive issues of the day. It was a daily display of verbal magic, and he was entrancing and empowering at the same time. The skill with which he took on the challenges of atheism and nihilism gave us a roller coaster ride between the "no-longer and the not-yet", the dynamics of a God who enters into history always to reclaim and restore the human soul. A preacher as well as a consummate teacher, Lehmann imbued us with hope for the world that God was at each moment bringing about.

The at-homeness I felt was physical; I felt more relaxed. Without much thought, I let myself be elected Treasurer of the Student Body, something that, seen from hindsight, was ironic in the extreme (I am not good with money, bankbooks and reconciliations.).

Especially in the first year of the Bachelor of Divinity program (later renamed the Master of Divinity), students were expected to do field work not just to earn money, but to add practical experience to their classroom learning. My first year I dallied around until there were few choices left and finally accepted an assignment to teach middle school children at Christ Church Methodist at Park Avenue, then under the leadership of Harold Bosley. I was still officially a Methodist, and was interested in this particular church because it had been for many years the pulpit church of Ralph Sockman, a famous preacher on the National Radio Pulpit Program, and author of several books, some of which I had read. Bosley, Sockman's successor, was a tall, middle-aged, well-dressed man from Nebraska who seemed to fit the class to which Christ Church, on Park Avenue, seemed to cater.

Not content merely to show up to teach Sunday School, I proposed to the Christian Education Minister, David Fisher, to conduct a poll in the church on the escalating Vietnam War. I took it to Bosley for his approval, but I had a bit of a chip on my shoulder: I was marching against apartheid in South Africa and against the war in Vietnam, and wanted him to come out more explicitly against the war with more grit than polish.

He had, in fact, traveled with a delegation of clergy to Vietnam who had made what I considered to be a tepid criticism of the war, and I wanted more from him. I suppose I wanted him to be angry, as I was angry. Lurking beneath my anti-war sentiment, however, was a barely concealed envy of the man's achievements, his self-confidence, and his position of power, none of which I would have acknowledged to anyone at the time. I am sorry to say that he became defensive amid my questioning, and my questionnaire went only as far as the class I was teaching. I was happy with the results though: my students were all against the war.

At Union, we were not merely involved in the moral issues of other countries; we paid attention to local politics as well. In October of 1965, the New York City race for mayor was heating up, with John Lindsay running as a Republican, and Abe Beame, the incumbent, a Democrat. Lindsay impressed many of us at Union as a light shining on the future amid a very dark and tired world of politics-as-usual with Beame. So we joined the Lindsay team and spent our extra hours knocking on doors of tenement apartments in Harlem, our mostly white faces gleefully encouraging the mostly Hispanic and Black residents to get out and vote, and telling them how to make sure they were registered.

One evening I went swimming at the Columbia Teachers' College swimming pool and met a young man about my age from Mexico named Raoul. I went over to his apartment from time to time until one afternoon his father came home, discovered us naked in the bedroom, and was outraged. Raoul had never told him. He was embarrassed. I was terrified and ashamed. I took Raoul's father's diatribe to heart as if he were my own father. I felt sorry for Raoul, who kept apologizing to me as his father continued his relentless harangue til I finished dressing and walked out. Later Raoul called and wanted to get together, but I was too mortified for fear of a repetition to meet again.

By the time Thanksgiving drew near, I was anxious to get out of the city. Frederic Hudson had become chaplain at Colby College in Waterville, Maine, so I borrowed the Monkmans' little black Morris Minor and drove to Maine.

The snow started falling as I drove through Massachusetts. By the time I hit the Maine Turnpike, it was coming down in thick, soft flakes that muffled the sound of the tires on the road. Ever since childhood in Illinois I loved snow and had missed it when we moved to Florida. The tall green pines on either side seemed to open like portals as I drove, welcoming me to a splendid, unknown, but enchanted country sparkling with diamond flakes.

The Hudsons were living in a small red Cape nestled among the pines only half a mile from Colby's campus. The kids were as excited to see me as I was to see them. By the end of dinner, Fred had regaled me with his latest enthusiasm, the Death of God movement. He was in the middle of writing an article about it that already had a publisher and a deadline, so he worked as we talked.

Sitting back in his desk chair in front of his high piles of manuscripts, Frederic spelled out the movement's beginning: "You're familiar with Bonhoeffer's *Letters and Papers from Prison*, right?"

"I've read some of it. I read his *Cost of Discipleship*, which you introduced me to."

"That was one of his earliest books. *Letters and Papers* was written in his last months before he was hanged for attempting to assassinate Hitler."

"Right."

"So, Bonhoeffer's main point was that humankind has now reached a stage of maturity regarding religion in which God is no longer necessary for people to feel safe and comfortable in the world; we no longer need the metaphysical assumptions about God in order to live meaningful lives."

"Okay, I kind of remember that, but are you saying Bonhoeffer was a 'death of God' theologian?"

"No, I'm not saying he was. But his idea of 'living without God—before God,' started many of us thinking where that led. The Death of God theologians—among whom I count myself--are going the next step in saying, in fact, however defined, God is no longer a pre-requisite hypothesis for a scientific world, and is therefore dispensable. Even more than that, to continue to talk about God as if there were some entity at the outer edges of the cosmos, is bad faith, indulging in illusion and idolatry."

He took out his quarter stem briar pipe, filled it and lit it. I followed suit with mine.

"All right, Frederic, let's say God is dead--- what then?"

"Religion, if it is to have a future, has to take God's death into account. Further, Christianity may no longer need to be a religion."

"Bonhoeffer himself asked what would a religionless Christianity look like, right?" I was getting the bug; no one at the seminary, as yet, was talking of the death of God movement, and I was both curious and excited. I felt totally tuned into what Frederic was saying. It seemed to speak to the very heart of my own struggles. I felt myself at some point of crisis in my life. As far back as I could remember, I had been drawn to religion. Church was where people talked about what I felt mattered: What's our purpose here on earth? Why is there suffering? What is the meaning and purpose of life? How should we live? Is there such a thing as love, or are we driven primarily by selfishness? What, ultimately, did it mean to be human? These questions burned within me, preoccupied me. But they led me in a very non-religious, not necessarily Christian, practically a-theistic direction.

Our conversation shifted as Kate joined us with hot toddies and filled me in on how the children were so much happier living in Maine. Finally, Frederic and Kate went to bed and I stayed up, refilled my pipe and lit it, and stared out the window at the snow and pines, reflecting on Frederic's ideas.

My conversion experience when I was nine reached so deep inside me that I felt my encounter with God was more real than life on earth. To me, it was an expression of a dimension of life that seemed also to be the source of life, and spoke to me of how life in the world could be and was intended to be. Was I wrong? Was I suffering from some psychological illusion, an infantile projection onto God and Jesus and the church? Or was the promise of the great *shalom*, the kingdom of God, in fact more real than the horror of Vietnam, the injustice of my brother and of all who suffer because of what someone else has done?

Ever since my parents sat me down to question my religiosity and warn me of hypocrisy, I'd been struggling with ambivalence about the very religion that meant so much to me. I had wrestled with these questions in high school by reading Albert Schweitzer and Bertrand Russell. I took them to my study of philosophy at Columbia, and yet felt no nearer to any answer. I never found any solace in the ancient arguments for the existence of God, because neither Plato nor Aristotle seemed to know the God I had experienced at age nine. I couldn't resonate with Augustine or Aquinas, either. It was only when I got to the existentialists—Kierkegaard, Jaspers, Camus, Sartre—that I found resonance.

Then, when I read Tillich's definition of faith as being ultimately concerned—it had opened a gate of hope, without which I would never have gone to seminary. But most church services made me angry; I found them supercilious, superficial and plain fake. Yet, again, something still burned deep inside me that agitated me and I couldn't let go of the questions any more than I could answer them.

"Wake up! Wake up!" Lisa and John-John hollered as they jumped on me in bed.

"You have to help us make a snowman!" Jeff said.

"Hey, please. A cup of coffee first," I pled, pulling the covers back over my head.

Two hours later, we had a big fat snowman, with a proper Allagash hat and an old pipe of Frederic's. Lisa'd made angels in the snow all around the snowman.

I picked her up and turned to view what we'd done.

"I give us an A+," Jeff said, standing beside me on the left. John John scooped up snow, packed it and threw it at us.

"No fair, John John!" Lisa hollered and squirmed down to make her own snowball.

I was suddenly weepy and thought, "I want this. I want children of my own." And then, "You have to be married. Where's the woman in your life?" A snowball caught me by surprise.

"Gotcha!" Jeff said.

Joining Frederic again in his study with coffee for both of us, I relayed my wee hour reflections.

"Well, I totally share your skepticism, as you know," Frederic replied. "Personally, I found atheism intellectually honest and refreshing, but somehow hollow and lifeless; it seemed to leave no room for wonder, joy and meaning.

What appealed to me about the death of God, was to think in terms of there having been a God, or at least what people experienced as God, but that that God was no longer 'there,' no longer available for humans to be in relation to. It was like discovering a dead body, and being left to make sense of a life that had been but was no more, and left to make meaning out of what was left. But what makes this different from your standard atheism is the feeling that what's left wasn't nothing, but, in fact, everything."

"But what is everything then?"

"Everything is all that's left except the God who once was and now is not. So this constitutes a story about God, a history of God, indeed, a biography of God, ending in His eulogy. But it's also the story of us, of our developing consciousness. Bultmann and demythologization did their job up to a certain point: we can do without the Biblical myths. But where do we go from there? That's where the death of God comes in and basically announces that the world, as it is, is our responsibility, and its not a sad story, it's a human beings coming-of-age story."

"That makes total sense to me," I said, now feeling my thinking aligned with Frederic. "We, as humans, are solely responsible and solely response-able for the fate of human life on this planet. No appeal to a God-beyond-this-earth to save us from what we ourselves can do."

"We can't in any way pass off responsibility for what happens to this God who presumably created us, because even if in some sense we had been created by such a God, that God is alive no longer, exists no longer. This is it. Sartre's depiction of the human situation in *Huis Clos*, translated as *No Exit,* was spot on. We are condemned to inhabit the space we are in and have to take responsibility for what we do with it. There's just us. Period," Frederic said.

I suddenly felt very somber. "There's another way in which the idea of living in the world without a father resonates very deeply with me," I said. "When I was four years old, I ran away from home and went to a corral at the edge of town in Mounds, Illinois, where they had horses. Both my parents were working, and even though I had a babysitter, I felt all alone. This feeling, of being alone without parents seems to be a core feeling, right at the core of my being. It is the mind and heart of the stranger. Of all the early Biblical stories, I identify most with Cain in Genesis 4—not that I slew my brother --but that I feel exiled, thrown out of my place of safety and pushed into the freedom of the homeless, no safety, no security; as Heinlein put it, a *Stranger in a Strange Land*. I always felt in some way I carried the mark of Cain with me, "a fugitive and a wanderer." In this sense my relationship with God is that of the alienated one, the rejected one; although my personal feeling is more that of abandonment than of rejection. Maybe that's why I'm resonating with the death of God. It's an inner feeling about loss and aloneness…not necessarily loneliness."

Frederic's grey eyes were looking at me over his glasses. It was a kind of "tell me more" look, and I wanted to tell him more.

"You know we're talking so theoretically here…abstractly. But this stuff is very real to me. All my life, my brother Bill's inability to walk and to learn things like reading and writing have stood as a challenge for me to the belief in a God who was all-loving and all-powerful. The usual answer was that God gave humans freedom; but I didn't see how humans were responsible for Bill's condition. There was no issue over which I so completely agreed in philosophy than Camus' statement, 'I refuse to live in a world where innocent children suffer and die.'"

Frederic nodded slowly, still looking over the rim of his glasses.

"Another place I connected to what you're saying is in relation to my own father. I was so incensed at his affairs and the likelihood of his leaving the family, his authority and his credibility have pretty much evaporated. I don't look up to him like I used to. I felt forced to claim my own rights and responsibilities as a mature man in the world because my father had so clearly failed to exercise his own responsibilities. Somehow that seems connected to the death of God idea."

"Yes, I can see why you'd connect those," he said.

"Sorry to interrupt you two theologians," Kate said as she poked her head through the door. "We need a father to carve the turkey."

"So to whom do we give thanks after the death of God?" I asked as Frederick led the way to the kitchen.

Two days after the turkey, I returned to Union filled with excitement about the new movement in theology. I wrote a short article about it for the student paper, **Balaam's Ass**. No one had yet finished a book on the subject; it was appearing mostly in journals and magazines. Through Frederic, I met Bill Hamilton, one of the Death of God Theologians, who taught at Colgate Rochester. I invited him to come to Union and speak to us about the new movement. He was a very hang-loose kind of man, relaxed but in a nervous kind of way that left him unable to sit still for long. He shared with us the basic parts of an article he was writing, which Union would publish in its Quarterly Review as "From Prufrock to Ringo: the New Optimism". And indeed, the Death of God Movement did tend to be an optimistic theology, replete with hope for a world to be accepted on its own terms without the imposition of theological assumptions and messianism.

Over the next few months, the writings of Western Protestant theologians such as William Hamilton, then at Colgate Rochester Divinity School, John A.T. Robinson, then Bishop of Woolwich, England, Gilbert Vahanian of Princeton, Thomas J.J. Altizer of Emory, and Richard Rubenstein, of Florida State University, sought to broaden the consciousness of churches and temples as well as seminaries. Within Catholicism, though certainly not a member of the death of God movement, Roger Garaudy pursued dialogue with Marxists and entertained the possibilities of an a-theistic faith.

When I approached Larry Jones, the Dean of the seminary, to see if there was any money available for me to attend a Conference on the Death of God in Ann Arbor, Michigan in October of 1966, I was told there were no funds available.

I felt deflated and joked to my roommate, "Maybe this was God's way of showing me he wasn't dead yet."

"Ummhmm. You'd just better listen when God's speaking to you!" he said with the voice of a more-knowing one.

However, a couple of days later there was a knock at my door and the president of the seminary, John Bennett, stood there in his typically rumpled suit and too-narrow red tie with a silver tie clip. He handed me an envelope and said he appreciated my writing about the Death of God movement, and though he disagreed with it, he felt it was important for us to know and understand it. So he wanted to support my going to the conference. He handed me an envelope.

I peeked into it and saw a check for $100. I thanked him profusely. I went back into my room and cried in gratitude and amazement at the generosity the president of the seminary displayed in supporting the pursuit of a cause with which he personally disagreed.

I couldn't resist showing the check to John. "Now what do you think God is saying?" I asked with a big grin.

So it was that, in the winter of 1966, I flew out to Detroit and then made my way to Ann Arbor where I roomed with Frederic Hudson in a dormitory. Somehow, Frederic already knew the major leaders of the movement. By following him, I got inside access to the real life thinking and personalities of these men whom I knew only through their published writings. Harvey Cox was perhaps the most down to earth and friendly of them all, very much a Baptist pastor turned theologian. Richard Rubenstein impressed me as a very troubled man, for whom the holocaust was a symbol of a larger life negation with which he struggled, I suspected, on personal as well as theological and academic levels. Tom Altizer was the most flamboyant of the group, showing up on stage to speak as loudly with his voice as his bright red socks showed, hands moving in gesticulation that appeared somewhat effeminate. I wondered if he was gay.

The voices of what were called "death of God theologians" differed greatly from one another, and there was no real agreement regarding the meaning of "the death of God." For Hamilton, faithfulness was still possible by following Jesus and giving up our dependency on a father God "out there." According to him, our task was to live, as Bonhoeffer said, "before God, without God." Altizer interpreted the death of God as an actual event, a radical kenosis, the self-emptying of God, which we had been loathe to accept. Rubenstein added a Jewish perspective to the group, and declared that, though there could be no God spoken of after Auschwitz, a psychoanalytic reading of religion could suggest a continuing utility for a religion without Yahweh. Others joined Vahanian in considering it a cultural shift requiring some updating of symbolic life. Some considered it a mere sign of people's unbelief and the sorry state of seminaries that produced such "faithless" theologians.

After the last session of the conference, Harvey Cox invited Frederic, Tom Altizer, Gabe Vahanian, Dick Rubenstein and me to join him for some brews at

The Blind Pig. Vahanian bowed out, claiming fatigue. We were given a round table, which was great for us all to be able to hear and be heard. Harvey sported a full beard, slightly more salted than Frederic's. Hamilton, Rubenstein and Altizer were clean shaven. While Altizer, in a Mexican loose-flowing shirt, had no tie, those of us who did, loosened them up after ordering two pitchers of beer, except for Rubenstein. He kept his tie in place and remained rather uncomfortably aloof, clearly someone who kept his own counsel, but took intellectual exchange as important.

Once the beer came and was poured, Altizer offered a toast to religion "*post mortem dei*," to which Frederic countered, "I'm not so sure about the religion part. I don't know that there will be a place for religion after the death of God."

"Dick," Harvey said, "I am fascinated that you find Christian communion so powerful….not many Protestant Christians feel so strongly about it, I daresay."

Rubenstein scooted a bit closer to the table, removed his black-rimmed glasses, and replied, "if you take Freud seriously, then you know we never outgrow our desire for the breast…and how much closer can you get to infancy than to let someone else feed you? Kneeling and sticking out your tongue so you can be fed seems to me an exceptionally rich ritual of letting go, returning to our infantile neediness, and being fed by the mother/father priest."

Altizer set his mug down after a swig, and said, "Some of us don't bother with such a symbolic gesture: I'm quite happy to lie back and let a real breast come into my mouth!!" He took an extra big gulp of beer for emphasis.

"Still, Dick may have an even more significant point: that through psychoanalysis, we may find much more in common among our religions than we ever imagined before," Frederic said.

Rubenstein finished a swig, set his mug down but kept looking at it. "You are all moving chairs on a Titanic that has already sunk. How can religion exist at all after the holocaust? My admiration for Christianity is only for the psychoanalytic meaning of its ritual….that does not make it a religion…There is no religion because there is no god."

"You seem to mourn the death of God….Could it also be a source of joy and freedom?" I asked.

Rubenstein glared at me. His face reddened, he retorted, "You...you are very young....you have no idea what we have lost.... What civilization ever lasted without a God? The death of the father God spells the unleashing of madness among the sons, as Freud said."

"....or their rise to a natural maturity," Bill Hamilton offered. "I think the death of God is the release of our innate powers for making the world more human."

"Yes, more human!" Altizer responded, slurring his words. "Kenosis means more flesh! Let's hear it for more human and more breasts!"

Frederic gave me one of his beguiling smiles, encouraging me to carry on.

I continued, looking at Rubenstein. "The death of the father God could mean a new level of conscious assumption of responsibility for our world...very Sartrean... .'l'homme se fait'.... "I don't see why Dionysian madness is the only alternative. This was Bonhoeffer's point, I think: it is our opportunity to grow up and move past an infantile dependence on the father God. Community and contract...communion, if you will, rather than dependency on an outmoded father God."

They were all looking at me and I felt embarrassed and didn't know what to say next.

"But that is precisely the limit of the virtue of the mass, you see," Rubenstein replied. "The value of the mass cannot be separated from the death of the Son of the Father God. The sons eat their guilt and drink their bloody absolution, because they are still plagued by what they have done. It's a repetition compulsion, not real freedom."

"I think the Indians have it right," Altizer offered. "You get together in a circle and smoke the peace pipe." He took a drag on his cigarette and blew a smoke ring for emphasis. "No need for the father...just men sitting around agreeing to live peaceably rather than kill each other! No mass, no father, just reality!" he said, slamming the table and spilling his beer. "Shit!" he retorted.

I thought of his red socks and his words of "just men sitting around...." "Like what's happening right here," I said.

"Here! Here!...haha!" replied Altizer. We all laughed.

I suddenly realized how good it felt to be in this place, hanging out with these men for whom deep and careful thinking was their life's work and I felt an odd closeness in being part of this conversation. With more experiences like this, would I lose my sexual interest in men because I was having intellectual intercourse with them? I must be getting drunk, I thought to myself.

The entire encounter with its formal and informal conversations was utterly exhilarating to me. I felt like I was on the inside of history in the making, and inside a circle of people who shared my concerns and lived it with the same ultimate seriousness that I felt.

I returned to Union all the more convinced that the Death of God was not a flash in the pan event, but an historical event whose meaning and implications the conference and all of us who attended it were only beginning to explore.

God's death made headlines in **Time, Newsweek** and **Look**. I wrote another article for ***Balaam's Ass***, trying to summarize the gist of the Ann Arbor conference.

The Death of God is the natural culmination of the deep self-examination theologians were forced into by the radical evil manifested in World War II. To understand how an allegedly Christian nation could try to exterminate an entire race and so many other ostensibly Christian nations could collude or ignore that evil requires a deeper look at the very source of theology itself: the human mind and the formation of consciousness and the unconscious. After Freud and Marx, we can no longer ignore the extent to which God is not only a projection of our needs for a father, but an expression of immaturity and bad faith, a diversion from taking full responsibility for what we as humans do.

Somewhere around 10 p.m. the night after my article appeared in the student newspaper, David Easter and I gathered with a couple other students at O'Malley's pub on Amsterdam Avenue. David sat across from me, the Beatles' *Eleanor Rigby* blaring in the background, took a sip of beer and said, "I really liked the article you wrote about your trip to Ann Arbor. The Death of God movement really speaks to me…makes me wonder why I'm at Union at all…" His brown eyes were big through his thick glasses. His blonde hair hung curved over his forehead to the left. His thick lips were voluptuous. David was one of the most insightful students in our class. He took in big theological ideas with ease and related them to real life issues such as the war in Vietnam and the poverty of Harlem. What David said sometimes verged on the revolutionary, but his manner was disarmingly gentle and unaffected.

"I also wonder why I'm at Union now," I replied.

In January, I went to Washington with Clergy and Laity Concerned about Vietnam, an organization founded by Union's president, John Bennett, Abraham Heschel from Jewish Theological Seminary and William Sloane Coffin from Yale. For several days at the end of January, we stood vigil in front of the White House in silent protest against the war. We slept in a church basement as we took turns keeping the 24-hour vigil. The snow and the cold were bitter, but the company was great.

One night, I had a conversation in the cold that perhaps reflected the debates across hard lines that were being drawn across America and dividing our country. A cab driver had stopped by and started challenging us on our position. I took the bait and tried to convince him of the rightness of our position. After awhile, he invited me into his cab to carry on the conversation, and three hours later, I realized I wasn't going to get anywhere with him. As I got out of the door, he exclaimed with frustration equal to mine, "you mean, after all this, I still haven't convinced you?"

Meanwhile, although there were obviously a lot of gay men at the seminary, and I was beginning to meet them, there was no one yet writing a new theology of sexuality. I was still not revealing myself. I had crushes on David Easter, Gil Winter and Nick Hodsdon that were never were voiced or acted upon. Indeed, the word "gay" had not yet entered the general public vocabulary. I learned from my conversations with Barry that sex has less shame attached when you can talk to the person and get to know each other, but the guilt, the internalized self-rejection, continued. I read everything I could on the psychology of homosexuality.

Until that year, 1966, the psychological perspective on homosexuality was dominated in America by Charles Socarides, M.D. and Irving Bieber, M.D., both of whom took a psychoanalytic reductionist approach, saying homosexuality is caused by an absent father and a domineering mother. They supported their claims by drawing on patients who had come to them to be changed. In other words, men came to them wanting to change their orientation because in a world which did not accept them, they felt bad, and those men were the basis for Socarides and Bieber to proclaim homosexuality a form of psychopathology.

Evelyn Hooker was the first psychologist to undertake systematic research of the psychological status of non-patient homosexuals, and to determine from a more objective study that there was no direct correlation between homosexuality and psychopathology. Psychologically, gay men were as likely to be as healthy or neurotic as straight men, neither more nor less. Although her work was reported in 1957 in a professional journal, it did not reach the broader public until the 1960's. I read of her work like a man in a desert being given a drink of water. The only other writer I came across who seemed to counter the pathologizing of homosexuality was Hendrik M. Ruitenbeek, a Dutch psychoanalyst.

Then, in the spring of 1966, I heard from the grapevine that a graduate of a couple of years before, Neil Secor, had written his M.Div. dissertation on a new appraisal of homosexuality. Shortly after, a friend of mine, Carl Schneider, wrote his dissertation on the same theme, expanding it and adding more recent material. I had no idea whether either of them was gay. Carl told me he was not, but that many people assumed he was because he wrote on the topic. I was so afraid of being found out, I did not dare even ask Carl to read what he wrote. But I felt the ground shifting slightly in a positive way.

As Spring break approached, Easter of 1966, I got a letter from my mother that my dad had moved out and asked her to file for divorce. In Florida at the time, there had to be an aggrieved party, and of course it was my mother. I decided within the hour to go down to see what I could do to head off what I considered a disaster. I arranged to get a ride from some other seminary students who were headed to Albany, Georgia to work on voter registration during the break. I planned to hitchhike on to Florida from Atlanta, since I had no money.

Six of us, two white, four black, piled into a '58 Chevy sedan, and headed south. As soon as we crossed the Mason Dixon line, the mood in the car became somber. The joking stopped. The radio music stopped. When we pulled over for gas somewhere in North Carolina, we were at a station where everyone was black.

"Get your head down, white boy!" Charlie said to me. His tone of voice said it all: we were in dangerous territory where white and black didn't mix.

Near midnight, approaching Atlanta, we pulled up to a small grocery store, isolated, one car. This one had a white man inside. This time, the four black students crouched down, and Joe went in for snacks. As we drove on in the dark, the lynching of civil rights workers James Chaney, Andrew Schwerner and Michael Goodman two years before in Mississippi came home to me like it never had before.

They let me out at a truck stop just about sunrise. I was afraid to stick my thumb out at first. I didn't know who could be trusted—white or black either one. Two truckers and nine hours later, I was walking up the hill and into our yard in Jensen Beach. I told Mom I'd been given a ride by students headed for Ft. Lauderdale on spring break and went to sleep for a good twelve hours.

The next day I asked Mom and Dad to meet with me and try to talk things through. I had a flashing thought that there was something off about my doing this. Since when do children try to step in to resolve their parents' problems? On the other hand, doesn't every child try to keep their parents together?

We sat at the kitchen table, the beige formica table at which my father had sat for hundreds of mornings, watching the sun rise across the hill, the Indian River and Hutchison Island, drinking his first cup of coffee before Mom or I awoke; the table at which Mom and Jeanne and I had waited so many evenings for him to come home from work so we could eat; the table where my brother ate when he came home and I cut up his food for him; the table that in fact I had bought while in high school to replace the one that was rusty.

Mom was dressed in her usual after-work outfit: beige pants and a flower print blouse. She poured coffee for all of us. Dad sat at his usual place at the head of the table, short-sleeved white shirt unbuttoned and tie loosened. Mom sat down at her place on his left. I sat where I usually sat, to her left. Jeanne was already in bed.

After they both spoke for awhile, delineating their respective complaints and disappointments, I finally spoke up. "I have been listening to both of you and I get different stories of what's wrong," I said. "I just wonder if you both heard each other and might consider whether you could find a way to work things out."

Dad pulled out a pack of Lucky Strikes and his lighter, reached across to the window sill where his ashtray still sat, and lit up.

"I thought you'd stopped smoking," Mom said.

Dad took a long drag on his cigarette and blew the smoke out in a quick burst, jerking his head toward her. "I don't need you getting on my case, Viv."

"It's just that...."

"Get off my back, okay?!"

I felt her flinch.

I had never seen or heard my parents fight before. Raised voices were never heard.

She turned to me, "You see, Bobby, that's how he's been...."

"You mean that's how *you've* been....I'd rather die from smoking than be a blimp." The year before, he'd quit smoking and put on 40 pounds. Now it seemed he'd trimmed down again.

"I just want you to take care of yourself, Henry. It's just like the money. Like you're hell-bent to have things your way, no matter who it hurts, including yourself."

"What's with the money?" I asked.

"Tell him, Henry. May as well let him know everything," Her mouth was set in that firm, thin line which always meant she was standing her ground, come hell or high water.

"I owe a lot of money, that's all," he said, looking straight at me.

"About $27,000 worth of 'that's all'--- we have no more savings, I am now paying the house by myself, and I have no idea where all our money has gone!"

"I told you it was for business, and for running for the school board. Don't worry, I'll catch up and make it up to you," he said. "Any other wife would have been more supportive...." He sucked in the smoke from his cigarette and blew it out in rings. No matter how hard I tried, I could never get the smoke to come out like that.

"How can you be out of money—you're both working!" I said. I recalled seeing the financial aid form they filled out for Columbia. Their combined incomes totaled $13,000 in 1960. I thought that was a lot of money.

Mom looked at me. "We may both be working, but we're not both making a steady income."

My father broke into a condescending smile. "Selling cars is like the weather—sometimes it's great and sometimes it's lousy."

"So you have money problems. I don't see why that means you two should separate; it'll be more expensive living apart anyway."

Mom got up, grabbed the coffee pot and started refilling our cups. She stared at the coffee as it poured into his cup, her cup, then mine. "You gonna make me say it, Henry? Haven't you told him what's been going on?"

I really didn't want to hear about it, not just because I'd heard it from each of them before, but because sons and daughters should not have to know about their parents' sex lives. For a moment, I turned away from the kitchen table, looked out the window, and let my thoughts turn back the clock.

When I was six years old in Bluford, my mother sent me to the hotel to get my dad and tell him to come home to dinner. It was probably half a mile on an oiled cinder road from our house. I got to the door of the hotel and painted on the door were the words: "No minors allowed." I wondered why they didn't want miners in the hotel…my uncle Joyce was a coal miner and I didn't understand.

I walked in and it was very smoky and noisy, but I saw my daddy sitting at a table with some other men playing cards. I saw the money on the table. I knew what that meant.

"Henry, isn't that your son?" someone at the table said.

My daddy looked up from the cards in his hand and stared at me as I walked over to the table.

"Mother said to tell you to come home. We're having supper soon." My voice sounded weak to me, but then my daddy ruffled my hair and told me he'd be along soon, and for me to go back home and tell her.

I went back home and as soon as I got through the door I burst into tears and knelt down sobbing into the red velvet platform rocker.

"What's wrong?" my mother asked.

"He was gambling," I said, and more tears poured out and my mother reached down and patted me on the back.

"There, there, it will be all right, but I think you should tell him how you feel when he comes home."

And so I did what my mother said I should, and I felt the worst kind of horrible: horrible that I saw my daddy doing something that I had been told repeatedly in church, in no uncertain terms, was wrong; and horrible that I, at the age of six, had to tell my daddy what I saw and thought-- to be his accuser, to betray him, when all I wanted to do was to love him.

"All our married life, every once in awhile, I would get this feeling and I knew your dad was out with another woman."

I turned back from looking out the window to my parents at the kitchen table.

Dad drew in long on his cigarette, exhaled slowly. "You think I'm the only one. You tell her, Bobby, men do things. Maybe it's not nice, but it happens."

"And that's supposed to make me feel better? You see how he talks to me, Bobby? And what did I do to deserve this?"

"Maybe you never really backed me up, Viv. When I ran for school board, you never stood by me and supported me."

"That's not true, Henry. I supported you. I just don't like being in public."

"Exactly my point. Soon as I try to make something of myself, get elected to the one position I really felt good about, you can't even be by my side."

"So that justifies you running around with other women?! How do you think I felt when people would come to me and whisper, 'Viv, how are you and Henry getting along? I thought I saw him at the causeway last night and somebody was in the car with him.' Or they'd say, 'Viv, I see Henry's been real tied up going to meetings, meeting a lot of people, must be like he's never home.' And I knew what they meant. They were telling me you had another woman. How do you think I felt then? I can tell you: I felt humiliated, my husband supposed to be working late, and then the stories came with bigger and bigger hints." She looked at him with a fire in her eyes I'd never seen before. "I know this, Henry Gunn," her voice loud and strong, her right forefinger pointing at him. "That's when you know who your friends are…when they tell you the painful truth that your husband is running around with another woman!"

"Look, I don't want to say things I'll regret in front of Bobby, but maybe you didn't do everything you might have as a woman!"

Tears came to my mother's eyes and her lips trembled. Now she was almost whispering to herself. "What was I supposed to do? With a man like him?"

Now it was my dad's mouth that was set in a straight line. "A man has his pride, you know. You can't expect to reject him time and again and for him to act like it doesn't matter. A man's got his pride…"

"Pride?" she said. "Seems to me you didn't have enough pride--couldn't even keep it up when you tried, no matter how hard I tried to help you."

He shot a quick glance at me, pushed his chair back, scraping the floor, stood up and walked to the door. He glared back at Mom. "You don't even know what humiliation is, or you'd never say something like that."

"That's right, Henry, just walk away." Then, "I'm sorry. I'm sorry. You're right. Sit back down, please."

I wanted to say something, find the perfect healing words, but I was struck mute. Just sitting silent at the battlefront of our kitchen table. Then, suddenly my mother turned from my father and faced me.

"Bobby, how can you just sit there and be so detached? Like you don't even care! I wish I could be as uninvolved!"

I felt like screaming at her, "why the hell do you think I hitch-hiked all the way down here?! Don't you know this is tearing me up inside?!" But I didn't. I couldn't give voice to what I felt, because I was trying to control an emergency, to stem a blood flow before we all died. Somewhere long before that night I had learned to hold things in, and that's what I did. "It's not that way, Mom," I said quietly.

Then my father went back to his chair, sat down, and looked at me. "You still think we can work things out?"

It was not a real question.

I was shaking. I had never heard either of them talk that way to each other… had never heard them shout or even argue before this night. "I don't know," I said. "You need help. Marriage counseling can help."

"Your mother went for help...can't say as I see it did her much good. Don't' see why it would help for both of us to go."

"Because you're in it together?" I offered.

"You blame me for my depression, don't you, Henry?" she asked.

"I'm not saying it's your fault, Viv. I know what depression's like. God knows I know."

I was surprised to hear this. I never thought of Dad as depressed. He always walked with a lively jaunt that, in earlier years, included whistling, but I hadn't heard him whistle, I suddenly realized, for a long time. My mother's depression was more obvious, in part because she would talk to me about what bothered her. I had begun to hesitate to sit down with her at the table after Jeanne had gone to bed and dishes were done, because she would go on talking until I felt worn out. It didn't seem to matter what the topic was.

"You never held a steady job!" Mom said.

"You never wanted to go out into the real world and so you just stuck at home!" he countered.

"Home? I wasn't home: I was working at a steady job!"

Each of their complaints came gushing forth and I could not control what was happening. I was paralyzed with the tension and torn up inside.

About 11 p.m., two hours or so into the discussion, my mother said she was too tired to think any more, that she would agree to file for divorce, as Dad wanted her to, and then she went to bed.

I felt spent and useless, and stupid, like a little kid trying to deal with adult problems. Somewhere inside I know I also felt mad. Mad at her for not trying harder to deal with her depression and sexual inhibition, and mad at him for acting it all out with affairs and now giving up.

"Want a beer?" Dad asked me. He had never done that before...never included me in having a beer or a cocktail. I was eighteen—legal to drink in New York, but not in Florida. He never used to drink in front of me. Sometimes with their friends when they came over. But I'd noticed when I'd come home for a couple of years that beer started showing up in our refrigerator-- about the same time he and mom began having problems.

"Sure," I replied.

He got up, pulled out a couple of cans of Budweiser, gave me one and sat back down. We popped the cans and made a slight gesture of a toast, as if we did this every day.

Dad heaved a sigh, then pulled over an ashtray, pulled out cigarettes from his pocket, offered me one.

"No, I'm still smoking a pipe," I replied, reaching across to the kitchen divider for my dark briar, straight stem pipe and tan leather tobacco pouch. We both lit up. "….just like you taught me."

"You know I knew when you and your friends used to stay out all night that you'd been drinking."

"I figured you knew," I said.

"Sometimes I thought about going out drinking with you, just to see if you could hold your own, try drinking you under the table."

I chuckled. "Like the time you tried to get me to stop smoking cigars by making me sick, but I didn't get sick?" I said with a smile.

He grinned. "Yeah, probably. Didn't work very well, did it?"

We took another gulp of beer. Silence. We drank again. I don't recall ever sitting at the table with him and there being silence. This wasn't uncomfortable. It was okay. I looked out the window onto the yard in the dark. A streetlight shined onto the area where the Sunfish used to be and I thought of the times we had spent sailing. You don't have to talk all the time when you're busy paying attention to a sail and the wind and the currents and the rudder. And now here, over beer, another kind of silence. We drank again.

"You know your mother has been more dependent on you than on me for a long time."

Perhaps imperceptibly, my jaw dropped. Holy shit, I thought. I've won the fucking Oedipal conflict without any real fight. I wanted to scream at him: Why'd you let me win? Take her back! She's your woman! Why didn't you say, 'She's mine!' Instead, I just looked at him and said, "What was I supposed to do about that?"

No answer. Then, "Gotta go to work tomorrow." He got up, emptied the ashtray into the garbage can. I stood up, put my hands in my jeans pockets and watched as he moved to the door.

"Good night, son."

"Good night, dad."

On my first night back in New York, just as I was still struggling with the dissolution of my parents' marriage, David Easter and I went for a beer at O'Malley's.

"I've made up my mind," he said. "Maude and I are going to get married, and I'm leaving Union to join the American Friends Service Committee, be their regional rep on anti-war and anti-draft actions."

"Congratulations on a new wife and a new job! That's great!" I said. "Wow! You've really launched your course!" David and I had talked about homosexuality in the abstract and I never felt any tension from him around the issue; he had such a highly developed feminine side—his softness of voice and skin, his ability to sense and be empathic with others. Once I saw him stand naked in front of the mirror in the shared men's room at Union: he was beautiful. I had had unspoken visions of a different future for him that included me.

He smiled really big, showed his brilliant but slightly crooked whites, and said, "Thanks! I want you to be my best man."

"I'd be honored," I said, while my throat clenched against tears. And so it was that I became chief architect, chauffeur and best man for his wedding. I made reservations for a honeymoon suite at the Hotel St. Moritz (now the Ritz Carleton). I escorted them to their room, wished them goodbye with a hug, and burst into tears as soon as I got outside their door.

The summer following David's wedding, I was back in Florida again, facing the end of my parents' marriage. I worked construction part-time, hauling cinder blocks from point A to point B, but I also worked part-time at the Stuart Methodist Church as a youth minister.

The pastor, Allen Stuart, was a "nice" man. Somewhat chubby, always grinning and ready to joke around, he was the quintessential Methodist pastor. Methodists were called that because, taking after John Wesley, the founder, they were exceptionally well organized, as in "methodical." Allen was extremely well organized and worked from a very nicely appointed office with leather easy chairs and a full high-back pale green swivel-and-tilt leather chair of his own.

One day during the summer, he called me into his office and let me know that he had special training in pastoral counseling and that he knew how to deal with a lot of issues people sometimes have, such as loneliness and homosexuality. If I ever wanted to talk to him, he would be glad to be of help. I did not flinch. I did not blink. My voice was as light and even-keeled as could be, as I said, "thanks, that's very kind of you."

To myself, I had always wondered about him, whether he might be homosexual, even though he was married. He had this way of looking at me very deeply, as if trying to see into my soul. I also said to myself, "you'd be the last person I would open up to about such a thing." He had been nothing but nice to me, but I had already read him as a professional minister, the kind who goes to seminary like musicians go to music school or doctors go to medical school or people go for MBAs: to learn a trade, to learn the skills to do a job.

For me, ministry, if it was worth its salt, was much more knitty-gritty than this well-dressed, slicked-back hair with a paunch of a preacher. Perhaps my mistrust or skepticism of Allen Stuart came from a sense that he had never suffered in a way that left him inwardly humbled. Still, why did I have such antipathy toward a man who had been consistently kind to me? I wondered. The question took me back to that night when my parents had the long talk with me about hypocrisy in religion. Perhaps I felt Allen's super-organized life had to be hiding something. All of this, of course, was the conjecture if not outright projection, of a seminary student ten years his junior.

There was one other person at the church there that stood out for me because he was the complete opposite from Allen. His name was Ed. Ed was probably in his 60's, pure white hair, Polish—second or third generation. To my mind he was the real thing --a dedicated Christian, one who found Christ and sobriety at the same time. Ed's edges were rough, too. Whatever else you might think of him, you knew he had suffered, and that he had earned whatever joy he was trying to pass on. One afternoon toward the end of the summer, just as I was going to meet Mom at the lawyer's office, Ed gave me a paperback edition of the New Testament, "Good News for Modern Man," which was fairly new at the time. Inscribed inside the front cover, he had written, "God loves you. I love you. Ed."

My "Good News for Modern Man" in hand, I arrived at my mother's lawyer's office with her for her to be deposed. I held her hand as she cried when telling of several affairs my father had had over the years, claiming those as the grounds for the divorce. It only took about twenty minutes. Since my father had agreed not to contest it, the divorce went through within a few days.

Less than two weeks after my parents' divorce was decreed, Dad called me and said he had someone he would like me to come over and meet. He gave me the address of a house in a very nice section of Stuart. I estimated its worth to be 3 or 4 times that of the house he had just left behind. He came to the door smiling and led me in to a sun porch with a table. He introduced me to a black-dyed-hair-held-high-like-a-pompadour woman with caked make-up named Betty. I knew this was not the woman I had last heard about several months earlier, who had had red hair. Betty was taller than Dad, and had thin, pinched lips, which seemed strained to form a fake smile. She looked older than my dad and certainly not pretty, to my mind.

I sat down as they offered me iced tea and told me their story. They had been dating for three months or so. Betty noted that she was a Bible-believing Baptist and would never have done anything to break up my father's marriage to my mother, but by the time she'd met my father, she could tell his marriage was over. So when the divorce came through ten days earlier, they had driven to Georgia and gotten married. Georgia had a shorter waiting period to remarry after a divorce than Florida had, she explained. She proudly showed me her ring.

"But you told me you weren't seeing anybody last month," I said to him.

"Well, at that time we weren't sure," my dad said. "There's another thing I have to tell you: we'll be moving to Jacksonville."

Jacksonville was 225 miles to the north. My brother was in Wood House in Ft. Lauderdale, some 75 miles to the south. At least 300 miles away from where Dad was moving.

"What about Bill?" I asked.

"We plan to see him as often as we can, Bobby," said Betty, leaning over toward me. "We'll make time to come and get him and have him spend time with us."

I wanted to slap her lying face.

"Have you told Jeanne yet?" I asked. I was fuming. I felt sick to my stomach. I wanted to leave.

"Not yet," he answered. "I wanted to tell you first."

I waited a moment, then said, "And how are you planning to tell Bill?" It was an accusation even more than a question, because I knew this would likely fall on my shoulders, by default. I think if he had looked me in the eye at that point, he would have seen my fury. But he did not. There was nothing more to be said. I silently seethed because my father had lied to me and was now going to move out of all our lives into his fancied dream. But I was as formally polite as a southern young man was supposed to be when visiting the house of a stranger. Though, when I finally got up to leave, at the door I hesitated a moment, wanting to wipe the fake smiles off both their faces by asking them, 'How can the two of you live with yourselves?' But I simply turned, without a word of good-bye, and left.

After that, I drove over to Stuart Lanes, a bowling alley off US 1. The bar area with a pool table beside it, was off to the side of the bowling lanes and somewhat enclosed. The jukebox played selections of your choice for 10 cents, or 3 for a quarter. It was mid-day and no one was there except for the bartender. Patsy Cline was singing "I Fall to Pieces" as I walked in and I thought, "How did you know?" I ordered a shot and a draft, racked the balls and picked a cue stick. I put back the shot then chugged down the beer, asked for another round, and broke the triangle into 9 scattered pieces.

When I finished my second round, I cursed God and then reflected on the fact that the Death of God Movement came at exactly the time when my own father's existence, as far as I and the rest of our family mattered, was in question. Indeed, it was as if he, too, had died.

I was playing rotation with myself, aiming to pocket the lower-numbered balls, moving up in sequence, but the numbers on the balls were already getting difficult to discern—was that a 3 or an 8?

Suddenly I felt stupid, but I felt my father was at least twice as stupid: he was stupid when he dropped out of college, and he was stupid when he had his affairs and finally ran away with another woman.

I scratched. Shit. How do you give your opponent an opportunity to get even when you're playing against yourself? But maybe that's what I'd been doing the whole time I thought I was trying to help my parents—just playing against myself, trying to fix my world for me. I racked them again. Broke'em.

Maybe I wasn't so innocent, so pure a heart trying to save a dead marriage. But my father wasn't innocent and neither was my mother. According to my dad, she had failed him sexually and failed to support his ambition in the public sphere because of her own difficulties with self-esteem. There are always two sides to every story, I thought, as I leaned against a bar stool, three sides if you included the third round I ordered.

The more I drank, the more the dimensions of my dad's betrayal came clearer into focus. Moving away—away from Jeanne, further away from Bill. And worst of all, lying about it. Lying about Betty-whatever-her-name is. Fact is, he's running away, wants to start a new life, new family. How can he want another family? I shot the ball so hard it jumped the table.

"Hey, easy on my table, lad!" the bartender said.

"Sorry," I said, though I was nowhere near sorry....

There's something about having a mother and father that makes the world feel secure, complete, whole. Maybe you don't realize it when you're fighting against one or both of them to grow up and make your own way in the world, but then, when the two are no longer one, and the family is no longer one but two or seven or eight, everything shatters, fragments.

I got all the balls into the pockets.

I looked at my empty shot glass and the empty beer mug. I looked at the empty pool table that I'd cleared, leaving all the balls in the pockets. I looked around the empty bar and felt empty.

I ordered another round and racked another set.

And then Wham! It struck me how each of us was alone, except the guy who split who is now supposedly yummy with his newbie. I was left holding the bag, and I couldn't trust anymore because he lied; and I couldn't be confident anymore because I couldn't trust myself if I couldn't trust him.

I stared at the balls on the table. So this is how you lose a piece of the fire in the belly because your mother's depressed and anxious because she's all alone, and your brother and sister are hurt and lonely and scared and crying and you have to be there for them.

I kept chasing the 7 ball without pocketing it...

I drained my glass, went for another.

I put another quarter in and played Patsy Cline again, three times.

I hate country music except when I like it.

I remembered the times when I was the one putting up the Christmas tree because Dad was supposedly working late selling cars; now I wondered whether he had been fooling around with other women.

Fuck!

If your parents have been married for 25 years and then break up, how can you trust yourself to hold out any longer than that in your own marriage? Even before this, I used to tell Maw Maw I was never going to get married. Was that because I kind of knew what was going on between Mom and Dad and that it wouldn't last? Or was it because I knew my strongest attraction was for people I could not marry.

If my own mom and dad couldn't keep it together with all the social and religious support they got, how could I expect to marry some girl and stick it out, especially when all I wanted was to find another man I could love. But even when I let my thinking go there, if heterosexual love was so flawed, how could I hope my type of "unacceptable" love stood a chance? Was I ever going to be able to put my heart on the line with any other?

The cue ball was beginning to have serious curves in every hit. When it jumped the table a second time, I quit. Drank the last bit of my boilermaker, returned the cue stick to the rack and left.

As I crossed the parking lot outside and then entered my car, I felt I was entering my future without God and without family, just as I had felt when I'd run out of the house into the cornfields in Bluford all alone when I was six years old.

I fretted a great deal about whether or not to return for my second year at Union. Quite a few people dropped out after their first year. David Easter left to work with the American Friends Service Committee. Another classmate went to Columbia Law School, another to the School of Social Work. Still another dropped out to sell BMWs. Another went into theatre as an actor. With the exception of David, without acknowledging the death of God or looking into it theologically, historically or psychologically, they simply stopped being interested in religion, and did their own thing. Of those who continued to be interested in religion, many were trying drugs, some finding what they considered a truly religious experience (usually on LSD or mescaline

But I felt no call to do anything else, and I was still interested in theology, *post mortem dei*. Also, perhaps I'd little or no momentum to explore options in the wake of my parents' divorce and my father's remarrying; so a part of me, almost by default, found it easiest to continue my studies.

So I returned to Union in the fall of 1966 where I roomed with Jack Quigley, who had a bright, quick mind and a body that betrayed him when he broke his neck body-surfing some four years earlier, leaving him a wheelchair-bound quadriplegic. He paid for my room in exchange for my helping him with his daily routine. That routine consisted of emptying his urinary bag and rinsing it morning and night, helping him don the condom-like sheath for the urinary tube, and helping him put on his pants, shoes, socks and shirt. We had one of the few suites in Hastings Hall: a large living room with a small bedroom on either side. It became a great gathering place for whatever events we concocted. He also had a VW van equipped to accommodate his wheelchair.

The help Jack required I did quite easily, for I had had years of practice with my brother, including managing bowel movements and bathing. Also, in an odd way, it was healing for me, taking care of another handicapped young man, as it made me think less of my own problems.

One day near the end of the term, while I was cleaning him up after an accident with the bladder bag, Jack remarked, "You know, for a white guy, you manage the shit-work of taking care of me pretty well."

"Well, I've had a lot of practice," I said as I drained and rinsed the bag, with a sudden hesitation, as I realized I had never told him about Bill.

"What do you mean?" he asked.

I put everything down and turned to look at him. "My younger brother had cerebral palsy when he was born, and has never walked. So I grew up taking care of him, bathing him, wiping his ass….his is smaller than yours, though!" I joked, trying to lighten the gravity I was feeling.

"You have a brother in a wheelchair all his life and you never told me!?" His black wavy hair fell down over his forehead, but his eyes were wide open. His elbows were on the deskboard attached to his wheelchair. "If I'd known that, I would never have asked you to be my roommate."

"And that's exactly why I never told you."

"But, shit, man….you should have told me." His mouth was set in a tight, straight line, his usual response to frustration.

"Any regrets, Jack?"

"No. No, man…it's been good. You're cool," he said.

"You've taught me a lot, Jack" Suddenly all the held-back feelings of what it had been like to go through the same physical motions of caring for Jack as I had done for Bill surfaced, and I struggled to hold back tears.

"Like what?" he asked.

"My brother, Bill, is more limited mentally and physically than you are. But you've shown me what it really means to take responsibility for your life, to make your life happen and have the determination not to succumb to lethargy or depression."

He gave me one of his biggest shit-eating grins ever. "That's cool. I'll take that!"

It was true; helping my roommate helped me, just as field work my second year with a high school group at Herkimer Street Dutch Reformed Church in Bedford Stuyvesant helped me to be busy and less self absorbed. The pastor was Lou Pojman, a white man about seven years older than I, about my height (5'6"). He was a fireball of social concern, which is what brought him to Bed-Stuy. He was equally anxious to discuss the politics of drug trafficking and what the church could or could not do as he was excited to talk about the meaning of Kierkegaard's *Concluding Unscientific Postscript*.

Lou had guts. He was white and his wife and child were white, and they adapted to life among Jamaicans, Puerto Ricans and American Blacks from the

South. I was not aware of just how the young people I led saw themselves and their world until I invited them to visit me for an evening at Union.

Most of them had never been to Manhattan. It was a Saturday night when we ended up eating pizza in my suite, with the stereo blaring out Otis Redding and Ray Charles. Never having ventured out of Brooklyn, they were worried about both the racist hate from white people and the turf lines of black gangs in Harlem. I, myself, was on edge, but in the end I learned more from these young people than I taught them.

In addition to helping my roommate and my field work, not to mention my studies, I made friends, and so kept busy, despite a lingering sense of loss I'd brought with me from Florida to New York that wouldn't go away.

Gil Winter was one of Jack Quigley's friends before I moved in. Gil had a face and a body straight out of the Hitler youth movement: gorgeous blue eyes, winsome smile and straight blonde hair that always fell seductively across his forehead. He had an energy that I fell totally under the spell of, and my heart would go pitter-patter whenever I heard his voice as he entered our suite.

Gil worked for a church sponsored educational program, Harlem Prep, that took dropouts off the street and gave their lives a structure and a purpose so that they began learning valuable life skills. The work was exhausting because it required guiding young men through getting off drugs or alcohol before any schooling could even begin. Gil was immersed so deeply in his work in Harlem that he barely kept up with his school work. I looked for excuses to be around him, though we never quite found common ground.

Soon after meeting Gil, he introduced me to Steve Anderson, a student from Columbus, Ohio attending Drew Theological Seminary. He was the least self-conscious person I had ever met. Steve's shirt and pants always looked un-ironed, but never unkempt…clean but without any thought given as to how he looked to others. He wore thick glasses and had a smile that conveyed utter sincerity when it appeared. He seemed equally at ease confronting issues and yet not stirring trouble where it could be avoided. He was essentially an autodidact. He steeped himself in psychoanalytic thought and somehow gained a perspective on not just Freud and Jung, but the entire panoply of the depth psychological movement to discuss the finer points with insight, and most importantly, to apply them to contemporary issues.

We would go to a movie—"Sunday with Cybele", "Rosemary's Baby," Fellini's "8 ½", Truffaut's "400 Blows," Antonioni's "Blow-Up".... The film would last an hour and a half, and then we would spend three or four hours talking about what it meant. Steve accepted the death of God as a western cultural event of profound importance, but he was more interested in the implications as drawn from Freudian psychoanalysis and Jungian analytical psychology, than in continuing to study theology.

Steve's assumption, with which I agreed, was that men in general are out of touch with their own feminine side, and therefore projecting onto actual women in their lives both their own inner alienation from the feminine, which Jung had termed the "anima," and their attempt to repair that "anima." Thus, according to Steve, the European movie directors such as Fellini and Truffaut sought to portray not only the damaged inner anima, but their quest to heal it.

"8 ½," for example, portrayed the difficulties a movie director had creating a film when his own marital life became problematic. "Sundays with Cybèle" portrayed a man's inner devastation at having killed a young Vietnamese girl during the French occupation of Vietnam, and his attempt to heal himself in a secret relationship with an orphan. For Steve, men's damaged connection to their anima amounted to a revised origin of original sin, a psychological "Fall," through which could be seen the origin of all evil, most especially the quest for power, on both individual and collective levels, up to and including the U.S. involvement in Vietnam. Steve himself sought to be conscious as he engaged in his own quest to connect to his inner anima, and this gave him a unique and well-thought-through perspective on just about everything.

Through Steve, I was introduced to Robert Theobald, a Harvard and Cambridge-educated economist. Theobald was a visionary who wanted to transform the world from an assumption of there not being enough to go around, to an assumption of plenty. His book, *Free Men and Free Markets,* maintained that the belief in scarcity, which underlay most economic policies, was a myth that perpetuated the gap between rich and poor which we accepted because we had neither the imagination or the will to dream up a means of improved and equitable distribution of resources.

For quite some time, Steve and I worked with Theobald in presenting his ideas to national church groups, hoping to enlist them in a new way of thinking of the future. Theobald represented the kind of optimism that was part and parcel of the death of God movement. For me, it was using the mind to imagine a different configuration of the world, without calling on divine supernatural intervention.

However, no matter how many brilliant and stimulating friends I made and surrounded myself with, something was still missing, and I was still at a loss to identify exactly what it was, just as I remained at a loss how to resolve my own internal struggles with God and my own sexuality.

John Elliott was one of the financial backers of Harlem prep. Gil worked for his field placement at Union and had been telling me about John. One evening Gil said John had invited both of us to dinner.

"Why me?" I asked.

"Because I told him about you and he wants to meet you."

That didn't really answer the question, but I was very interested in meeting someone who had money to put into an experimental program in Harlem.

I wore my latest Brooks Brothers suit, a gray and blue pinstripe, white button-down shirt and blue rep tie.

"You look nice," Gil said as I climbed into Jack's VW van.

"Thanks," I said. "So do you." He was dressed in a casual sport shirt. "Am I overdressed?"

"Anything is fine with John. We usually eat in the Village near his apartment. Casual or formal will be fine."

We headed down the West Side Highway to Perry Street.

"John's homosexual, you know," Gil said as he blew his cigarette smoke out the window.

"Well, no, how would I know that?"

"Right, of course not. He may talk about it or not, but…just so you won't be surprised."

I had never discussed homosexuality with Gil before. I assumed he was straight just because I didn't pick up anything otherwise, except my attraction to him. But I was fast learning that what I felt was absolutely no reliable indicator of another person's orientation.

"Okay," I said. "How old is he?"

"Late thirties, I guess…"

"Okay."

"And he always pays when we go out to eat, so don't bother even offering. He's got plenty and he knows we don't."

As Gil was telling me about John, all I was thinking was how incredibly sexy Gil was whenever he did anything. Even the way he just sat in the car. How can anyone have such power? I mused. But then, before I said anything supid or uttered anything that might expose my internal thoughts, we'd parked the van and were at John Elliott's apartment in the Village.

"Welcome. I'm John," the man said, extending his hand to me. His grasp was firm and strong.

He was about six feet tall, clean-shaven with a ruddy, chiseled face. His smile was immediately engaging and his eyes twinkled. He was beginning to bald, but a small wisp of hair at the front of his head gave him a somewhat impish appearance. He was dressed in jeans and a denim shirt.

Bookshelves along two walls spilled over with books and magazines onto the floor and coffee table. The ceilings appeared to be about 9 feet high and he had several large pieces of African sculpture. From brick walls hung several scrolls of Asian calligraphy and paintings. Two large Danish black leather and teak chairs were set at an angle to each other.

John pointed to one of the chairs for me and asked what I'd like to drink. "I'm having scotch," he said.

"That would be fine," I said. Gil asked for sweet vermouth.

I sat down where John had indicated. Gil sat on a settee on the other side of what was obviously John's chair, replete with a pack of Camels and an ashtray on the side table. I looked at the chairs more closely. Mahogany, not teak.

Gil watched me taking in the plethora of books and art, and smiled.

"Take off your jacket and tie," John said to me, as he handed us our drinks. "I like art," he said, noticing my looking at one wall, then another. "And I like to live with it, so I can touch it, feel it and have it around me, not just store it in a museum." He picked up a fist-sized black object, handed it to me. It was heavy and very hard. "A petrified head of one of our ancestors from Africa," he said. "About 4,000 years old."

"Wow," was all I could say as I felt its heft. I handed it back, then took off my jacket and tie.

He stood up, gestured for me to follow him as he walked over to the brick wall with scrolls. "My pride and joy," he said as he pointed to one of them. It was a painting of a large mountain with a small boat on a river, a man at the helm.

"Southern Sung China, 9th century," he said.

Next to it was a long scroll that had some calligraphy but nothing else except, at the bottom, with a single stroke, the barest image was created of a man sitting.

"Eighteenth century Japanese Zen monk."

Beyond his work on Wall Street as an investor, he told me he studied humanitarian projects around the globe and supported those he felt were most worthwhile. He was especially fond of education and development programs among Southwest Native Americans. But his deepest love was Chinese and Japanese scrolls of painting and calligraphy.

After a couple of drinks we walked a few blocks to a small Czech restaurant below street level. He ordered a bottle of wine for us. When the food came, he took a fork, scooped up rice, and said, "Take a bite of the rice before anything else."

I did and chewed it slowly.

"Ever tasted such texture?" John said. "Just the right cooking. You can't find this quality everywhere....that's why I come here."

Two hours and two bottles of wine later, John insisted we try their version of baklava with Armagnac and espresso. I'd never heard of Armagnac before.

We returned to his place and I thought Gil and I would leave immediately, but John asked Gil to put on an LP of his choice of music and asked us whether we wanted more Armagnac or back to scotch. We both asked for scotch.

"Robert, mind coming in here while I fix the drinks?"

"Sure," I said and followed him into his small galley kitchen. I loved how he called me Robert. No one ever called me by my formal name in conversations.

He leaned over the marble kitchen countertop like a man stretching before running, turned his head to me and said, "I'm glad Gil introduced us tonight. He told me you were a very special person, and now I see why. I would like to continue to get to know you better and for you to know me. So, there is something about me I want you to know. I don't like the word "homosexual" and I don't like the word "queer." Since you're in seminary and have studied philosophy, I'm sure you know the Greek word,"philio" or "philia," meaning friend or lover. I like to think of myself as homophilia, a friend or lover of men." He looked at me for my reaction.

"I like that way of putting it," I said. "Homophilia. Yeah, I like that."

"Okay, good," he replied, standing up and reaching for glasses, then ice.

"And I would very much like to get better acquainted," I added.

"Good," he said, with a quick glance at me as he pulled out ice cubes.

"What are we hearing?" I asked Gil, nodding to the hi-fi as John and I returned with drinks.

"Beethoven's Triple Concerto," Gil answered. "Like it?" Gil's huge smile again.

"Fantastic!" I answered as I took in the melody from the violin.

"The line, that's the thing," John said, sipping his drink. "A superb piece."

Conversation meandered. I was feeling the alcohol a bit, a happy satiation.

As we left, John stood at the top of the stairs and shook my hand. "Thank you for coming," he said.

He had just treated us to a great dinner with lots to drink; how does he manage to convey gratitude to me for receiving what he has given? I asked myself.

"Thank you," I said with emphasis. I leaned forward and kissed him on the lips as if it were something I did every day, and it was only as I turned back and caught Gil looking at me that I wondered what the hell I had just done.

"So are you glad you met him?" Gil later asked as he drove us back to Union.

"Yes, indeed. Thanks for introducing us," I said with a smile.

One Bright Pearl

One winter evening, soon after I'd met him, John called and asked if he could come over. I was taken aback by such a surprise visit, but said, "sure." A short while later, he walked in bundled up in a long coat, stocking cap and wool gloves, carrying something in a paper bag.

"I was walking through Harlem and thought I would stop by. I want to show you something," he said, as he pulled a box with Chinese lettering all over it out of the bag. Then he opened the box and pulled out a gorgeous blue and white vase.

"It's beautiful! It also looks expensive."

"Fifteenth century Ming vase," he smiled.

"And you were carrying that through Harlem?! You're out of your mind."

"Hey, it's just a paper bag. I had to stop by Harlem prep and see how they were doing after I met with my seller. Care to join me for dinner downtown?"

And so I, of course, jumped at the chance to spend more time with this intriguing man alone. Over dinner, John mentioned that he was quite skeptical of all the "do-goodism of you Christians" at Union. Yet, he was impressed when anyone put his body where his ideals were, as Gil and others were doing in Harlem. John had first gone to Harvard, then transferred to Princeton. I had no idea what he saw in me, but when he spoke to me critically of others for what he considered their "inferior education," I felt he was indirectly approving what I got out of Columbia.

That night, after we had dinner, I stayed over at his place. I remember that first night he came to my bed. He sat on the side of the bed the way he stood and the way he sat at dinner or wherever else he might be: as one thoroughly at home. There was no self-centeredness in John. Individual people mattered. Art, history and music mattered, not in an intellectually abstract way, but as part of what mattered in life. As he had said the first night I'd met him, he liked having his art around him to touch and feel as well as view, a part of his daily life. He lived in a larger world and I felt larger being with him.

We did not have sex that night, but I fell under his spell, something between enchantment and love. He started calling me "Big Shot," a play on my name, I suppose, but when he said it, I felt taller, more capable, wanted to live up to his standards and his view of the world. I was in love, but unlike any other way

I'd felt before. There was no concept in my mind nor- as far as I knew, in the culture of 1967-- of being a couple, because we were two men. All I knew was that I wanted to be around him, to enter into his world and learn from him.

John began calling me every few days. No big conversations, just some comment about what he was doing on Wall Street, or when he'd be leaving for Paris or Munich for business. When he was in town, we had dinner nearly every week. I rarely called him. Perhaps out of a reticence I'd picked up from my mother who never felt comfortable with more affluent people. Yet, I did feel comfortable with John, because I was totally interested in every aspect of his life; however, I never thought of him as a peer in the way that I thought of Gil as a peer. Gil and I were students; John was a well-established businessman, twelve years older than me. I had no idea why John gave me his attention, even as I was thrilled to receive it. To me, therefore, calling John during the middle of the day with nothing particular to say would have felt like I was imposing.

I had no problem relating as a peer to another strong, but very different, personality I encountered that same semester of my second year at Union-- Jim Bigham. Jim was an organ student in the School of Sacred Music, which, at the time, was part of Union Seminary. We met one day in the laundry room. He was tall, skinny, with a killer smile and seductive, twinkling eyes. He was an assistant organist at Fifth Avenue Presbyterian Church, and when I heard him play, I realized he was very good.

One night, after too many drinks, I found out he was also very good in bed, and made sex playful in a way I had never experienced before. He was from South Carolina and his accent was completely beguiling. Jim was also a lot of fun to be with. He was almost always upbeat; he would regale any current event with enough flourish to create high drama. He was the first gay friend I had who would certainly have qualified for a high level of "bitchiness." He could be quite searing whenever he chose to, and utterly delightful in his ability to see large, dramatic themes in everyday life.

However, I never told Jim about John, nor John about Jim. Like the other fragments of my life, it seemed to me one relationship had nothing to do with the other—despite myself being the common denominator. Jim was fun; John was something deeper and, hopefully, more lasting.

When John and I did have sex for the first time, it was simply an extension of our conversation, and I had my first insight into the Biblical reference to sex as "knowing." The movement from talking to physical contact and making love felt like one seamless motion, like the development and resolution of a symphony's theme.

My nights and days were also fragmented. It was often difficult for me to go from having sex in the evening, just because it was so exciting, to getting up the next morning for Bible study with Bill Webber. That fall semester of my second year, Bill taught a course on "Bible Study in the Local Church". He was one of the founders of the East Harlem Protestant Parish in Spanish Harlem. He was a model of humility and simplicity. He insisted we call him Bill. He would come in, white hair with a small shock falling over his forehead, take his coat off, loosen his tie and roll up his sleeves, elbows on the table, head in his hands and give an opening prayer. I don't think anyone ever prayed at the beginning of any of my other classes at Union. He was the real thing.

But so was sex, it seemed to me. But sex and the Bible—that is to say, sex outside of marriage and especially sex with a man—just did not compute. In order to engage in either sex or Bible study, I felt I had to eliminate one. But I couldn't.

The more I thought about this either/or split in my life, the more I thought about taking a year off, as many students were doing, for an internship somewhere, an extension of what Erik Eriksen called "the psychosocial moratorium" for young people who don't have enough sense of who they are to get serious about a life direction.

I began looking at the possibilities. I interviewed for a one year position as chaplain at Blair Academy, a boys' prep school in New Jersey, but as I looked around at the cute high school kids, the more it seemed a set up for torture or trouble. I was offered the position, but decided to turn it down.

One night, as I tried to focus on studying while my mind kept going back and forth between my sexual life with John and my questions about God, I received a call from Frederic Hudson. The Director of the Student Union at Colby College in Maine was going on a sabbatical the following year, and Frederic wanted to know if I might be interested in filling in the slot as an internship. It would give us a chance to work together more closely, he explained, and he had a couple other people who would be working as chaplain's assistants that he thought I might enjoy being with.

Maine is different from New Jersey I quickly said to myself, and college kids are different from high schoolers. Plus, I already knew the Hudsons and would love having Frederic to talk with about my struggles. I said yes, I was definitely interested and would like to be considered. I had fallen in love with Maine when I drove up the year before, and was excited about the prospect.

Two weeks later, I flew to Augusta to be interviewed for the position, was picked up by the Dean, Joe Rosenthal, and given a tour and an explanation of my responsibilities. In addition to serving as interim director of Roberts Union, I would have the opportunity to teach two sections of Introduction to Social Science. By the time I left to return to New York the next day, I was offered the position and accepted it, to start in September of 1967.

When I returned from Maine, looking forward to the year I would be spending there starting the next fall, I faced the end of my spring semester at Union with mixed feelings. Tired of my own internal struggles, I suddenly found myself preoccupied with external problems which took me away from myself.

In that early spring of 1967, many of us students were working hard, organizing, planning and participating in public debates and marches from Union down 5th Avenue against U.S. banks' investing in apartheid in South Africa. But we were frustrated that our own seminary was slow to divest itself of holdings in the same banks we had singled out as key to the maintenance of apartheid.

Conversations we had had with the administration didn't seem to be going anywhere. After much debate among ourselves about next steps, we decided to take over the office of the president of the Seminary, John Bennett. Bennett was a teacher of social ethics, one of the most renowned ethicists on international economics and politics of our time. We all felt he would be understanding of our actions and, in fact, be sympathetic. So one morning, before anyone quite arrived to their offices, we entered the president's office with a key from our Student Body president, Peter Johnson, wrote out our list of grievances that formed the basis of our action, posted it on the door, and then barricaded ourselves in.

Our self-confidence in our cause weakened, however, when Bennett came to the door. The upper half of the door was glass, so he could see us and we could see him. He read our grievances and he started to cry. We weren't prepared for this response. We could have withstood his anger or argument; that's what we expected. But this cut us to the quick. We all knew he was a softhearted man, fierce but fair. We certainly hoped for sympathy because of his dedication to fairness, but how could we face his tears?

After my experience with Bennett the previous year over the death of God, I knew this soft side of him. But we all utterly failed to see how personally he took our invasion. We took away the barriers that blocked the door and spent the next couple of hours talking with him. He agreed to call the chair of Union's Board of Trustees to meet with two of our representatives, Charles Powers and Al Sharpe. We wanted to win over the Union Board and then make our case to the National Council of Churches to create a nation-wide ecumenical force putting pressure on the banks to change their support of apartheid. After a date was agreed upon to meet with the Trustees, we relinquished the room.

Gradually, the goal we set of exerting enough pressure from churches to change major corporations policies in South Africa was met. We did not expect that it was sheer economic pressure that forced the change; multiple factors were at work. We did feel, however, that we had established in the public eye a link between where we invest our money and the maintenance of unjust policies.

Meanwhile, during this time, one of my classmates, Bill McFee, from Nova Scotia, was deep into his studies of ancient church fathers and the Christian mystical tradition. He chided those of us who were caught up in the political concerns and said, "just wait….the day will come when you'll see that meditation is more powerful than your protests!" I replied, "If that day ever comes, I'll buy you dinner!"

Another outcome of our protests at Union was the opening up of coursework to include student-initiated courses. Along with Peter Johnson, our student body president, and Jack Quigley, I initiated a course on Freud, Marx and

Nietzsche. We made our own reading list, invited faculty to spend an evening with us on each of the men, and had our own discussions in between.

Robert Neale led us into Freud; Hans Höekendijk, a theologian from Holland who had lived through the Nazi occupation, led us through Marx's *Economic and Philosophical Manuscripts of 1848*; and Paul Lehmann guided us through readings of Nietzsche. In addition, we put together a course on The Future of Technology and Theology, featuring Robert Theobald's writings, led by Robert Lynn who taught in Union's Education Department.

The power and the excitement of both of these courses made all of us recognize the importance and value of an educational process that begins with one's own questions, creating a commitment and an interest that could hardly be matched by a curriculum that was entirely constructed many years ago by someone unknown.

On April 4, amid all our protests, marches and meetings, Martin Luther King, Jr. came next door to Riverside Church to "break the silence" on Vietnam. I went with Jack, and several others from Union to hear him. We went early to find a spot on the outside aisle of the nave because of Jack's wheelchair. I had never seen the church so fully packed, including the two balconies and sides. It was a thrilling moment. We felt we were in the middle of the making of history.

His address, "Beyond Vietnam—A Time to Break Silence" was a landmark position paper, drawing a direct connection between the issues of race, poverty and war. Sadly, he was deeply criticized and lost supporters from those within his own ranks for moving beyond the racism battle. But the connection had been assumed for those of us who had marched against the Vietnam war and in favor of civil rights. His speech made the connection between racism at home and racism abroad in a foreign policy in which we were trying to bully and control another racial minority and their country, and taking money desperately needed by the poor at home to spend on destroying another race.

Moreover, as he made clear, the majority of the U.S. troops going to Vietnam were Black, those who were too poor and less educated to have jobs that would exempt them from service. For most of us, it was the natural unfolding of the implications of the dream he had begun articulating at the March on Washington in 1963.

King's speech seemed to me such a powerful, clear statement about the intermingling of politics and the military-industrial complex, completely in accord with what I'd learned in my Peace Corps training as well as what we talked about at Union, I wanted to do something relevant for the summer before I went to Maine. At the same time I was concerned about my mother and how she was adapting to being without my father, so the closest I knew how to combine both my socio-political concern and my family concern was to go to Florida and live at home with my mother and sister, and to teach Head Start in Stuart.

Before I left New York, John and I met for dinner in the Village.

"So you're going to save the poor people, eh?"

"Well, I don't know about saving them…but I think it's a good age to try to spark a love of learning."

"Well, Big Shot, I admire your effort. If nothing else you'll probably enjoy being with all those kids with all that energy!" He took a long sip from his glass of the Chardonnay he'd ordered with our Shrimp Scampi, set it down and looked me in the eye. "What would you think of my coming down to spend a few days with you, meet those kids, and, of course, your parents."

"Wow! That'd be great! But, won't you be bored? I mean, Jensen's such a small town…no place to go, nothing to do."

"You have a beach, and you mentioned a Sunfish. I can see you in your element!"

No one had ever taught me how to teach, but the student-initiated course we'd devised with Robert Lynn on education and technology had led me to think I knew what preschoolers needed, despite my never having prepared a lesson plan. My book of the day was A.S. Neill's *Summerhill*, which outlined the basic principles of the school he'd founded in England. His method was to place emphasis on what the child him/herself wants to learn; the teacher's role was more to be midwife to the inner interests that arise from the child, than to impose the teacher's own values on the child.

To apply A.S. Neill's child-centered approach to preschoolers who were coming from strong authority-minded parents for whom corporeal punishment was simply an assumed form of discipline, however, proved chaotic at best. My classroom was noisy, the children were often out of control, and sometimes the assistant director stepped in to impose a discipline that I didn't believe in, but to which I had no effective alternative.

In the middle of the summer, John came down to visit for a week and stayed at our house. Never was the difference between my family's culture and John's more obvious. John thought nothing of making omelettes with Swiss cheese and scallions for breakfast, or squeezing lemons to make fresh lemonade. But these were not Gunn family fare, and despite John's very polished manners, I think my mother felt intimidated and useless. Despite my own trepidation, I invited John to meet my dad and go sailing together.

My father, whom I had seen as most knowledgeable around sailboats as well as the inboard we'd had, suddenly seemed very inept, while John seemed to know exactly how to manage the little Sunfish with ease. It was even more painful being on that Sunfish together, with John searching for things to talk about and my father simply not knowing how to respond.

When John and I went to the beach, he wanted to snorkel and I, who'd never had a mask and snorkel, felt intimidated and bowed out. I was simply tense and anxious at John's meeting my family, partly because I didn't know how to explain who he was and how we could be friends when he was twelve years my senior. Also I was nervous because there was the obvious gap in class and life experience between our backgrounds, so I was naturally worried about what John thought of my family. Sex seemed impossible for me; the plaster walls of my bedroom were way too thin. I worried that John would lose interest in me.

John came to my Headstart class for a couple of days and surprised me by how nonchalant he was with these preschoolers. He related to them the same way he did with most people- naturally, neither aloof nor condescending. He took special interest in the same young boy I did, named Sean.

"Quite a young man, there, Big Shot. Smooth milk chocolate skin, perfect head, inquisitive, eager eyes," John said to me quietly. "Above the rest."

On the way as I drove him to the Palm Beach airport for his return to New York, however, he was in a good mood and let me know why: "I've just become a millionaire with my own money. You must take a few days before you start at Colby to come to my family place on Mt. Desert, okay?"

"Oh, that'd be terrific. I haven't seen the coast up there yet." I hesitated but knew I had to bring up the divorce situation. "Sorry to bring my family problems up, but my father agreed to buy my mother a car in the divorce settlement, and now he's saying he can't. Mom and I have talked about whether to take the legal route of his failure to keep the agreement, but we just can't see putting him behind bars. Now that you've shared your good news, it may seem I'm suddenly seeing you as a sugar daddy, but I was thinking of this much before and was just wondering if you could loan my mother enough for a car."

"How much does she need?"

"About $1400."

"No problem. I'll send you a check from New York. It'll be to you, no interest, no timeline, just repay when you can."

"Thanks, John. I'm sorry to ask, but really appreciate your help."

As the summer neared an end, with John's loan, my mother purchased a '64 Chevy sedan and I bought a 1960 aqua four-door Chevrolet Impala for $200 from my dad. With my new wheels, I drove from Florida to New York, where I piled all my worldly goods into the Impala, and set out for Maine with John. It was mid August of 1967 and my job at Colby was to start right after Labor Day.

We broke the trip up by stopping at an elegant old inn in Massachusetts that went back to the days of mail carried by men on horseback. After setting our things in the bedroom, we donned jacket and tie to have dinner at the adjoining restaurant. Old wooden beams supported a low-hanging ceiling. Candlelight on the tables and wall sconces, linen tablecloths and baroque music in the background cast an aura of quiet civility.

"Are you good for your half of a bottle of wine?" John asked me as he perused the wine list.

"I think so," I replied modestly. We usually were good for two between us. I had pheasant. John had veal. We both had St. Emilion.

The bed was a double. Whether John chose it to make sure we were close or because that was all that was left, it felt perfect. We undressed each other and slid under pure white sheets and a down comforter. It felt like the first time ever, there was no one looking over my shoulder—no mother, no father, no roommate—there was no danger of being caught in bed with a man. And John, as a man of the world, older and of the wealthy privileged class, was no ordinary man. I felt safe with him leading the way.

Everything seemed so natural that I did not even stop to think how we might have appeared to our waiter or the woman at the front desk. I was happy. John was happy. And over the next hour, I experienced more mutual emotional and physical intimacy than I ever had before.

The next morning, John bolted out of bed and said we had to get a move on in order to reach Grand Pré, the family place, in time for dinner. We made a mad dash to unload my things at Roberts Union at Colby, then continued to Mt. Desert.

When Mt. Desert finally appeared, as we drove out of Ellsworth, I took in all its splendid pined glory, the deep blue of the bay, the dark green of the trees, and the clear blue of the sky above. Then, after we parked at John's family home and walked up the driveway, the smell of the sea greeted us. The house's entrance was through the kitchen, which was filled with the smell of freshly baked blueberry pie. Madeleine, the grey-haired buxomy cook, wiped her hands on her apron to welcome John, then me. Ellen, as John called his mother, came into the kitchen and, after exchanging kisses in the air with him, she turned to me. John introduced me and we shook hands. She had a surprisingly strong handshake for a woman. She stood slightly shorter than I, and had an erect carriage, as if a rod held her head and spine in a straight line. Her black and grey hair was pulled back in a bun, leaving her face open. Her eyes twinkled as she continued introductions.

We were ushered through the dining room which had a large, wide-planked floor, well-worn and well-polished, and a hand-hewn long, dark wood table, beyond which a series of windows gave a 180 degree view across a large lawn (the "big meadow" as in Grand Pré) to Somes Sound, sparkling in the summer evening. Then we were led upstairs to the living room where people had begun the cocktail hour. After more brief introductions, we picked up our luggage.

John led me up to the third floor where the bedrooms were to freshen up before rejoining everyone. His bedroom adjoined mine, separated by a glass door.

"Convenient," I said quietly.

"Of course," he said and gave me a brief hug.

"What should we wear?"

"It's informal tonight...just a sport shirt." His voice was barely more than a whisper. "Also, when we're up here, we need to be extra quiet. Ellen's bedroom is right next to yours and we don't want to disturb her."

"Got it."

We changed shirts and went back down to the living room.

Since we were the latecomers, we drank our scotches rather quickly then went downstairs for dinner. After we sat down at the table, Madeleine brought in a large tray of steamed and steaming lobsters, one of which she gave to each person. I was introduced into the fine art of eating Maine lobster, which I found far more succulent than those in Florida. John poured *Pouilly Fuissé* all around.

I was being lulled into a sense of comfort, despite myself, that I was one of them, with my Maine lobster and my glass of Pouilly Fuissé, and my plush seat beside John. Unlike the experience of years earlier at Dr. Andre's pool, where I was certain I didn't fit in, here, with John, I felt I belonged. I sat between John and a man in a brown Franciscan habit who introduced himself as Brother David Steindl-Rast.

John's brother was the other David at the table, and described his plan to develop real estate at strategic locations across the state of Maine. John asked some questions about his long term goals. Although I, of course, had no money to invest, I listened as attentively as if I had.

Ellen interrupted. "Oh please, boys, let's not talk money at the table. Brother David, you're working on a book these days, yes?"

Brother David said he was writing a book about his recent trip to Southeast Asia. As he spoke of his experience there, he managed somehow to convey his compassion for the people of Vietnam and Laos without stepping on the political toes of anyone in the room.

I was not so careful: "Then aren't you saying that the countries of Southeast Asia ought to be left to work things out among themselves without our interference?" My own voice surprised me; I sounded very loud to myself.

"I do not know politics," Brother David answered quietly. "I do think it is extremely difficult for people outside a culture to understand what is good for that culture."

"Exactly. We have no business there. We'll only destroy what we say we're trying to preserve," I concluded.

David Elliott interjected, his voice rising, "We're not there for them. We're there for us and the world. We're there to prevent the domino effect of communism."

At that, Ellen lifted her little bell to ring for Madeleine. "I think we're ready for dessert, are we not? David, will you help clear the table while Madeleine brings the tea and coffee? Who will have which?"

Ellen's question seemed particularly pertinent to me about all the unanswered questions in my life: who will have which? A man or a woman, sex or God? War or peace?

After dinner everyone retired to the living room except for Ellen and Brother David, who asked to be excused. John poured drinks for his mother, David and me.

"Bob, John tells me you're from Florida. Do you have family there?" asked Ellen.

"Yes ma'am. I have a sister and a brother- both younger than me, and my parents."

"And you're studying for the ministry?"

"Well, whether I actually go into the parish ministry is an open question. One of the reasons I'm going to teach up here at Colby College for the year is to think about whether I want to continue my studies at Union Seminary. There are so many important issues in our society today; I'm not sure the church is really ready to deal with them- or that it's capable of making any significant contribution to people's real needs."

"And what sort of needs do you think those are?" she pressed.

"Poverty, racism, the growing gap between the haves and have-nots, the war in Vietnam, the increasing fragmentation in society and the lack of anything to believe in to make commitment and sacrifice worthwhile."

"Those are problems that have always been with us," David said impatiently. "There will always be the poor- Jesus said so. And there has never been a time without war. And there is no such thing as equality. You can't change that. Religion is to help people cope with life's pains, not to change the world into something it never was and never can be."

"Well-" I shifted in my seat, took a sip of scotch- "to me that makes the church pretty irrelevant. It turns religion into a long-term hand-holding operation. If the church can't really address the issue of social, as well as personal change, I think it's pretty useless."

I looked to John for assurance. He gave me a smile, which seemed to be his way of saying, "You got yourself into this...let's see what you're going to do with it."

"You sound more like a radical than a minister," David added, taking another sip of his scotch.

Ellen expanded, "I think people need hope. And most people have all they can do to cope with their every day lives. I'm not very active in our local church, but I find it comforting to know it's there. I think you have a very compassionate demeanor about you, Bob, and I would hope that you wouldn't disdain the holding of suffering people's hands. You probably would be quite good at it. At any rate," she said, rising, "it's time for me to call it a day. Bob, we thought the best way to introduce you to Mt. Desert would be to take a tour tomorrow of the entire island, taking in the main points of interest."

"How thoughtful of you," I said.

"We'll leave after breakfast then," she replied.

The men rose as Ellen did and shook her hand good night, David and John adding a kiss on her cheek.

"Big shot, would you put another log on the fire?" John asked as he freshened our drinks.

It seemed strange to me that every time I talked about religion with people outside of seminary, they had a very strong belief that religion's role in society was a passive one, and that it should not stir up trouble about injustice and war. Ellen certainly was right about being compassionate to the elderly and sick, but if someone is setting your whole house on fire it's not really compassionate to hold their hand while the flames engulf both of you.

"Boy, I hope I didn't offend your mother," I said after tending the fire.

David was lighting a cigarette and John, who was pulling one from a Camel pack, smiled at me. "Not to worry."

I sighed and leaned forward in my chair. "This is a beautiful place, this house, the area here that I have only had a glimpse of so far, is breath-taking and inspiring. I just think it's easier to take your position when one is comfortable than when one is actually having one's home and family napalmed off the face of the earth. Vietnam is a beautiful place, too- or at least, it was."

David stood suddenly, scowled, and pointed his finger at me. "You know what your problem is- you don't know what you're talking about. You not only don't understand anything about politics and economics, but you don't understand manners either!" He whirled around, stalked over to the drinks table, poured a quick dash more of scotch into his glass and ended with, "I'm going up to bed. I've said too much. I guess I've had too much to drink. I'm sorry."

After David was gone, I turned to John, this time for absolution. "I've really fucked up the first night, huh?"

"Again, not to worry. I can assure you Ellen is unbruised and David will have shrugged it off by morning. We seldom have guests who say what they think, and who challenge our assumptions. I think it's refreshing."

"I thought your mother was refreshing! I can't talk about politics in my family at all."

"We don't usually back away from heated controversy. My father raised us to meet challenges head-on."

"With the exception of one topic, as I understand..."

"Mmm. Yes. True," John conceded. "I need to pee," he said.

"Yeah, me, too."

John stood, walked over and opened the door to the veranda. "Let's go out here."

The full moon had passed the midway point in its arc and, with no clouds, it lit up the land between the house and water, silhouetting the mountains on the other side. John started peeing. I tried but couldn't. My mind was too busy drawing comparisons between John's family and my own, his history and mine.

What would it have been like to grow up with this as a summer house, to have gone to Harvard or Princeton, to travel easily around the world, speaking French, German or Chinese according to which friends I was with? What would it have been like to have a father who died bequeathing so much, rather than a father who divorced your mother and couldn't even pay for a car for his ex-wife? What would it have been like to have a brother who was capable of managing investment properties? Who was a playmate, or a mate on a boat, rather than...?

After John was finished and I still hadn't gone, he reached over. "Let me help you." He slowly jiggled my penis. "Relax."

"This always happens when someone else is around. I think it's because it's confused about what it's supposed to do, pee or get hard."

Scarcely had I gotten into my room upstairs when John opened the connecting door.

"Undress in there, and muss up your bed, then come on in-- where you belong," he whispered, smiling, and gave me a quick kiss.

I shivered when I lay down naked beside John.

"Are you cold, Big Shot?"

"No," I said. "It's just that -- I don't know. I'm a bit tight. I can't take it all in, so much beauty, not just in the land here, but this place. And your family- I'm not used to...I don't know.... I feel welcomed, but it's like I'm also so out of place, like I don't belong. Just like you and me and what we're doing. On the one hand, you're making sure we enter separate bedrooms and I make it look as if I'm actually sleeping in mine, like there's a reason to be ashamed. And on the other hand, once we're in here, you're totally loving to me, affectionate and... and sexy!" I kissed John on the forehead, smiling, but with a furrowed brow.

"Sounds like Vietnam to me," John rejoined, his hand on my naked buttock.

"What!? What're you talking about?"

"You're into either/or. You think things should be one way or another: no mix, no compromise, no paradox."

John ran his forefinger gently over my eyebrows, trying to erase my tension. "Can I make love to you?"

I answered by hugging him hard, giving him a kiss on the lips, then turning onto my side and backing into his larger body, spoon-fashion, pulling up the covers and turning off the light. Although I felt comfortable snuggled against him, it still felt like a letdown, after having had our night of freedom at the inn in Sturbridge, to come now into his family home where we had to be careful not to make noise and I had to muss up the bed in the adjoining room to pretend I had slept there, rather than here, with John. Why can't we just be "us?" I mused.

The next morning John was shaking my shoulder saying, "Get up, Big Shot," and I saw pine trees and blue sky out the window. After dressing, we started downstairs, but I stopped at the view in front of the house. The front yard consisted of a gently sloping green lawn that ran some two or three hundred yards down to the sea. A small stand of white birch trees was on the left, where the shoreline came in. The waters sparkled with the sun's rays.

"Good morning John, Bob. Everyone else has eaten already," Ellen said from the head of the table. "Please help yourselves."

We were treated to Madeleine's "Maine Lumberjack breakfast," consisting of large plates of eggs, sunny-side up, and scrambled, piles of pancakes, a pot of coffee and pitcher of orange juice, and enough honey, jams and jellies to feed a large crew.

After breakfast, Ellen, John, David and I got into her Pontiac. John drove, David and I took the back seat.

"We're going to Cadillac Mountain first, so you can get an overview of the entire island," Ellen said. "It's the highest point on Mt. Desert."

"Why is it called Mt. Desert?" I asked.

"It's the name given it by Champlain when he discovered the island in 1604," Ellen answered.

"But why did he call it a desert?"

"When you get to the top of Cadillac, I'm sure you'll see," she replied.

I was enthralled with every change of scene: Somes Sound seemed everywhere, Echo Lake on the left. So many different wild flowers, and pine trees. Grey and pink granite popping out of cliffs and water. I kept turning my head in different directions to try to take in everything.

One Bright Pearl

When we finally reached the top of Mt. Cadillac, I realized it was one humongus bald pink granite rock! No trees on the very top. Just rock. And what a view! What Cadillac lacked in height, compared to western mountains, it made up for by the breadth and extent of the view: 360 degrees of ocean and bays, smaller islands all around. The blue of the sky and the darker blue of the water, the white of the clouds, moving so swiftly because we could see their movement by the shadows they left on the lands below, lighthouses dotting points of land, sailboats near and far.

I wished I could be alone with John at that moment, even wished that his family would leave us alone here, to share it together, make it an experience of "ours," of "us." Of course, for John, this spectacular view must've felt common and ordinary. I walked over to him, where he was standing looking out to the eastern horizon, in khaki pants, rumpled checked shirt, hands in his pockets. His wisp of hair blowing in the breeze, accenting his own bald spot at the top. He looked at me with his blue eyes and it was all I could do not to hug him or hold his hand.

"This is amazing."

"Yes, it is. It always is."

Then, suddenly, Ellen came over and began pointing out the villages on the island, including Southwest Harbor and Fernald Point. Before I knew it, we were back in the car, driving to Thunder Hole. Once we got there, I also understood how Thunder Hole got its name. It was an exciting spot where huge, rolling ocean waves entered this crevice in the rocks, smashed against it mightily, then sucked itself back out, only to return again and again, with huge roars and spattering sprays of saltwater you could taste on your tongue. The excitement lay in the very real danger of the place. The granite, wet with spray, was slippery, and one could easily imagine falling into the crevice and being pounded by the waves, unable to escape. Signs and a cable fence warned visitors that the danger was real.

"Someone got too close and fell in, just last year," David said. "They didn't make it out."

Next we went to Jordan Pond House, a gorgeous valley replete with yellow, white and blue wildflowers under the Bubble Mountains, on Jordon Pond.

There we were served tea with fresh, hot croissants and jam. I had not had croissants before. Delicious!

We drove leisurely on the way back, explored Northeast Harbor with some of its "cottages," summer homes of the long ago wealthy, and it was then that I suddenly saw the Elliotts in a new light. They were the relatively new moneyed family. The great cottages of Northeast Harbor, considerably larger than "Grand Pré", were built by older money. So, like the east side and west side of New York, even here on this incredible island, there was a division of those with more and those with less.

Whether from the somnolent effect of the tour of Mount Desert or an unspoken agreement that we not get into another argument, conversation at cocktails and dinner was rather subdued.

"Bob, perhaps you would like to follow up our tour by car with a day of sailing tomorrow around the southern shore of the island," Ellen offered.

"I'd love to go sailing," I replied. "My father and I used to sail quite a bit in Florida."

"Then we shall," she said, "so I'm turning in early tonight."

After Ellen left, David followed her upstairs moments later, leaving John and I alone.

"Let's go for a walk outside," I suddenly suggested to John.

He stamped out his cigarette in the ashtray, stood up smiling and we walked out the door onto the great expanse of lawn with the moon casting shimmering light on the sea. We walked down toward the shore, both of us with our hands in our pockets.

"Are you cold, Big Shot?"

"No, it's nicely cool," I replied.

I looked around at the shoreline, all rocks and clam shells, no real place to sit. A dinghy was pulled above the high tide line but didn't seem suitable for sitting on land. The Lightning sat bobbing in the waves some 30 yards out. So we just stood there, staring out at the moon and the water with our hands in our pockets, the small waves lapping the shore. My thoughts went back to a time when my family still lived in Illinois and I stayed the night at Johnny O'Connell's and we were both eleven years old and we sat looking at the moon and I had this strange warm feeling of wanting to be close to him, to hold him, but not understanding why, and he made a remark about wishing he had a girlfriend. And I thought of the time in Florida when I was camping with the Boy Scouts on the North Fork of the St. Lucie River and it was a full moon and we went swimming without our suits and there was a lot of splashing and joking around, and when Billy Roberts and I went back to the tent, he talked of wishing we had girlfriends to cuddle with and I was glad we didn't and we jerked each other off and held each other through the night until light made us self-conscious and we pulled apart. And as I stood beside John, wondering whether we would do anything, I kept thinking, this is the same moon I watched with Johnny and Billy, and now it's John.

But we didn't do anything there and we turned back up the knoll to the house and I wondered if something was wrong, but as soon as we got into his bedroom, he made it clear that nothing was wrong—nothing at all.

"I'm looking for the eagle's nest," Ellen said. She'd brought along a pair of binoculars and was scanning the shore as we passed.

That morning, we'd left early. Now we were sailing south in the *Blue Sprite*, their 19 foot racing sloop.

"It's a bit further on, mom," David said.

"There!" she shouted shortly after, and pointed to a nest atop a tall pine tree. She handed me the binoculars and pointed. With them, I could see the eagle's moving wings and hooked beak.

"Yes, I see." I handed the binoculars on to John. "Beautiful!"

"It's an American Eagle," Ellen said. "There's a nest of a bald eagle...I believe on the further side of Northwest Harbor."

I leaned back against the cockpit, felt the warm sun on my arms and neck, and looked at how the gorgeous sunny day, the dark blue water and the clear blue sky gave a vivid depth to the color of the pines, the houses, the pink and grey granite rocks covered with brown and yellow seaweed. I looked at John as he continued to survey the land. When he was in Florida, he'd said, referring to me, "It's important to see a man in his own element. To see how his own sense of place makes him come alive." John certainly appeared "alive," completely at ease, on the water, in his family's boat, their island, in his home. "What a sense of place," I thought. "Does everyone fall in love with this place?" I asked aloud.

"It gets under your skin," Ellen replied, "Edward discovered this island during the depression. He came upon Grand Pré and decided immediately to buy it. Quite without asking me! But I am oh so glad he did!" The way she was looking out to sea gave me a profile of her face. She looked splendidly happy with the slightest trace of a smile.

After that, I lost track of time as we sailed along peacefully, listening to the water and wind without speaking. Then, suddenly David hollered, "Ready to come about," as he swung the tiller to starboard. Ellen ducked and John managed the shift of the sail as we set a course north to return.

I felt as if I were in a dream. As if magically I had been given entrance into this family that lived indeed on an enchanted island. And I wondered what it would have been like to have grown up with their assumptions about "place," not just geographic, but social, economic and cultural. It seemed to me that they lived in a larger world than I did and that, in some important sense, perhaps, one's world is the size of the places to which you have the power to go.

At that point in my life, I had managed to come to New York, and now to Maine. Briefly I had been as far west as Denver. John had travelled to London, Prague, Amsterdam, Paris, Beijing, Hong Kong, Taipei and had lived in the Sahara desert. I would have loved to go to those places, but I knew, even as I dreamed of such travel, that I was being led by something inside of me rather than outside of me. My mind was always ready to dream up possibilities for travel, for career, even for a relationship. But when it came down to specific decisions, I knew I made them based on something in my gut, an inner necessity that pulled me into seminary with no more clarity than the question Bonhoeffer raised in *"Who Am I?"*

It was like one night weeks earlier in his apartment. I was saying how much I loved John's Chinese scrolls with the calligraphy, and wondered what it would take to have one. "All you have to do is save your pennies," he said. "But really—how much does a scroll like this cost?" "A small one like this—around $7,000." It would not have mattered to me had he said $1,000,000. I knew instantly that I would never own such a scroll…that saving money for such a thing, regardless of how much I loved it, would never be a determining goal for me, that I was under the power of other concerns.

"What a marvelous day!" Ellen declared when we dropped sail and anchored back at their home. "Did you enjoy it, Bob?"

"Oh, yes ma'am. Very much so," I replied giving her a huge grin, catching John's eye. "Thank you for all of this."

Back at Grand Pré, Madeleine greeted us with the message that Gil Winter called to say that he and Jack Gallahue would be arriving for dinner.

"Jack?" I asked John. "Jack Gallahue?"

"Yes. Do you know him?"

"Yeah, but I didn't know you did."

John looked at me with curiosity.

"Well, I mean, I just didn't know," I said.

"He's a smart man," John said.

"He's a very smart man," I replied. I had never heard John call anyone smart before. Jack certainly deserved the kudo. I had sat in on conversations with friends at Union where Jack was holding forth. He was an ex-Jesuit, and had a mind that covered leagues of territory and circled back to the starting place such that you felt near exhaustion from the intellectual tour you'd just had. However, there was not much dialogue with Jack so much as there were intermittent responses to what he had to say, which, I had to admit, was usually brilliant. "The last time I'd heard him, he was spelling out the implications of Herbert Marcuse's *Eros and Civilization* and *One Dimensional Man* for American society and why the Vietnam war was both inevitable and disastrous. Jack had little time, however, for those of us at Union who were actively opposing the war through teach-ins, protests, demonstrations and vigils such as I had done the past January."

What I didn't say to John was that, for all Jack's brilliance, I didn't like him. Maybe it was because he was a sloppy dresser, and he was such a big man, probably around 6 feet 4 and 300 pounds, he could easily have played "Little John" in *Robin Hood*. He was loud and domineering. Maybe I was just jealous and intimidated.

"We certainly should have interesting conversation tonight," I added.

"An ex-Jesuit, a Franciscan priest, a Protestant minister and a non-believer," John said.

"Did you plan this?" I asked.

He smiled. "No. Just happened. Gil will sleep in your room in the other bed. Jack will take the bedroom next to Brother David."

There was another reason to my reaction to the announcement of Gil and Jack coming: Gil. Gil had introduced me to John and I was utterly grateful and glad, but I still had an attraction for Gil that was very different from my feelings for John. I wondered what it would be like for me to be in the same room with both of them for the first time since Gil introduced me to John. Even more, what would it be like to have Gil sharing the bedroom that I wasn't really using? I had never seen him undressed, but I had certainly fantasized about it. Something inside was jarred by the prospect.

The uncertainties that came over me when I thought of being with both Gil and Jack overwhelmed me. In the space of twenty-four hours, I'd come to feel I might belong with John's family in this idyllic corner of Maine, and here were these shades from New York invading. Would they disrupt the calm I had only so recently achieved?

I knew that Jack didn't think highly of me and might be competitive. Gil, on the other hand, was a man I was attracted to, but I had no idea if he was gay. And I certainly had never said anything to him about myself, but he'd seen my first kiss with John that first evening. But even if Gil was gay, I had no idea whether he would've been interested in me. All of my interactions with Gil remained risky guesswork. Added to all of these considerations, or really at the center of them, I didn't want anything or anyone to disrupt the bond I felt with John.

At cocktail hour, Gil filled us in on his latest work at Harlem prep. "These kids, we get them off the street, help them get off drugs, get organized and give them some tools for coping. But there's a rise in the Muslim movement, even more since Malcom X was killed last year. They tend to be totally separatist—no white men allowed!" he said with a grin. "I feel we're part of bringing some real hope and also teaching that the races can live together....but it's hard earning their trust. And I have to admit, they have to earn mine also."

After a stellar dinner of *Chateaubriand*, we returned to the living room. Gil lit the fire and David Elliott served drinks around. Jack had been –uncharacteristically, as far as I knew him—quiet. Perhaps Ellen's presence affected him, I thought.

John pulled him in. "Jack, what have you been up to lately?"

"I continue to work on my dissertation at Columbia."

"What's your topic?" Brother David asked.

"An Examination of the Role of Religion in Post-modern Consciousness from a Psychoanalytic and Marxist Perspective," he said. "I'm suggesting first of all, that religion needs to take seriously the work of both Freud and Marx if it wants to be a contributor to the development of consciousness going forward into the future, and that insofar as religion—whether protestant or Catholic—engages in that self-reflection based on Feuerbach, Freud, and Marx, the differences among the various religions will tend to dissolve and they will find their common ground in practical service to real human needs."

"Quite a task you're undertaking," Brother David responded. "I love the idea of religions being able to transcend their differences. I have been working in that direction with Buddhists as well as with Protestant Christians."

"Well, part of my thesis is that, to the degree that religions engage in this consciousness expansion, they will cease to exist as religions *per se*. This will be a natural development of secularization."

"So you're in agreement with the Death of God theologians," I said.

"I think their starting point and mine is basically the same: there is a fundamental change of consciousness in the world that recognizes the power of human projection in the creation of religions, and that, as that secular consciousness reaches more people, there will be less need for religion and God," Jack replied. "As far as the Death of God theologians are concerned, they're a pretty ragtag, motley crew as far as I can see."

"And you're not?" I felt like saying, but instead said, "they are all very serious about doing theology with or without God. I attended the Conference on the Death of God in Ann Arbor last October."

"Gentlemen," Ellen said, rising, "I'm afraid I have to call it a day. I'll leave you all to decide whether there is a God or not. Meanwhile, I'll continue to go to church and enjoy the Eucharist."

Brother David also rose to leave. "I hope to talk to you more perhaps tomorrow," he said to Jack as he shook his hand.

When they'd left the room, John passed out Churchill-sized cigars. "Cuban," he said. By the time we each cut and lit them, a noticeable sigh and relaxation of mood was apparent by the focus on the taste and smell of the cigars. I thought of Native American peace pipes.

David opened up. "You guys are very, very smart, I'm sure, and way more knowledgeable about religion and consciousness, whatever, than I am. All I have to say is: 'This is a great cigar!' A toast to good cigars!"

"Here! Here!" we all echoed and lifted our glasses and drew in deep breaths and blew out a lot of smoke.

About an hour later, after we'd finished our cigars and we'd all already had too much to drink, Jack picked up where he'd left off earlier, speaking as if he'd just left off moments before.

"Freud said civilization is only possible by the repression of man's erotic desires. And if you don't repress them, if everyone is completely dedicated to sexual gratification, there will be no motivation to create empires, much less art and music. Marcuse raises the question of whether we can, through retaining intentional- not unconscious- sublimation and an increased culture-wide consciousness, build a non-repressive civilization as yet unknown in history."

"Sounds like fun to me," David said, beginning to show the effects of his scotch.

"The death of the father God releases all the pent-up sex and aggression, as in Dionysius' bacchanals," I said.

"Correct, that's why you get the hippie movement," Jack replied. "But then Marcuse goes on to raise a question which to Freud would have been inconceivable: is it possible for man to reach a level of consciousness in which we choose the higher good in a Platonic sense, choose to share wealth, to create art, to sacrifice immediate gratification of erotic desires in order to enjoy the higher satisfactions of the intellect, of peace, art and human community."

"So Marcuse takes us back to Plato's *Republic*?" John offered.

"Not exactly. Marcuse is not in favor of government by an elite, however configured. Instead, Marcuse said we cannot have meaningful change just by managing our morals or our government. There has to be systemic economic change. His book, *One Dimensional Man*, argues that capitalism is built on a lie – apologies, John—his theory--- he says capitalism is built on the lie that there are limited resources in the world and that therefore conflict among people for control of resources is inevitable. If people understood that in fact there is enough for everyone, there would be a revolutionary demand for a government that was truly of, by and for the people, in which resources and ownership were shared by all."

"Total bullshit," David declared, rising to his feet. "I think that's my cue to call it a night, gentlemen. Good luck solving the problems of the world." And with that, he left the room.

After his brother was gone, John turned to Jack. "And by what force of law or the holy spirit are the powerful supposed to relinquish their power to support the revolution?"

"It would require a revolution in consciousness," Jack replied, "born of those who realize that their current investment in capitalism has left them "one dimensional men"—men who have myopically focused on getting money at the expense of all else that comprises being human."

John, Gil and I were looking at Jack. There was finally a silence, but a silence poised over an abyss.

"What does Marcuse really know about money—not economic theory, but money: how it's made, what you can do with it." John's tone had a quiet fierceness to it, unlike anything I'd heard from him before, like a lion being roused from slumber. "Without the profits of private capitalism, where would the great museums of the world be? For that matter, where would great art or great music come from? Without wealthy subscribers to support them, the arts would not exist. I think your friend, Marcuse, is an idealist who has never been to a ballet or a museum in Moscow or Beijing. Communism—which is where it seems to me he's headed—systematically killed all culture and all genuine science. Creativity in the arts and the sciences is *dead* in Russia and China."

"I don't think you're an example of Marcuse's *One Dimensional Man*," I said to John, trying to siphon off the tension in the room.

John pushed on: "I suppose you're another one of those anti-war protesters," he asked Jack.

"I'm not a protestor," Jack said. "I'm dedicated to clarity and consciousness. That's a big enough job. I leave the demonstrations and protests up to Gil and Bob." He nodded and grinned at Gil and me.

"Not me," Gil said quickly. "I'm too busy."

"Well, okay. I'll be the token protester here," I said, draining my glass. "Yeah, I've put my body on the line." I was beginning to feel the effect of the scotch and brandy. "I mean, these are real life and death issues. People are dying over these things. It's not an ivory tower exercise. This is why we're in Vietnam: to defend capitalism."

"You mean fight communism," John interjected.

"Same thing: fight communism, defend capitalism. I mean, every day we see more and more Americans bleeding and dying—we don't even face the Vietnamese wounded and dead; they evaporate into 'body counts'. It's hard to watch, even more when McNamara intones his spiel about numbers in his obfuscating lingo." I felt tight all over. "I mean, who are we to control a country on the other side of the world?"

"Big Shot," John's voice softened, "it _is_ about control. It's about power. With power comes responsibility. You can't have democracy just by surrendering power. You have to use power in responsible ways. You may not like the domino theory, but if we let Vietnam fall into the hands of the communists, we will have given up all of Southeast Asia. That would be a disaster politically and economically, on a world scale—much larger than your seminary friends have any idea of."

I felt admonished, rather than responded to. I suddenly smelled the stink of our burnt-out cigars. "Refill?" I asked around to break the awkward moment.

"Yes, scotch would be great, Big Shot," John said.

"I've had enough," said Gil. "I don't want to be hung over tomorrow, but I'll help you, Bob."

As Gil put ice in new tumblers and I poured, he whispered to me, "Nice job, Bobby." Gil was the only person since high school that called me Bobby, and somehow, coming from him, I loved it, because it was full of affection and made me feel intimate with him, like John calling me Big Shot.

"Well, I could use a little help here," I said. "I feel pretty lightweight." I was undone. Between butting heads not only with Jack but now John, and then feeling this huge wave of turn-on to Gil with his calling me Bobby, I gulped half my scotch still standing at the table.

"Sorry, but I just don't understand all this. I'm against the war, but I get lost in theories," Gil answered. "Also, my head's spinning. I'm turning in."

After bringing fresh drinks to John and Jack, Gil said goodnight and headed upstairs to the bedroom we were ostensibly sharing. After he left, I suddenly felt a wave of disappointment, knowing Gill would be asleep by the time I went upstairs. I felt a sense of a missed opportunity. But even as drunk as I was, I knew it was for the best. I was, after all, with John.

As John, Jack and I worked on our scotches, I filled my pipe, llit it, and tried to forget about Gil. "You know, I was just thinking….why is it that we can get so heated up talking about Vietnam and politics and economics—we haven't even gotten to religion yet! Like, what's our investment in the conversation?"

"I think you said it awhile ago. These are issues of life and death. They affect how we live, what our goals are, what our commitments are," John offered.

"Issues of life and death—I've never felt them so keenly as I have since turning forty. Especially, I find myself thinking of death," Jack said. "When you're younger it doesn't seem so important."

"I've thought of it seriously all my life," I said.

"Yeah, but it doesn't hit you like it does at forty," Jack said.

"It's very real of course. But when you turn forty, it carries a different valence," John insisted.

As I listened to Jack and John, I realized I was getting annoyed. They were condescending to me because of my still being in my twenties, assuming I could not have felt any more on the issue of death than they did at my age. Maybe I was crazy to feel as strongly as I did, but still— Had they watched three of their own dogs die before the age of six? Had they seen the dead bodies of three great grandparents and a grandfather in coffins in the parlor of their own home before they were ten years old? Had they grown up with a brother whose legs never developed and couldn't walk, making them wonder what could happen to their own legs or hands? Had they compared penis sizes with their cousin one month when they were thirteen and seen him lying in a coffin the next month because of a sudden bout of polio?

My reverie was interrupted by Jack. He was saying goodnight and then going upstairs.

When Jack was gone, John winked at me. "What do you say, Big Shot- time to turn in?"

I nodded, then struggled my way out of my chair, and took his glass and mine to the drinks cart. John emptied the ashtrays into the wastebasket and then we turned out the lights.

Once in bed, the arguments about war and cultural consciousness, oppression and denial, evaporated, and our bodies did what they wanted to do.

The next day was Labor Day. Before we got out of bed, John kissed me and said, "Thank you for coming, Big Shot." It was his personal goodbye. He was never affectionate in public. I was feeling sad as I drove him to the Bangor airport for his return to New York. As I waved to him getting on the Delta flight to LaGuardia, I felt instantly alone, a kind of abandonment, even though I was the one who had chosen to spend the year 300 miles north of him. But as I drove south to my new job at Colby and replayed those few days I'd just spent with John on Mt. Desert, I felt that my sadness itself suggested, whatever the coming year brought, my future had both John and Downeast Maine as part of it.

Once I got unpacked, I drove down Mayflower Hill into Waterville where the Hudsons had moved. Frederic had called an organizing meeting in his home on the Tuesday after Labor Day for all the interns and students who would be working with him on Lorimer Chapel affairs. In addition to myself, there were two couples, Jerry and Linda Boren and Homer and Melody Page, who were there on internships for the year under Frederic's direction. Each of we three men would be teaching Introduction to Social Science. Jerry and Homer would be Assistant Chaplains for the year, while I was Director of Roberts Union, the center of student affairs. I also planned to teach a course on the Death of God Theology in the Adult Education Department.

Frederic introduced Susan McFerren as Chair of the Dance Department. She wanted to help plan the chapel program because she often created liturgical dance for chapel services. Single, with short brown hair, and very lean, she stood out from the group by her posture. Even sitting cross-legged, her spine was erect and seemed to center her. She wore a bright blue turtleneck that enhanced the blue of her eyes. Frederic had told me about her before the meeting in a suggestive way. Although he always gave people full freedom not to follow his suggestions, so that he could not be accused of manipulating people, he nevertheless was usually busy trying to underscore the latent possibilities of relationships from the most personal level to the level of careers and politics.

Frederic's none-too-subtle suggestions that Susan would be a great catch would nonetheless have fallen on deaf ears were it not for the thousands of other voices, reflecting centuries of Biblical tradition and social consensus, bouncing around in my head that said, "you should be with a woman", not to mention the Levitical injunction, "thou shalt not lie with a man as with a woman. It is an abomination."

At Frederic's prompting, Susan began talking about liturgical dance. Her voice was articulate without an accent that I could detect; it was not so much forced as conscious, the voice of someone who had been trained how to speak perfectly. Nevertheless, having been to a performance of the New York Ballet that I had trouble relating to, I was intrigued to see what Susan's own style of dance might be like.

There were about a dozen students also at the meeting who were interested in helping out with chapel programs. Frederic had been hired as Chaplain because there had been a dying off of interest and attendance at Chapel, and he was replete with new ideas, born of his critical perspective on God, theology and the church. More students were participating in chapel because he drew out of them what they were interested in and their own perspectives on their spiritual quests, just as he had done with me.

It was no surprise, therefore, when, after discussing drama and dance in worship, the subject of protesting the war in Vietnam came up. Whether to hold demonstrations in downtown Waterville or somewhere on campus settled into a focus on action in Roberts Union and a protest against the ROTC (Reserve Officer Training Corps) program that would soon be visiting. Frederic made it clear that this had to be a student-led and operated event. Neither he nor any of us interns would actually participate in the demonstration. We were to be perceived as knowledgeable about the students, but not as having directed them. I would be telling Dean Rosenthal about what I had heard, and take a sympathetic view of the college's concerns to maintain order.

One of the most vocal and articulate students in the conversation was a young man with a full brown beard, wearing an ivory cable knit turtleneck sweater. He had a great sense of humor and vitality about him that was expressed in the twinkling of his eyes and a grin that seemed somewhere between mischievous and wicked. His name was Richard Shippee.

"I'm going to be in your Social Science class," he said as the meeting was breaking up.

"And also in my dance class!" Susan said as she walked up to us and added. "I'm Susan."

"Yes, Frederic told me about you."

"All good, I hope…?"

"Of course."

"I'm having my dance students over for a little barbecue Friday. Rich will be there and several others from this group. Would you care to join us?," she asked. "It's a way of kicking off the new semester with some fun before they get engrossed in studies."

I glanced at Richard.

"Sure, come!" he said.

"Well, yeah, okay." His encouragement was all I needed.

"Do you need a ride back to the campus?" she asked.

"No, thanks. I brought my car," I replied.

"Oh, then could you give me a ride back?" Rich said to me.

"Of course."

"Room for one more? I'm Amelia Rosenthal," a young, lithe, long brown haired woman asked. "I'm also from New York," she added. "Well, Brooklyn!"

"Sure, it's a big car. Anyone else?" I said to the room.

In the end, five students piled into the Green Machine to head back to Colby and so I had no chance to speak with Rich alone or clarify my own thoughts about Susan.

That night the phone rang. "Hi, Big Shot."

"Hi, John."

"Have you found any Adonises up there yet?"

"No, I wouldn't say so. Well, maybe one."

"Who's that? What's he like?"

I told him about the meeting at Frederic's and my reaction to Richard.

"Does he have a head on his shoulders or is he simply a hunk?"

"Oh, he definitely has a head with something in it. He made some astute comments about the war and a possible student demonstration."

"All for God and country," John said. "Sounds irresistible!"

"You don't need to worry. He's a student: nothing will happen."

"Just read the *Symposium* in class and see how he reacts."

"I know, he'll be my Alcibiades and I'll be his Socratic troll of a mentor."

"Big Shot, it will take many years before you qualify for that title."

"You know what they say, at 27, it's all downhill physically."

"Two more years to go! Plenty of time to sow your wild oats!"

"Yeah, right," I said sarcastically.

"I've been thinking—at the end of your year there--- do you have any plans yet?"

"Are you kidding? I don't know whether I'll even return to seminary, much less have planned anything else."

"So how would you like to go to Iceland together—take a freighter ship—live like the crew, spend a few weeks?"

"Iceland?...Why Iceland?" I was shocked. I recoiled from the idea as if I'd been tossed a hot potato.

"It's a place I've never been. Great glaciers and mountains. It's off the beaten path. Extraordinary beauty. And tundra—and lots of sunlight in summertime!"

"Uh, yeah. Sounds interesting…" I didn't know what to say. I suddenly felt as though, if I went on the trip with John, I would be completely exposed, like, everyone on the boat would know we're queer, and worse, that he's twelve years older than me and paying for everything.

Later, when I got off the phone, I poured out a glass of Johnny Red, lit my pipe, and imagined being on a freighter with John where everyone would see us as a couple. I could already hear their taunts and jeers: "Faggots! Queers! Fairies! Fruits!" The two of us alone with a ship full of fishermen—I imagined being beaten up in our bunks while sleeping. They could throw us overboard and claim we fell and drowned before they could pick us up.

"Gunn, you're being paranoid," I said as I puffed on my pipe. "....which doesn't mean they're NOT out to get us," I countered to myself.

Nothing made sense. I had just spent five days with this man, sharing his bed, his family, his idyllic life. Now, suddenly I was frozen inside. Somehow all our time in his apartment, at Union, at restaurants in New York and at the country inn in Massachusetts and the house on Mt. Desert—all of it seemed like an idyll—a mystical experience that took place out of ordinary space and time. And then his suggestion of Iceland came crashing through the idyll, shattering it, leaving him and me exposed to public view, like the pictures Bill Wertheim showed me in sophomore year at Columbia of Jews in Buchenwald after they had shed all their clothes, standing naked in front of Nazi dogs and guns. Shame and fear filled me as I tried to argue my way out of those images. Nazis singled out homosexuals, not just Jews, I said. Yeah, but this isn't Nazi Germany. Then why did I get called all those names and get beat up in every new school I moved to in Illinois?

Stop it! Just stop it! I said to myself, and put on Beethoven's Triple Concerto with Rudolf Serkin—an LP John had given me. And Goering went from the gas chambers to his home where he and his family listened to Mozart and Beethoven, not Mendelssohn! I took the record off. Poured another scotch.

The next morning, Wednesday, I put a sign out in front of the open office area at the entrance to the Union, giving the date and time of the meeting I would hold to discuss what to do at Roberts Union. The Union had been run for some thirty years by a now-elderly couple who had no sense of connection to students, and discouraged innovation in favor of order and predictability. Students were ripe for a chance to make the place "theirs" and I was happy to be a facilitator. The next few days I was prepping class materials and settling in, then it was Friday.

The barbeque Susan had invited me to when I met her at Frederic's was set for 5 p.m. I picked up Rich, Ken and Amelia, all three students in both Susan's dance class and my social science class. Rich wore khaki shorts with a beige tank top that revealed his hairy chest. As we drove in, several other students were already milling around in the side yard. Susan was squatting at the small charcoal grill where hot dogs and hamburgers were sizzling. She was dressed in white Capri pants, sneakers and a short sleeve blue and white striped shirt hanging loosely over her hips.

She hollered out to us all, "Soda and beer in the cooler. Help yourselves. Hot dogs and hamburgers just about ready!"

It was 1967 and The Doors' "Riders on the Storm" was blaring out of an upstairs apartment window.

Rich introduced me to the students I didn't know. One student stood out by being the tallest person there. His also had brilliant red hair, and so, fittingly, was called Rusty. He was a senior and seemed to me to have an ample dose of narcissistic self-confidence. Very outgoing, he seemed accustomed to being the center of attention. In contrast to the other students there, Rusty seemed obviously to be "that way." Not heavily effeminate, but having the self-consciousness of the performer who is never off stage in his own mind. He was, he let me know, the principle dancer who partnered with Susan.

A young woman with large dark brown eyes and a smile with big full red lips came up and introduced herself to me. "I'm Cathy Pagano. I'm from Long Island." Her eyes and bearing exuded passion and intelligence.

"Tell me, are all Colby women smart?" I asked.

She looked around the yard. "In this group, yeah."

We both chuckled.

Rich and I chatted as we ate. He told me about life at Colby and his family who were from Pawtucket, Rhode Island. After everyone had filled up on hamburgers and hot dogs and had some of Susan's superb homemade cheesecake, she gathered us all into a circle.

"We've been given a grant by the Maine State Commission on the Arts to go around the towns as far north as Caribou and downeast to Calais to introduce dance into the schools," she began.

Applause and hoots all around.

"Do any of you know 'Carnival of the Animals'?"

Three hands went up.

"It's a musical suite by Saint-Saens, and we'll be choreographing it as a dance. We're the only dance program in Maine, so this is a great opportunity. We'll probably be the first live dancers these students will have ever seen." More cheers and applause.

"That's quite a coup for you," I told her later as people began to leave.

"Yes, I'm very excited!" she replied with a big smile. "It's a chance to cut through some of the prejudice against the arts in areas where people don't see live performances. And since we do modern dance, it will also counter some of their images of ballet as the only kind of serious dance."

As we all carried the food and utensils upstairs to her apartment, she pulled me aside and said quietly, "How would you like to have a home cooked meal sometime? Food at Roberts Union can be pretty dull fare after awhile."

With other students passing by the narrow passageway in her apartment, our bodies were pressed together. The faintest whiff of perfume. She was slightly shorter than me, had small breasts and a nice butt. Kind of boyish, like Mary Martin in *Peter Pan*. "Sure," I said.

Returning to campus, Cathy and Charlie joined us. Rich sat up front in the middle beside me, Cathy on the passenger side. Charlie, Ken and Amelia in back. Rich's hip and thigh pressed against mine. Was this an overture, I wondered? Or just someone who felt comfortable with me? I was feeling some physical response to the contact. What was his story? How could I have just made a date with Susan and be having this reaction to Rich?

When they'd all piled out and gone to their dorms, I pulled the Green Machine into the driveway at Roberts and went upstairs, poured Johnny Walker Red over rocks and put my Jefferson Airplane lp on the stereo. After "White Rabbit," these words resonated through me:

don't you want somebody to love
don't you need somebody to love
wouldn't you love somebody to love

The meeting at Roberts Union came and went. Many wanted some sort of pub. Richard and Charlie Abbott (who had also been at Frederic's and Susan's) just wanted a hangout. Since alcohol was definitely forbidden, the group focused on an empty room to the side of the first floor of the union, and decided to turn it into something beyond a coffee house, since there was already a coffee house in the chapel. They wanted to show old movies of Charlie Chaplin. They decided to decorate the place with newspapers all over the wall, and so decided to call it "The Paper Wall." They brought in large cable spools from the phone company that made great tables, and, over the next few weeks, peanuts whose shells littered the floor became *de rigeur*. It soon became a thriving place, especially during movie nights. It also became the center for all serious political discussions and non-alcohol partying.

My apartment was just above the Paper Wall, and often students, of course including Rich, would come up and hang out after the Paper Wall activity was done, sometimes socializing, sometimes talking about serious things in their lives. We would drink beer or Johnny Walker Red or Cutty Sark and I would smoke my pipe or a cigar, and when I felt the conversation was dying or when I got tired, I would collect the ashtrays and stop offering more to drink, and pretty much everyone got the hint.

In the meantime, once the semester started, I discovered that I loved teaching. We read essays by Marx, Lenin, and Mao. I was surprised to find how much I and many of my students agreed with Mao about the nature of true education, or the importance of "experience," over theory, by which he meant people should become more aware of their actual economic and political reality, paying attention to who controls whom and who owns what and how that shapes freedom and its limits.

In class, we also discussed the situation in Vietnam and their situation as students in a private prestigious college grappling with the ever-looming possibility of being drafted, while wondering who had power over their lives (parents, college, Selective Service). This also led to the students evaluating who limited their freedom, and many found it hard to cut through their rationales to think beyond the existing limits within which they were living.

As the possibility of demonstrating against the presence of ROTC at Colby became more and more real, the class divided fairly quickly into those for whom it was unthinkable, because of what their parents and Colby president Robert Stryder might think, and those who felt free to take such a risk. Many people throughout America favored the war, believed it was necessary, truly "to make the world safe for democracy." But many of my Colby students who wanted no part of the demonstration didn't feel strongly about God and country; they didn't care about the moral issues; they were concerned mostly about what those in authority might think. Still others, many of them, just didn't want to be drafted and risk getting killed.

During all these classes, Rich would follow everything with his twinkling eyes and his impish smile, always checking in with me to see what my own reaction was. He was clearly thinking on his own and yet his thinking and mine so coincided that, before I would even say anything, he had already expressed the thought to the class. He was, after all, my student, and therefore not to be pursued in a romantic way. Of course, I said nothing of my feelings for him to him. But we were constantly looking at each other in ways that I worried (and also was thrilled to feel) might have been suggestive. Still, it was more of a psychological and intellectual attunement, and I had no idea how to break through the ambiguity.

One day, as my Social Science class ended and others cleared out, Rich came up to me, grinning big.

"What's that shit-eating grin about?" I asked.

"Oh, nothing much. Just wondering when you're going to take Susan out." The grin again.

"Are you trying to play matchmaker or something?"

"Mmm. Maybe." He hesitated until I looked at him directly. "She really likes you."

"Really?" And how do you know that?"

"After our dance rehearsal yesterday, I heard some of the girls talking about the eligible bachelors on campus. Your name came up, and they were saying how handsome you were and Susan walked over to us, poked her head in and said, "and sexy." She totally blushed, then said, "Well, I mean he's very smart, too!" And everyone laughed and her face got even redder."

"And what do you think?"

"I think you should go out with her. She's really cool—with a beautifully moving body!"

"No, I mean—what do you think—about me?" I looked over at the blackboard and deftly grabbed an eraser and started wiping out Mao's points about education as action. "Sorry, no, never mind."

He laughed. "Now you're the one blushing! Omigod! You <u>do</u> like her! Go for it, man!"

I dropped my book and papers.

"Shit!" I bent down to pick them up and Rich bent down to help. As he handed pages to me, our eyes met and the world stopped for a long second. I was on the verge of tears and I looked into his dark brown eyes that seemed so completely open I could walk right in. I shifted my gaze to the lips I wanted to kiss but couldn't.

"Sorry, thanks," I said and we both stood up. His grin was gone.

"Well, time for lunch," I said.

We started walking out.

"About what do I think about you---"

I was skipping down the steps fast, two and a time. I didn't want to hear any more.

"—you're handsome and smart—and I'm no judge about sexy because you're a guy, but, yeah, that too." He was trying to keep up with me.

"Thanks for the vote of confidence," I said, matter of factly.

"What—did I say something wrong?"

When I wasn't working with my Colby kids in Social Science and being distracted by Rich, I was also enjoying teaching the course on Radical Theology and the Death of God to adults. In middle age, the seven students in the class were all women—four Catholic, one atheist, two Protestant. Even apart from the identified atheist, they were not particularly religious in terms of going to church, but they were very serious about their quest for personal meaning. If church members could be half this interested, I thought, a parish pastor might be a very cool thing.

When I went to Susan's apartment for dinner, I was nervous, though I couldn't say why. Though I was living in perpetual conflict about my sexuality, I still oddly expected myself not to be nervous during a "normal" thing, such as a date. She served me Cutty Sark and played a new Leonard Cohen album. When it got to "Suzanne" we listened intently while she turned over the steaks. He sang:

> Suzanne takes you down to her place near the river…
> And you know that she's half crazy
> But that's why you want to be there
> And she feeds you tea and oranges
> That come all the way from China
> And just when you mean to tell her
> That you have no love to give her
> Then she gets you on her wavelength
> And she lets the river answer…

Susan served steaks and corn on the cob with a bottle of Beaujolais. She played an album by the cellist Janos Starker, of whom I'd never heard, but he was extraordinary. In the doorway, after I thanked her for a great night, I found myself kissing her, and I let the kiss linger a moment longer than a polite brush of my lips, uncertain if I was doing this as I felt it was expected or me or because I'd really wanted to. As I drove home in the dark, I did wonder what the difference was between being mesmerized and being drunk.

A few days later, Susan invited me to hear Alice DeMille speak in the Colby auditorium. Alice was the niece of Cecil B. DeMille, the famous movie director who had made "The Ten Commandments" and other epic movies. As she discussed her own life as her uncle's niece and then her involvement in the arts around the world, I felt my own world expanding. She made music, film and literature come alive in an utterly inspiring way. After we all gave her a standing ovation, Susan took me by the hand and pulled me to the podium where DeMille was greeting students.

Susan introduced herself and said, "You make me feel proud to be a dancer... like there's a real purpose served in the culture at large."

"You should be proud, because you create unimagined possibilities for all of us," DeMille said.

They talked on a bit as I stood by listening and watching. Susan standing there talking to Alice DeMille was in the world she belonged to, the world of the arts. She was absolutely one of the people DeMille had been talking about, someone who opens up the senses, the mind, the heart, the imagination. But Susan was also opening up something in me, in fact, and I was intrigued. More than that, I felt proud of her, or more honestly put, proud to be with her. In a sense, she was doing in her way what John had done in his way—expanding my own world, and I felt closer to her for that, and suddenly I could see our lives mixing well together.

After watching Susan speaking with Alice DeMille, I was confused, wrestling the old, familiar tugs in competing directions for a few days, but doing my best to conceal my confusion. Then, thankful for the distraction from my own internal dilemmas, I watched as the students staged their sit-in against the war, in Roberts Union, right across from the ROTC recruiting table, much to the consternation of the Dean, Joe Rosenthal, and the president, Robert Stryder. I was standing on the sidelines with Susan, worried that at any moment it might turn ugly. It was, however, an entirely peaceful event. No one got into a fight, though there were snide remarks tossed back and forth between the demonstrators and some jock types. The ROTC officers maintained their cool, and there was nothing to warrant the arrest that some had feared. Within three hours, the demonstration was over and students talked about it mostly in terms of who went and who didn't and who wanted to but made excuses.

Oddly enough, after the demonstration, Susan left and I found myself bumping into Don, the manager of the bookstore which adjoined my office in Roberts Union. It was clear to me and anyone else who mentioned him, that he was homosexual. He had a dark red beard and hair, and eyes that always seemed to me to stare vacantly, as if he were trying to see you, but just who was the him inside seemed unclear.

After a few moments of small talk about the demonstration, Don invited me to dinner that night, and, with no thought of Susan or even if I really wanted to have dinner with Don, I accepted. Just why I accepted so suddenly, when I wasn't really attracted to Don and I was just starting to enjoy seeking Susan in a new light, I cannot explain. But that night, I went to his place. Don had one half of a duplex house in Oakland, only four miles from Colby. He served drinks, we had supper, struggled to maintain a conversation, then after a couple more drinks, he began to make some physical overtures which I politely declined. He politely accepted my refusal. Was that dinner a part of me testing myself? Or was I simply wanting to know if Don was an interesting person quite apart from being gay?

The first time I saw Susan dance was in November, just as the weather was turning colder. A sculpture called "The Whole Man," had just been installed at Colby. It consisted of a tree about twelve feet tall made of bronze and silver branches with leaves intertwining. Created by Clark Fitzgerald of Castine, Maine, he had asked Susan to create a dance around the sculpture to celebrate its installation. The music was a piece called *Three Synchronisms* by Mario Davidovsky. Once the music started, I was transfixed, watching Susan's lithe, slender body wind itself in, out, around and through the branches of the "Burning Bush" in an astounding way. I had never experienced modern dance to be so entrancing and, somehow deep inside me, seductive. I felt something was opening inside me.

Once, as a freshman at Columbia, when I was studying harmony, I had a dream of notes going in and out of a music staff—three-dimensionally—and it was completely erotic. I had an erection and came, waking up from my sleep. I responded to Susan's dance in a similar way, though I wasn't physically aroused...it was more of a psychological thing for which I had no words at the time. I felt it more in my abdomen than in my crotch.

After the dance, Susan introduced me to Clark. He was a wonderfully warm, engaging man in his 50's who looked very much like an old man of the sea—large wrinkles on his face, weathered, seemingly, by the seashore where he lived. He was quite interested in the fact that I was studying theology, and said he loved Paul Tillich, and invited us to come visit him and his wife sometime in Castine.

Jim Carpenter, Chair of the Art Department, held a reception in his home for Clark and for Susan after the performance. There I met other faculty, including Paul Perez, the Chair of the Psychology Department, Harriet Matthews, the resident sculptor on campus, and Bill MacKinnon, Chair of the Math Department. As I talked with these people, I got a picture of the life of Colby faculty: they taught, they all had homes near the college, and most of them had weekend or summer cottages either out in the country or down on the coast; several had places bordering Reid State Park in Georgetown. What a life! I thought. Maybe I'll be a professor, but of what? The whole question of my future was at least as open as the question of my sexuality, and I couldn't see fitting in as any one thing, whether as a pastor or a professor.

A few days after Susan danced for *The Whole Man*, we went to the local movie theater to see "I am Curious Yellow," a Swedish film that had been banned by courts in both Boston and New York for its explicit genital depiction of a man and woman having intercourse.

It was a powerful critique of bourgeois Sweden and showed clips of Martin Luther King when he was in Stockholm, and Yevgeny Yevtushenko reading *Babi Yar*. It captured the essence of the revolutions going on: the protests against war, the concern for the poor, the breaking free of sexual inhibitions, the explosion of art, music and dance, the connection between sex and the natural environment. They climbed trees and frolicked in wheat fields. The twenty year-old woman lead was beautiful and seductive. The man was completely unattractive to me, but I was fascinated by the inclusion of sex as a normal part of a story. The movie made me curious about my own heterosexual possibilities.

After the movie that night, as I drove Susan home, I asked her what she thought of the movie.

"It was good," she said.

"What did you think of all that nudity?"

"It seemed very natural to me," she said matter of factly.

"Making love in the woods?"

"Yes," she answered, then yawned.

"What'd you make of Martin Luther King showing up there?"

"I didn't understand why. I guess he was there for the Nobel Peace Prize, right?" She seemed only slightly interested in keeping up her side of the conversation.

"Well, actually that was in Norway, not Sweden. But, yeah, I think he was in the film for the same reason Yevtushenko was…a voice of freedom against prejudice and oppression. King won the Nobel for his civil rights leadership, Yevtushenko decried the Russian Revolution."

Susan was silent. I wanted her to say more, to respond, to be as engaged by the movie as much as I had been, at least intellectually. It was, after all, a social breakthrough in America. After a moment of frustrating silence, waiting for her to continue the conversation and then realizing she would not, I asked her, "Are you okay?"

"Just tired, sorry."

My own "curiosity" and enthusiasm fell thud to the floor. What else could I say?

I saw her to her door and kissed her good night. As I drove home, I realized I had wanted her to be excited because, in fact, I had not been. I had not found the woman in the movie attractive with her big breasts, nor was the man attractive to me, so my own actual erotic feelings never got triggered, so I had gone intellectual about the whole movie. Perhaps Susan had succumbed to my own lack of enthusiasm, rather than counter-balancing it with some of her own.

Back at Roberts Union, I went upstairs to my place and poured myself a drink. Soon, there was a knock at the door. It was Rich, who had just closed up the Paper Wall.

"Hi, I saw you drive in, and thought I'd just say hello."

How much I wanted to hug him, touch him all over. "Want a drink?"

"Nah, nothing. I have to study. Just wondering how you're doing."

I motioned him to sit on the couch, took my usual chair.

"Well, I just got back from seeing "I am Curious Yellow.""

"Wasn't that great!?," he declared. "Sexual liberation, complete with Martin Luther King and Yevtushenko! It's happening all over, man! Totally anti-war and egalitarian! Just like we're reading about in class!"

"Yes, exactly!"

"And then she cuts the guy's dick off because he cheats on her! Whoa!! Men better watch out!" His impish smile was ear to ear.

"Yep, I reckon!"

"I loved all those interviews she did of people on the street, basically telling them they're bourgeois and why do they vacation in Spain where Franco's such a dictator! 'Collaborators! You're all a bunch of collaborators!' What a line!"

"Yeah, he's the ultimate symbol of oppression and censorship."

"She told it like it is, man, just like it is."

And I did not tell it like it was, how turned on I felt by this painlessly easy, grooving-on-the-same-track conversation with this sexy man, so much more sexy than the dud/dude in the movie. I kept it all inside but totally enjoyed the intellectual intercourse. My own curiosity had to be kept in check. But I longed for more.

Susan and I were both invited to the Hudsons' for Thanksgiving. It felt somehow very natural to appear as a couple in the context of the Hudsons' family, complete with three kids. There was a certain comfort in normalcy: setting the table, cooking, drinking, playing games with the children. I realized how deeply I longed for family, a sense of wholeness that I hadn't experienced ever since my parents' divorce.

In early December, John came up for a visit on a Friday night. For the first time ever, I felt a certain anxiety about his coming, though I didn't know why. I had consciously arranged my schedule so that John would not meet Susan during his visit. He stayed with me in the apartment and shared my bed. We mussed up the bed in the second bedroom, just as I had done at Grand Pré, for the maid's benefit. He had asked if I wanted anything and I mentioned I was out of Peterson's Mixture No. 700 pipe tobacco, which I usually got by the pound. He arrived with three canisters of Peterson's house blend in a large cardboard tube with his office address. He had had it messengered to him before leaving. I was so impressed at this gesture of thoughtfulness, I was delighted and told him so.

He also brought three books I'd never heard of before "to fill your time as winter stretches on up here," he said. They were James Barr's *Quatrefoil*, and Mary Renault's *The Charioteer* and *The Last of the Wine*. All three were serious novels, not pornographic at all, about homosexual romances.

John's very gifts, however, left me non-plussed. I had no idea how to reciprocate. I felt I had nothing to give. Even in sex, I was, from my point of view, being given to. I recall at one point during his visit, John was going down on me and I thought it amazing that this millionaire would find me so desirable as to place himself in a lower power position in sex. I had only begun to think of power issues in sex, but I had not yet brought my usual democratic egalitarianism into the bedroom, nor questioned my assumption of the inherently greater masculinity entailed in being sucked rather than sucking.

When I introduced Rich to John, I found myself wrestling with an odd mixture of feelings. I was showing John the Paper Wall, and Rich was on duty, serving snacks and sodas. I felt my love for John and was glad to be introducing him to Rich. And I also felt my bond with Rich and wanted him to know John. But in that very moment, I knew who I wanted to go to bed with more, and I felt guilty.

"Rich is in my social science class," I said to John after introducing him to Rich.

"Yeah, Bob's a great teacher," Rich added with his utterly charming smile. "By the way, how was Thanksgiving for you and Susan at the Hudsons'? I haven't had a chance to talk to her yet."

"Very nice. Big turkey and lots of dressing. How was yours in Pawtucket with your family?"

"You know. Same ol', same ol'." Turning to John, he said, "So how long are you up here for?"

"Just a couple of days. I wanted to see how Bob was making out up here."

"I think he's doing great!" Rich said, glancing at me, then back to John. "Some of us probably keep him up later at night than is good for him." He winked at me.

"Oh, God, if only..." I thought to myself.

"You didn't tell me you were dating a woman," John said when we got back to the apartment.

"Well, I wouldn't call it dating. We've gone out to some Colby events...and a movie. That's about it."

"You're a very busy man, Big Shot," he said in a kind of "go get'em tiger" way.

I smiled because he was trying to make light of the idea that the man he'd just slept with might be headed in the other direction and I, too, wanted to keep it light. But inside I wanted him to grab me and take me away somewhere even if it was as crazy as Iceland.

As I drove John to the Augusta airport to return to New York that Sunday afternoon, I suddenly remembered how I felt five months earlier when I drove him from Mt. Desert to the airport in Bangor, for him to fly to New York and for me then to go to Colby.

It had still felt like summer then, with the bright blue sky and full sun's warmth. On that occasion, he seemed to say goodbye as if we would meet again the next day. But I felt a gap somehow opening up as we'd shaken hands and he'd said, "Goodbye, Big Shot." I had felt abandoned, which didn't make sense to me; I knew I would see him again. So I dismissed the feeling, which seemed both small and deep, and focused on my work at Colby.

But now, as we drove through snow and ice to the little tarmack in Augusta for him to return to New York, I was feeling abandoned again, but more strongly. Absorbed in my own murky feelings, I didn't stop to think what it must have been like for him to see me focused on another man and a woman—not on him. Who was abandoning whom?

Perhaps the net result of his visit was something like the exacerbation of a previous injury, but, whatever it was, as I watched his plane lift through the snow, I knew I felt empty inside. As I drove back to Waterville and snow thickened around me, I thought of the time in Bluford when I had my new puppy, "Brownie." The afternoon when I was in the house and suddenly heard Brownie squeal and squeal came back to me. How, when I ran out the door, Daddy jumped out of the Black Chevy coupe and there was Brownie, under the tire, unable to get out. I'd screamed out "Brownie! Brownie!" and then ran toward him. I could still hear how Daddy had hollered at me: "Get back in the house, son!"

"But...!"

"Get back!" he shouted again, pointing to the house. Then, "Viv! Take the boy back in the house!"

Had something I loved died between John and me? As his plane lifted off the tarmac, why did I hear the sound of a puppy squealing? The more I thought about the shift in my feelings for John between our time on Mt. Desert when I felt totally together and intimate, and my feelings since coming to Colby, the more it seemed to me that Mt. Desert and my place in John's life were now somehow a step outside of time and space, an embodied fantasy that had brought me healing and strength, but was now not a place to stay or live. "Two men don't live together in the real world," I said to myself. Or was I suddenly fleeing in terror from a long-sought love I was afraid to have for fear of losing?

Over the weeks after John's visit, I inhaled the three books he'd brought me. In *Quatrefoil*, the beloved kills himself in the end because of the impossibility of him and his lover being able to live with their love. *The Charioteer* was based on Plato's dialogue, *Phaedrus*, in which the love between two men was depicted as originating in the separation of the soul in two, each longing for the other half. The action was set in England in World War II between a soldier and a pacifist Quaker. (Only later did I learn that John had spent two years in Europe working with the Quakers as a medical attendant.) *The Last of the Wine* was one of a series of Renault's historical novels that were set in ancient Greece from the time of Socrates to Alexander, all involving homosexual relationships. In both her novels, however, homosexual attraction remained unconsummated, as partners refrained from expressing their love physically out of deference to notions of propriety, and the supposedly higher good of masculine ideals of virtue, stoicism and honor.

I was so enthralled to read serious novels that explored gay relationships in the context of a search for meaning, that I barely noticed how depressed they left me. The message was clear: homosexual relationships never lasted and the most virtuous way of handling them was with philosophical sublimation, stoic restraint and a carefully cultivated silence.

After his visit to Colby, John kept in touch by phone, every week. He wanted to be with me. But I couldn't make the leap. I was so self-absorbed in my own level of conflict that I totally failed to appreciate how much John truly cared for me—was, in fact, in love with me. He gave himself to me sexually in a way I never reciprocated, and that bothered me.

It was not just that he was my mentor: it was that there was a continuing inequality in his giving to me and what I felt I had to give back, which was nothing. It did not seem to be a problem for him, but it bothered me that I felt huge urges to jump Rich's bones in a way I didn't feel for John.

In spite of John's very real signs of care and affection, neither of us ever said the "love" word. Paralleling my romp with David in high school when I resisted his kiss, John and I only kissed upon greeting or parting, never during sex. Neither of us seemed even to think about it.

I told myself that if it had been Rich with me, I would have had no hesitation to kiss and reciprocate every sexual gesture. But I couldn't put him to the test. In the dance between desire and the censure of desire, emotional truth, which is the basis of all intimacy, is stillborn; all the rest is gesture, eye contact, innuendo, ambiguity, interior drama. In the midst of all this, I wondered if I could trust my own attractions when everything and everyone I knew suggested I could not. But then I wondered further if my own internal battle over the acceptability of my sexual desire might be a mask for my avoidance of a love of anyone, a love that could be entirely giving, taking risks and suffering consequences?

After New Year's, January of 1968, the temperature hovered for days between 15 and 25 degrees below zero and the Green Machine would not start. The motor wouldn't turn over because the oil was solid.

Then Phil Merrill showed up with a car I'd never heard of: a BMW. I knew about their bikes, but not about their cars. Phil himself had the BMW bike, but he said the cars were only now beginning to be imported to the US. It was very cute and compact. Then he took me for a ride. It was incredibly fast and cornered just like a sports car! I wanted one. There was only one place to get them on the east coast, and that was in Long Island City, New York, where he got his, he told me. I flew down to LaGuardia, took a cab to the dealer in Long Island City, picked out the car I wanted and sat down to complete the papers. The cost of the car, with tax, came to $2675. I had brought $500 with me.

In the end, I called my soprano from the Methodist Church in Inwood and she agreed to co-sign for the car. Then, within just a few hours, I was driving a new beige 6-speed BMW 1600 back to Maine. It was an absolute thrill to drive.

I had confirmed with the salesman that, in contrast to American cars, the BMW did not need a breaking-in period. It could be driven flat out from the showroom, "as on the Autobahn," he said. As much as I could, I kept it in the 90-100 mph range all the way up US 95 and the Maine Turnpike. A trip that usually took 10 hours was reduced to 6 ½. I wished for curvy mountain roads rather than the boredom of the turnpikes; but to take even turnpikes at that speed with no sense of strain on the motor, and to see people staring at you as you come up from behind and then slip quickly and quietly past them when they're doing 75 or 80, kept the drive interesting.

The day after I returned to Colby with my new BMW, Susan and I drove up to Castine for dinner with Clark Fitzgerald and his wife, Leah. We drove down their road to a white clapboard house next to a lighthouse on the edge of a bluff overlooking Penobscot Bay. As we got out of the car, a light fog brought up the smell of the sea and we could hear the rush of waves on rocks below.

Clark and Leah greeted us at their front door. Both their faces had tanned creases earned by many hours of sun and sea. For both of them, their hair was between gray and white. Entering the house, I noticed large picture windows, offering a great open view onto Penobscot Bay.

As we sat down, Clark asked for drink orders. I asked for scotch. Susan and Leah wanted white wine. Clark toasted Susan's dance performance and then, turning to me, said his sculpture Susan danced in, "The Whole Man," was based on Paul Tillich's sermons in his book, *The New Being*.

"I told him he should have stayed with Tillich's title, 'The New Being,' or at least called it 'The New Person.' But he didn't listen to me," Leah said.

"Leah's concerned that I'm perpetuating sexism…but 'person' just sounds very lame to me," Clark replied. "I still think in the old language, I guess, the King James version of Paul's 'new man in Christ'. I think of myself as a symbol maker, trying to re-evaluate old ideas. That's what I was trying to do with that piece, express the essence of what Paul was referring to."

"I think you did that exceptionally well," I said.

"It seems to me that Tillich was the ground-breaker for an entirely new way of understanding God. 'The god beyond gods,' and 'the ground of being'…. If we have to resort to words, I think that's as good as it gets. I try to express that without words....just pieces of wood or metal, to create a new symbol that mediates the transcendent to man. Oops, see, there I go again!"

Leah stood and invited us to move to the dining area where she brought out plates of broiled haddock and green beans and we began to eat.

"I read his *Dynamics of Faith*," Susan said as we walked to the table and sat down. "I liked the idea that doubt is a part of faith."

"You didn't tell me you read that," I said to her.

"Well, I don't tell you everything!" she mumbled with her mouth full.

"I would love to hear you and Tillich talk about your work," I said to Clark.. "Did you ever meet him?"

"No, unfortunately.... Did you?"

"Leah, superb!" Susan said after her first bite.

"I heard him while I was at Columbia. He gave a lecture series in Low Library. Great thick German accent in the echo chamber of the rotunda. It was often hard to understand him. But I've read most of his stuff. It gives me hope for theology, especially after the death of God."

"He once said that to be an artist is to be at the early-budding edge of consciousness, creating new expressions and forms in culture that open up greater awareness in society, breaking out of what we call tradition into new forms. That's what I hope I am doing."

"Beautiful, beautifully said. And I think you are doing that very well!" I lifted my scotch as a toast and looked around the room. Sculptures stood on the floor and tables. Paintings by Leah adorned the walls. The whole room was warm and earthy, yet open entirely to the sky and sea. "What a poignant place to live!" I said. "On this fantastic bluff over the Penobscot...and you're right in the middle of a town dedicated to the art of war while you create art of consciousness."

"Nature is my greatest source of ideas," Clark said, looking out the window into the black night. "Kind of like the Old Testament. The whole history of the human enterprise is there, every psychological problem man has ever faced, it's all right there."

"Clark talks about his sculpture as "doing theology," Leah said. "For me, my painting is just painting—it just is whatever it is."

"I'm with you, Leah," Susan spoke up. "I dance and express what I feel in response to music or sculpture or whatever. But the dance is just that. The dance of the moment. Movement of the moment...nothing solid."

"So is this a male/female thing?—women focused on the concrete, men into their theological abstractions?" Clark asked.

Leah laughed a deep belly laugh, somehow full of irony.

"You remind me of Sarah," I said.

"Sarah who?" Susan asked.

"Abraham's wife. God told Sarah she would have a child at 75, and Sarah laughed," I answered. "That's why they named their son Isaac, *Yitzhauk* in Hebrew. It means laughter." Turning to Leah, I continued, "You had such a hearty laugh, Leah."

Leah dropped her smile. She swirled the wine in her glass and stared at it. After a moment, she sighed deeply and spoke. "I was forty-six last year and although I hadn't totally been through menopause, we were completely convinced I was beyond the possibility of getting pregnant. Then one day I woke up, ran into the bathroom to throw up, and we said, 'no, it can't be,' and we went to our doctor. He said, 'Yes, it can—and is!' So I call it my 'Sara moment'... except I wasn't really laughing, just incredulous. And then one morning two weeks later, I woke up with this agonizing cramp and...." Tears came down her eyes, sparkling in the light. "I—it—I don't know why or how—but it or he—it was male—aborted himself.

"I'm sorry, I had no---"

"Of course not, Bob." She turned to me as she brought the wine glasses back. Her eyes were wet with sadness and fury. "How could you know anything of this?" She and Clark locked eyes.

Tears were falling down Susan's cheeks. I offered her my napkin. I felt like crying too, but didn't. Clark's face was very soft as he simply beheld his wife. After some silence, Leah said, "I'm sorry. I've forgotten to host. Would you like some coffee?"

We sipped at cups of coffee briefly after that, tried to make small talk, but it seemed like Leah's story was the completion of a movement. After coffee, we thanked them, shared hugs warmly and left.

On our drive back to Colby, Susan and I were quiet for awhile. Finally, she said, "I guess nobody's life is easy."

"I'm all the more amazed. They're both very raw, but open about it. They both have a lot of guts." Suddenly I took my eye off the road for a moment and turned to look at Susan.

"You want children, don't you?"

"Yeah, sure."

"Me, too."

As we drove on mostly in silence, I had this distinct feeling of "being a couple," and I wondered what life would be like with Susan, a life with friends like the Fitzgeralds and the other couples I had met at Colby.

There was something about being a couple that was on a different plane than being just myself or just her, like, 1 plus 1 equaled more than 2, and I wasn't thinking of children—not yet, anyway. But the thought was too new and was even threatening to me, something that I both wanted and feared. I turned on the radio and searched for any station with clear reception. The Doors came on, singing, "People are Strange."

Over the next few days, I felt my conflict deepening between where my gut instinct ran and the thought of what married life could be like. It was the fourth day of April, spring already, and soon, summer, and then? I called John. I tried to convey how intensely I felt conflicted inside, and said, "I just don't know what to do."

"Big shot, come down and let's talk about it. This is too important to deal with over the phone. Grab a plane and I'll reimburse you when you get here."

By 6 p.m. we were having dinner at Giordano's. At 8, we were at the Eugene O'Neill Theatre for a new play in from London, "Rosencrantz and Guildenstern Are Dead," written by a new playwright, Tom Stoppard.

After the play, as we exited the theatre and walked to Broadway, newspaper vendors were waving an early edition of the *New York Times* and shouting out "Martin Luther King assassinated! Get the latest here!"

I was numb as I bought a copy. John read the paper over my shoulder as we rode to his place. John had issues with Martin Luther King in general, as if his work rattled John's old school view of "decorum." Also, he especially did not agree with

King's stand against the war in Vietnam. John's view was what I considered very Wall Street: conservative, assuming the obligation of America to defend our values against the communist threat wherever necessary. I wondered how anyone so smart could see things so monolithically; he wrote off my point of view to what he considered my Christian naiveté. But tonight I did not want to engage in an intellectual argument. My heart was heavy with the news about King, and yet I also had come down to talk with John about something else.

As soon as we were inside John's apartment, John poured Absolut over rocks for each of us, then we sat in the black leather and teak Danish chairs set at an angle to each other. John lit a cigarette, I lit my pipe. He reached over and put on an lp of Wanda Landowska playing the Well-Tempered Clavier on harpsichord.

"So, Big Shot, you're in a quandary."

"Yeah, and I don't really see a way out. I mean, I know I'm attracted to men, but where can you go with that?. Sometimes I want nothing more than to have a family, have a house, be normal. I love kids. I would love to have kids of my own. Up at Colby, I'll be in the same room with Rich and Susan. What I feel for her is not the same as what I feel for him. But where is there to go with a guy? Not to mention that I don't even know if Rich feels about me the way I feel about him. The basic thing is, I can't trust my own feelings. Psychoanalysis says homosexuality is a perversion. Theologians say it's a sin—punishable by death. That's heavy shit to be carrying."

"Funny you mention 'shit.' You may find it hard to believe, but there was a time when I also struggled with my sexual proclivity. I remember the first time I ever had sex with a man, coming home on the subway afterwards, I had this distinct sense of smelling like shit--not shit around me, but that I myself smelled like shit. It stayed with me the whole night."

"Thanks, John. That's helpful."

"Sorry, maybe this will help. You have to think of it as the Greeks did. For them there were no such problems as we face today. You Christians changed the moral compass after ancient Greece and Rome lost their power. In antiquity, there was an honoring of the male bond. Women had little place in society except to bear children and cook. If men were physically intimate, it was considered a natural extension of their life on every other plane."

"Yeah, but we don't live back then. I don't know how to live with myself no matter what I choose—or whom."

Whenever I spoke to John about something that bothered me, I always felt I had his full attention. He stayed totally focused on what I said. His light blue eyes listened to me with care—perhaps, even love. He shifted his chair slightly closer, leaned toward me and continued.

"Another time, about ten years ago, I had a dinner party here, and one of the guests was this incredibly beautiful blonde German girl with very large breasts named Beatrice—good name, right? Brings up thoughts of Dante, no? Well, we all had too much to drink, and I realized at one point that everyone had left but Beatrice. She knelt down before me and said she wanted to convince me that I could love a woman. She was voluptuous. Any normal man would have given a lot to be approached by her. I nevertheless felt frozen...or rather, felt nothing. She unbuttoned her blouse and exposed these enormous breasts—and I felt nothing. I was humiliated, but I didn't want her to feel that way. 'I'm sorry, Beatrice. But it just doesn't work for me.'"

Suddenly I saw the inklings of an unaccustomed vulnerability in John. The lines in his face were softer, and the little boy he once was—an unknowing child--suddenly appeared. He leaned back in his chair and sighed.

"That's the last time I was ever personally near a woman where sex might have happened. I just couldn't. So I've learned to accept that this is simply who I am. You, on the other hand, don't seem to have a problem thinking about being with Susan sexually."

"I don't know. We've never, you know, done anything."

"Okay. But sounds like the idea is not necessarily repugnant to you."

"No. And sometimes, like when she dances, I feel something, not like a physical turn-on like I feel with Rich—or with you. But something."

"Big Shot, my advice to you is, if you can manage to marry and have children, do it. Your life will be richer, more emotionally complex, not easy, mind you, but you'll have rewards and satisfactions that some of us can never have.

Children certainly bring a whole different perspective on a man's life. Expands his sense of being a part of the world, a part of history."

"Wow. But what about this other part? What about my attraction to men? What do I do with that?"

"People do different things. Some simply try to suppress it, deny it, try to forget it's there. Some people try to sublimate it—spend the energy cultivating a creative life. Like Leonard Bernstein. Others accept the fact that they will always want men in their lives and they design an intentionally divided life: travel on business or develop interests that take them places where they can find satisfaction."

"I don't think I could do that—deliberately cultivate a separate life. I'm too much like an open book. I don't think I could live a lie." I looked John directly in the eye and he returned the gaze.

"Doesn't have to be a lie. Some men tell their wives and they simply have an agreement, an understanding."

"I don't think I'm capable of that kind of deliberate slap in the fa…."

"It's not a slap in the face if you tell her up front and she accepts the terms of the relationship. The idea that people should marry for love is a rather recent idea in human history. Marriage has more often been an arrangement based on economic or political considerations."

"But how could I not have sex with the one I'm supposed to love, and have it with someone I'm not supposed to?"

"Sounds like some Christian 'supposed to's'."

"Guilty. Guilty as charged," I said.

"Can't help you on that one, Big Shot. You're at a tricky place in your life."

"I don't know, John. Tricky sounds like an understatement. I just feel completely torn inside between two different ways to live. The thing is, the last thing I want is to be like my father: get married, have kids and then decide I don't want my wife and abandon them for someone else – no matter which gender. That's the last thing I want to have happen."

" In big decisions, Big shot, there's nothing without risk, and no matter what you decide, you'll make mistakes. You're not going to get out of this one without losing something, regardless of what you choose."

The next morning, on the plane from LaGuardia back to Maine, my thoughts were racing. Although John's feedback was clear, I wasn't certain if it applied to me. He said, "If you can manage to marry and have children, do it." I knew I wanted children, but I wasn't sure I could really have sex with a woman, much less enjoy it. So John's advice had an implicit condition I wasn't sure I could meet: enjoying sex with a woman. I wasn't sure how I felt about that prospect, but it was intimidating. Nevertheless, his care in inviting me down and his open-heartedness in telling me about his experience with a woman, drew me closer to him and somehow helped calm my own tumultuous mind—somewhat like adding ballast to a sailboat so it can engage the shifting winds more fully.

Without being able to resolve my feelings for John and Rich, and my hesitation toward Susan, when the stewardess was offering newspapers, I took one and my thoughts went back to the death of Dr. Martin Luther King, Jr. Since the news broke, Dr. King's assassination had already triggered riots in New York and Los Angeles. What would be the next step? The entire Civil Rights movement had already been in upheaval, as King was attacked for not being radical enough by people like Stokeley Carmichael and Malcolm X, who were secular radicals, and did not follow the lead of Jesus or Gandhi as King had. Both Carmichael and Malcolm X were angry young men, impatient with nonviolence because, they reasoned, they had already suffered enough violence. Out of their insistence on change had come a new name to convey the difference in consciousness: Black. No more "Negro," no more "colored." Affirming their Blackness and reclaiming their pride with its roots in Africa before slavery, was the basis for seizing power over their own lives, and thus "Black Power" became the new language. Many white people were clearly afraid after King's assassination. And, as the plane touched down on the tarmac in Maine, I wondered, if you're a white man teaching Social Science in a white preppy college such as Colby, what do you do?

In a way, teaching rescued me from myself, from my own internal torments about my sexuality and my future. I turned instead to concern about the future of America. The question I posed to my Social Science class was: what are white people who grow up with the privileges of their whiteness to do to create a better world? The earlier part of the Civil Rights movement had a prominent participation of white folks in the marches, protests and demonstrations. Many whites were beaten and arrested, some had even been killed, along with ever so many more Black people. Clearly among the Carmichael/Malcolm X groups, white people were now told to step aside and let Black people determine the shape of the movement.

I felt that what white people should be doing was not to tell Blacks how to achieve their own liberation, but rather to deal with ourselves, our own consciousness and conscience. Specifically, we should deal with our own racism and our participation, on the institutional and governmental levels, in the structures of racism.

The discussions in class were lively and energized, with some students echoing the all-too-common resistance to the new consciousness, and others quickly getting the points articulated by Malcolm X that racism is a white man's problem, and the sooner white people started educating themselves about their own prejudice, the sooner justice would be served.

Near the end of the semester, Rich raised his hand.

"Isn't it kinda difficult for us to be talking about racism when there are no Blacks in this class, and only about three in the whole college?"

"Excellent point! Any ideas why that is?"

Pete Roy raised his hand. "Because there are almost no Black people in Maine?"

"And why is that? There are about as many people here from other states as from Maine, " I said.

"Low SAT scores," another student said.

"No money," said Tony.

"And if it's true that Black people tend to have lower SAT scores and less money, why is that?" I pressed.

"Racism," Rich said. "It's built into our whole society. From the get-go they have less advantages than white people. They make less money, have poorer schools, get less education and so they keep on making less money, generation to generation, than their white peers."

Silence in the room. Rich and I locked eyes for a moment, then I pulled my thoughts back to teaching. I was sure that there were students who might have voiced less-enlightened points of view, but I was grateful for Rich's comment which showed that at least the notion of racism was beginning to sink in, for some of my students, as something real.

The excitement of the class continued as it drew to the end of the semester. I proposed that we pick up the challenge and devote a weekend, after school was out, to studying white racism. Word got out of what we were doing and both Jim Carpenter and Paul Perez offered their "camps" in Reid State Park to house those who would give their time for such a commitment.

The number of people from my class who were interested and able to come was small enough that we opened it up to anyone who wanted to come. Rich Shippee, Cathy Pagano, Charlie Abbott, Ken Didsbury, Tony Burkhart, Anne Pomeroy and Amelia Rosenthal—all people who were connected either to the Paper Wall or the Colby Chapel, comprised the crowd. Susan joined in and volunteered to take charge of food and cooking.

Over the time since I'd returned to Colby from my visit with John in New York, I'd continued to see Susan, taking in movies together and visiting with friends, but we still hadn't slept together. Still, I was finding myself more and more at ease, just being with her, perhaps appearing as a couple, though whether we actually were or not remained a question.

"Oh, God!" Susan exclaimed.

"Oh shit!" I said. My heart sank. My hands squeezed the steering wheel.

Susan and I were driving her Mustang to the weekend on White Racism retreat and just turned on the car radio and heard that Robert Kennedy, who had just won the Democratic nomination for president in California, had been shot at 12:15 the night before as he was leaving the Ambassador Hotel in Los Angeles. He was listed in critical condition.

My mind flashed back to the time he visited Columbia and stood on top of a car on 114th Street, his loosened rep tie hanging down his white shirt, sleeves rolled up, hair tousling as he spoke into the megaphone telling why we should vote for him over the incumbent, Ken Keating.

"He can't die. He just can't," Susan said.

"Turn it up!" I said, impatiently. I had a thought and stopped myself from saying it: John and I leaving the theater in New York only two months ago and hearing vendors shouting "Get the news! King is killed!" But I hadn't told her I'd gone and certainly didn't want to say why.

"Jack. King. And now Bobby," I said. I felt like the wind had been knocked out of me and I was driving slower as I listened to the car radio. Somebody honked behind me when I hesitated at the stop sign onto Route 1 in Wiscasset. It was as if I felt that if I slowed down enough, it would give Kennedy more time to make it. I suddenly felt very old.

As we drove on, I recalled my excitement in reading Bobby Kennedy's book, *To Seek a Newer World*, which felt to me as if it had been written with true compassion. Suddenly I began quoting from the poem that Kennedy had used to begin his book, Lord Alfred Tennyson's poem, "Ulysses." I looked around at the sea surrounding the islands. By now, we were driving slowly down into Reid State Park. I began,

> "Come my friends,
> 'tis not too late to seek a newer world.
> Push off, and sitting well in order
> Smite the sounding furrows; for my purpose holds
> To sail beyond the sunset, and the baths
> Of all western stars, until I die."

I'd been doing pretty well, until that last phrase, and then I lost it. Tears rolled down my face. "He can't die. He can't," I muttered as I punched the dashboard of the Mustang.

When everyone arrived and was settling into their cabins, Susan and I started setting out lunch: pita pocket bread, egg salad and raw purple onions and raw vegetables, and iced tea. As she was cutting the onions, I stepped back and looked at her. She was wearing jeans, a sky blue turtleneck that emphasized the blue of her eyes. Her hair looked brushed by the sea wind. She looked like she belonged here, on the ocean rocks, salt air bringing a liveliness to her complexion.

"Very health-conscious, aren't we?" I said.

"Well, what kind of conversation about white racism would we have if we started off with the wine?"

"I agree with you, teacher," I said, and smacked her butt lightly.

"Be careful, teacher, your students may be watching," she countered.

"And? So what?" I bent around and kissed her on the lips. It happened quickly and naturally. Just like the first kiss I'd given John. Was I just fickle? Just responding to the person I was with or was there something genuine, albeit different, in how I felt toward Susan, John and Rich?

After lunch and cleanup, everyone was lounging around for our first session. Someone had put on a Simon and Garfunkel record:

> *It's a still life watercolor of a now late afternoon…*
> *And we sit and drink our coffee,*
> *Casting our indifference like shells upon the shore.*

I asked Rich to turn off the hi-fi.

"But we are not indifferent," I began, "We are here 'seeking a newer world,' as Bobby Kennedy was fond of quoting. Is there something ironic and contradictory about dealing with white racism with only white people present, enjoying the privileges of our white affluent status as we consider the crisis our society is in? Absolutely! But there is no more important job for white people to do than to look within and acknowledge the racism in our minds, as well as how it is structured into the institutions of our society."

We started going over the significant sections of *Black Power: the Politics of Liberation* by Stokely Carmichael and Charles Hamilton. I tried to get us to focus on the reading, but during our breaks, someone would immediately turn the radio back on and we would listen. By five, we'd exhausted all the energy we could give to white racism for the moment.

Susan and Amelia pulled out some lobsters, and started steaming them. I pulled out ice and set up drinks: iced tea and wine. The mood remained somber and we were quiet, all talked out of serious conversation.

Some people went to bed early; others of us stayed up late, keeping vigil as news came over the radio of no change in Kennedy's condition. Prospects seemed dismal. About midnight I went out on the rocks to be by myself.

The stars were out in all their splendor, clear on the moonless night. Waves lapped the shell-strewn shore. I thought about what John had said. Though we hadn't been to bed, Susan and I travelled easily together. In this situation, we had our respective roles of teacher and chef, and yet shared a common concern about racism. My blood still raced when Rich was around, but although he obviously enjoyed being with me and we shared an intellectual and emotional resonance which I did not have with Susan, Rich seemed interested in Cathy. Of course, I probably appeared similarly interested in Susan, which I was, but...

"And what has God to do with all this?" I asked myself as I stared at the stars. "I don't know," I answered. "And worse, I'm not sure it matters. People matter. That much I do know and believe."

Fully aware that my vigil would not make a serious difference in Bobby's life, around 2 a.m. I left the beauty of the dark night to get some sleep.

I awoke to the muffled sounds of students pouring coffee, speaking in hushed tones of Kennedy's death at 4:44 a.m. Eastern time. I suggested we have something to eat and gather for an informal memorial service for him before we took up the issue of white racism.

The effect of Bobby Kennedy's death on us was hard to name. We certainly felt knocked down by it and the loss of such a charismatic personality who seemed very much the man of the hour for "seeking a newer world." But at the same time, we all recognized that, in the words of Jack's inaugural, "God's work must truly be our own." This remained the persistent theme of the rest of the weekend concerning white racism.

As we ate more lobster and took in the beauty of Reid State Park, Rich brought to our attention how different other segments of society must be reacting to Bobby's death: the poor, whom he had championed; the disenfranchised; the under-employed. Class made a difference in our society as well as race. How would our personal aspirations on the socio-economic status ladder affect our willingness to sacrifice for the "newer world?"

For me the issue was deeply personal: I was very aware of how my brushes with poverty and the sting of watching our new car getting repossessed when I was in first grade created in me an urge to have more, to become affluent like I imagined my Columbia peers. What contradictions swirled inside me! Here I was, in seminary, contemplating a life devoted to God in whatever form that took, while seeking the most thrilling car I'd ever driven. Was that the secret attraction I felt toward Bobby Kennedy, that he could be affluent and still stake out a meaningful plan for social change?

I felt very sad leaving the group when we finished up on Sunday. I realized I loved these students, loved teaching and engaging them. With no meaningful prospects for teaching going forward, I hoped that my relationship with the students at Colby would not entirely disappear; there was something deeper than a usual student-teacher relationship with several of them. I don't think I was alone in feeling the edge of sadness permeating our goodbyes. We were returning, to some degree, to a different world—not the "newer world," of which Bobby'd spoken, but a world with less hope, less optimism, more unknowns than before.

With school out at Colby, after the retreat on White Racism, I packed most of my stuff into the BMW, left a few things with the Hudsons, and drove down to Madison, New Jersey. I'd decided to spend the summer of 1968 with Steve Anderson and three of his friends from Drew Seminary: Ed, Bob and Dan. They had been living together for two years as an intentional community dedicated to looking at themselves from a psychoanalytic perspective.

In addition to sharing chores and expenses for the upkeep of the house, everyone committed to a group sharing process of dream analysis and interpersonal as well as personal analysis. The goal was to provide psychological support for a deeper personal consciousness. I trusted Steve enough to be willing to try it for the summer. I knew three of us- Ed, Bob and I—would support ourselves financially for July and August by working as camp counselors and driving vans for the children to and from the camp in Leonia. However, I didn't know what I would do at summer's end. What I did know was that I needed a safe place to try to figure out my next move.

My last exchange with Susan had been in the form of a letter she handed me in a sealed envelope when I'd already loaded my car, had the engine running, and was about to leave for New Jersey. She had written me a letter while she was in northern Maine, laying plans for another performance of her Colby dance students, and knew I'd be leaving for New Jersey.

"Don't open this til you get where you're going," was all Susan said as she'd passed the envelope through my open car window.

"What is it?"

"Just a letter," she'd said. "But wait till you're settled in New Jersey before you read it."

"Okay, I replied, not knowing what else to say or what to make of her mystery envelope, then I took it, kissed her through the open window and we said our good byes. Of course, I pulled over at the next parking area of US95, tore open Susan's envelope and read her letter.

> Dear Bob,
>
> It seems I could have seduced you and that it might have been the best thing I could have done for you. Instead, I felt my physicality frightened you or perhaps it is your own that you can't handle.
>
> However, by trying to be patient and unphysical or something which I thought would be easier for you to cope with and bring you to an easiness/spontaneousness in your own time, I was being not fully myself in that I tried to be what I thought you wanted.
>
> Do you remember the Leonard Cohen song playing the first time you came to my place for dinner? It was "Suzanne." I'm listening to it now as I write this letter, and it seems to be saying,
>
> "When you want her tell her and when she pulls you down in the grass plunge into her not for "ever" but for "now." It is a very "now" type of thing I am thinking of and you must come back to plunge until you know and rejoice in that now. You must laugh and "not be up tight" if you don't find satisfaction in every encounter.
>
> There is no commitment in the act for a future but for a now. It is the affirmation of yourself and another that goes forward—sometimes together, sometimes not—the affirmation persists...

> *Divorce- people come together and go away, but it is not as if they had never been. Your hurt and confusion over your parents made the "forever" looming dismal future more strongly than the "now." I can't say "forever" but that seems what you need but can't trust. Take the affirmation of now.*
>
> *A physical affinity is not enough forever, but you mustn't assume that all else comes first or that at some point all logical reasons become clear. That would be stagnant—besides, there must always be something of the unexplained—whatever that is.*
>
> *People talk in bed.*
> *Love in the now.*
> *Me.*

After I put her letter away, started up the engine and soon found myself speeding south toward New Jersey, I imagined the reply I would write to her letter:

> Dear Susan,
>
> Can you really affirm me- with all the uncertainty I have about myself? You see, fundamentally I am afraid of love- of loving and being loved. Everything in my experience says that change is the only constant. And you tell me to rejoice in the now. Essentially that's why I was first attracted to you: you had the spontaneity and vitality and the now-ness which I wanted and tried so hard to believe in. But over time, is that enough? The real question is whether I can share my deepest self with you-whether I will <u>let</u> you know me.

As I kept driving down the Maine Turnpike, I knew I would never include that last line, because I knew it opened the door to my secret. No, I thought, when I was ready I would write back non-commitally, but underscoring my belief that a relationship of love had to include time for separateness as well as time for togetherness, then wait and see how she responded to that.

As the long drive wore on, my thoughts wandered. My uncertainty didn't stop with my relationship to Susan. I was completely ambivalent about returning to Union in September. As many people understood the death of God, ministry *post mortem dei* would be divided into either social action and service (law, medicine, protest, politics), or psychological and social understanding and healing (various forms of psychotherapy and group work). There seemed to be no need for theology. So I didn't see any point to finishing my B.D., since its primary purpose was to prepare people for parish ministry, which, in spite of Joe Matthew's and Saul Alinsky's efforts to turn churches into agencies of social transformation, didn't appeal to me personally.

I had failed chemistry and thereby given up the possibility of medical school; I had given up law as a possibility because everyone I knew going into it was interested in political economics. And since Cyril Richardson declared that my B- average disqualified me for doctoral work at Union, I assumed all doctoral programs were forever closed to me.

After my experience teaching at Colby, I was definitely interested in a teaching career, but without a doctorate, how could I teach? And what would I teach anyway—the death of God? (Would that come under history, anthropology or religion?). So I was driving to Madison, New Jersey needing desperately to find some clear clues to my future.

At the time, I saw no connection between my vocational uncertainty and my sexual uncertainty. I never said a word to Rich about my feelings for him. And yet we shared and acknowledged a very powerful connection that we labeled as somewhat psychic. He said his family considered psychic phenomena a fact of life, and that his mother sometimes engaged in séances with friends. Jung, of course, considered psychic phenomena real and brought his clinical analysis into his personal and professional experience of paranormal phenomena. Rich and I often felt we each knew intuitively when the other one might call or come over. I, of course, felt it was simply an expression of my wanting and needing to see or hear from him.

By the time I drove into the driveway of the house in Madison, I felt just about all aspects of my life were uncertain. In a glance, I took in where I would be spending the summer. It was a shabby colonial, graying white, long overdue for paint. After getting out of the car, on the porch I saw a faded, overstuffed-with-its-stuff-falling-out, club chair and an old rocking chair. I couldn't see anyone through the torn lace curtains on the door, so I rang the buzzer, but couldn't hear whether anything rang. I knocked. Finally I heard footsteps and Steve appeared, barefoot, in shorts and a t-shirt.

"Hey, great! We just started," he said, reaching to grab one of my suitcases. "Come on in."

"I have quite a bit more…"

"No, leave it. Come on down and join the group."

"Ed was just about to tell us his dream from last night," Bob said, turning to Ed. "Do you want to repeat it so Bob—the new Bob-- can know what we're talking about?"

We'd just been introduced to each other quickly and then I'd taken a seat. Ed glanced around the room, then rested his gaze on me. "I don't really know you…. I don't feel safe talking about important personal matters yet in front of someone I have no idea about."

There was a moment of silence, during which I looked around at the group. Bob was pudgy and shirtless, leaning back and tilting his chair on its back two legs. Dan had a white T-shirt and shorts that seemed very neat and tidy, matching somehow his thin lips and carefully short haircut. Ed wore a Drew Theological Seminary T-shirt, had black hair and black horn-rimmed glasses.

"Ed, trust me," Steve broke the silence.

"It's all right, Steve. I understand," I said. "What would you like to know about me, Ed?"

"Anything would help," he replied, leaning back and shifting one leg across the other thigh.

"Well, I just drove down from Maine where I spent a year at Colby College teaching and directing the student union. I was born in southern Illinois, went to high school in Florida. One brother, one sister- both younger."

As I talked, Ed looked at me intently, nodded his head in a slow rhythm. "And---?"

"And I'm here because I don't' know what the hell I'm going to do next in my life and I'm hoping that the kind of group process here, as Steve described it, will help me figure it out—"

"All right. All right." Ed tilted his head down so he could see me over the black frame of his glasses. "But why should I trust you?"

"I don't know. For that matter, why should I trust you? I don't think we start out with trust--- trust has to be earned—both ways."

"The thing is, I'm feeling pretty raw about this dream. It's way deep," he said, checking out everyone around the table. "—and I don't know where it's gonna take me."

Bob and Dan nodded. Ed started speaking, slowly, in a flat tone.

"It seemed to be nighttime and I was walking along the George Washington Bridge toward Manhattan from the Jersey side, and all of a sudden I decide to jump off. As soon as I jump, I realize I'm on my way to death, and I say to myself, I don't want to die. Then suddenly I pull this rope that I have in my hand and shift the direction of my fall, so that I swing back over to the railing of the bridge. Then, with a huge, huge effort, I manage to hang onto it and pull myself over the rail to safety." He glanced around the room, as if we could mirror back to him what he was feeling that wasn't getting expressed in the way he related the dream.

"So what do you think?" Dan asked.

"Beats the shit outta me," Ed replied. "It's dammed scary, that's what."

"What's the George Washington Bridge mean to you, Ed?" Steve asked.

"My dad used to go over it every day to go to work in Manhattan."

"You were living in Bergen, right?" Dan asked.

"Yeah, ever since we moved up from South Carolina."

I was completely wrapped up in my own meaning of the GW Bridge and the thought I used to have as a freshman of jumping off it because I was attracted to other guys. I couldn't even think of anything to say or ask because I sure as hell was not ready to trust these guys with that part of me.

"So maybe it's something about your father," Bob offered.

Ed shook his head. "There's a lot of shit about my father, but I don't think it's in this dream. This was just me." He pushed his glasses high up on his nose.

"What was going on for you in the dream that made you want to leap into the river?" Steve asked.

I froze, as if he had asked the question to me.

"It just seemed like a good idea—like I was going swimming from a high dive. But then as soon as I did it, I realized I was headed to my death, not just going for a swim—and of course swimming in the Hudson would be suicide enough in itself!--" he chuckled. "...from that height, the river might as well be concrete."

"Well, you hit water from 500 feet up, that's about what it would be like unless you could completely enter feet or hands first," Dan said.

"Actually, I hear most people die of a heart attack they're so scared before they even hit the water," Bob offered.

"But then you, like, wake up and tell yourself you don't want to die," Steve said. "So is there a part of you that wants to die?"

"Hell, no!" Ed declared.

"What about the rope?" I blurted out, surprising myself. "Where'd that come from?"

"Nowhere. It came totally out of nowhere."

"How are things with Marilyn?" Dan asked.

"Okay. Nothing special." Ed shifted his leg back to the floor, leaned over his coffee cup, picked up a spoon and started tapping it.

"Could you be a bit more specific, Ed? I mean, you were back and forth for months before you even decided to ask her out. Now you've been seeing her almost every night. I don't buy the 'nothing special' bit," Dan said.

Ed stopped tapping the spoon, put it down.

"Like out of nowhere the rope appears," Bob offered.

"Fuck you.... Fuck it all..." Ed's face was flushed; he was sweating; tears came to his eyes. "I don't know whether getting into the relationship is like jumping into the river ..... or whether she's the rope saving me from myself."

"Maybe it's both," Steve offered. "You have to let the ego die, stop holding back..."

"Falling in love is still falling...." Dan said.

I was totally taken in by the tone of everyone's talking. There was a gentleness and a real caring here. I felt my body relax and soften, the tension of the long solo drive had melted away, and I felt totally relieved that the personal meaning of this dream had nothing to do with my own associations to it.

Bob put his hand on Ed's shoulder.

Ed wiped his eyes with a napkin. "Shit! Fuckin' bullshit!" he said, smiling. "You wish!" Bob laughed.

Two weeks after I'd been living in New Jersey, a letter arrived from Susan, a response to the non-committal letter I'd finally actually written to her expressing my belief in love that also included times for separateness. She wrote back with an assurance that she agreed with me, and that anytime I ever felt crowded in the relationship, all I had to do was say so, and she would give me all the space I needed. That was tremendously reassuring to me, and opened a small crack in my door that was closed to a relationship with a woman.

I put an ad in the *New York Times* to sell the BMW for the balance I owed on it. Within a few hours of the paper coming out, I got a call from a man who came out, drove it briefly and gave me a check for it on the spot. I hated to see it go, but on a camp counselor's salary I couldn't keep up the payments. Besides, who knew where I was headed at the end of the summer? I realized when I bought it that my ownership would be short. But it was very sweet.

Despite Susan's place in my life, my attraction to men remained as strong as it had always been, however, I felt no sexual attraction to anyone in the group I was living with. Still, that did not prevent me from being inhibited with the group and much less than fully open or forthcoming with my own issues when it came time to have one of my own dreams analyzed.

My "big dream," as we had come to call dreams that seemed to express the deepest currents of the psyche, was at the beginning of the second week of August, only two weeks before the end of the camp and the end of my summer with the group. I had come to know each of the men individually and achieved a comfort level in groups analyzing the dreams of the others, but when my own dream teetered into unknown territory, I became excruciatingly uncomfortable.

"I'm kneeling in a church surrounded by clergy in robes for my ordination. I feel the press of their hands on my head, hear the shush of their robes rubbing against one another. In somber tones, the Conference Minister invoked the God of Abraham, Isaac and Jacob, and the God of Jesus. The choir is singing 'Almost Persuaded' and as the Conference Minister declares the confirmation of my ordination to ministry, a black robe is brought out and I rise and realize that I am totally naked. End of dream."

"To ordain or not to ordain, that is the question," Dan offered.

"Well, yeah, but, I mean, I'm totally ambivalent about seminary, even more about ordination. I can't figure out why I'm in that position in the first place—kneeling, others laying their hands on me, that's just so far from where I am at nowadays."

"Consciously, that is." Steve offered.

I was pleased that they were picking up on the ordination part; it was Br'er Rabbit's briar patch, the safest place to go even though others thought it was the most dangerous.

"Church just doesn't make any sense to me, that's all. Why get ordained if you're not going to work in a church?" ('Puhleeze don't throw me into that briar patch!' Br'er Rabbit cried out to Br'er Bear and Br'er Fox.)

"But on some level, it all makes sense, right?" Bob said. "I mean, it's your dream. Something in you is putting it out there in front of all of us for all of us to see."

"Yeah, I agree with Bob," Ed added. "What about the part of you that <u>does</u> want to be ordained?"

"When I was nine years old—a month before I turned ten—back in Illinois, I had a conversion experience. You guys are Methodists from Drew, so you should understand what I mean."

"We're from the north, man, you better tell us yourself," Bob said.

"We're not <u>all</u> from the north," Ed added, emphasizing his southern drawl.

"Yeah, well, why don't you tell us, Bob," Dan said.

"They were having this revival in our church all week, the church where my grandpa on my mother's side used to be the preacher. I had been there a couple of nights and now it was Sunday, September 13, 1953, and the preacher, Rev. Ragsdale, was shouting about how it was our last chance to come to Jesus, and everybody was singing and I was getting a lump in my throat, but I didn't want to cry, so I kept reading the words of the hymns, 'Come home, come home, ye who are weary, come home…see on the portals he's waiting and watching, calling O sinner, come home!' Still, I kept fighting back the tears, and then they started singing 'Almost Persuaded'—'almost persuaded, seems now some soul to say, 'go sinner, go thy way', some more convenient day…' I didn't wanna let go, but I did want to, because it seemed like Jesus was calling me to join him in heaven with God and like that was where my true home was, but I was afraid. Then they started singing, "Just as I am, without one plea, but that thy blood was shed for me." And suddenly I broke into sobs and ran down the aisle to the altar rail and knelt down and Rev. Ragsdale put his big hand on my shoulder and I felt its warmth and just totally let go and cried and cried and prayed to let Jesus enter my heart and I gave myself to him. I knew I was gonna be a preacher. A couple of other men came over also and put their hands on me, giving me comfort, and I began to feel lighter inside, and happy and peaceful. I felt I had just been called to the ministry." I stopped speaking, breathed a big sigh.

"What's the sigh about?" asked Steve.

"I feel exhausted, just telling you the story, wondering how you'll relate, feeling kind of naked to tell this story," I said.

"Kind of like you were naked at the end of your dream?" Dan asked with a soft laugh.

"I don't know about that," I dodged his question with a shrug.

"What happened then?" Ed asked, then, "Wait! I want to hear about what happened after your experience in church."

"I went home to tell my mother. I was so happy, I was sure she would be proud of me, and Paw Paw too."

"Who's PawPaw?" Dan asked.

"He was my mother's father, the preacher who used to preach there."

"And?" Ed pressed.

"I ran into the house, this big house where I had my own bedroom on the second floor and Paw Paw had a bedroom up there too. Mother was at the sink preparing something to eat, and I told her and she looked worried instead of happy for me."

"What'd she say?" Dan asked.

"She said, 'Well, if you still feel that way in a few more years, then maybe you will become a preacher. But Bobby—' and she put her hands on her hips—'let me just tell you this: if you can do anything else, you should do it. You should only enter the ministry if nothing else can make you happy.'"

"Wow. How'd that make you feel?" Bob asked.

"I was like—stopped in my tracks. All the enthusiasm just drained out of me. It was like getting slapped. I felt like crying again, but not like at the altar. I felt like crying because I felt I had just experienced the presence of God and Jesus and now, instead of being happy with me, my mother ---I don't know—it was like a shock. But all I could do was say, 'yes ma'am,' 'yes ma'am.'"

"Jesus Christ! No wonder you're ambivalent!" Steve said.

"Yeah, I reckon," Ed said.

"Whew!" Dave sighed.

On one level, they had led me to the right place: the part of me that wanted to be a preacher was that child who knew the peace and love of God as unconditional and eternal before he was ten years old. On another level, they'd sniffed out the other part of me, which was the source of my ambivalence in my mother's frigid reception.

"But, you have to understand why my mother greeted my conversion with such ice; it was because of her father, Paw Paw. He used to beat the living daylights out of his oldest son with a razor strap in his self-righteous anger. Later in life, he took refuge in prescription drugs for his "arthritis and rheumatiz" while he was chronically crying and complaining and saying he wanted to die. That's the preacher my mother knew from the inside, and that's why she didn't want me to become a preacher. Of course, I didn't know this on the Sunday of my conversion."

"Yeah, and knowing it now, really knowing it, can that change the effect her reaction still has on you from that time?" Dan asked.

Everyone was silent. Dan had essentially asked the ultimate question upon which the utility of all psychoanalysis rested. Meantime, to myself, I felt a bit of relief for having gotten through the dream and still having avoided talking about what I didn't want to talk about. Namely, how the image of myself naked while men had their hands on me left me alone with my fear of having my homosexuality exposed.

"But why naked?" Steve suddenly asked. "Why, at the very moment you are about to receive the robe of ordination, do you stand up and realize you're naked?"

Everybody looked at me with a new keen interest.

"I don't know," I answered, as I looked at the floor.

"Everything you just told us is very, very spiritual," Steve continued. "But then the body comes in. How does your body fit in with your death of God beliefs and seminary and ordination?"

"Or maybe to cut to the chase, where's sex in the story?" Ed added.

"Bobby, are you blushing?" Bob said with a shit-eating grin. "What aren't you telling us?"

"Absolutely nothing!" I retorted. "It's just that I haven't had any for a long time," I said. "Sex, that is. If anybody here knows what I'm talking about. Shit, nobody here seems very 'embodied' to me. We're all in our heads the whole fucking time!" I pushed my chair back, crossed my legs and arms.

"Bob, it's your dream, not ours," Steve said.

"It's 'just as I am,' guys. Without one plea. Just like in my conversion experience: just as I am. Unconditional love. Unconditional acceptance. That's what ordination means to me."

Ed nodded.

"That's what St. Francis did. Told his father he didn't need him or his money, took off all his clothes and walked away a free man," Bob said.

Dave just looked at me.

"Yeah, sounds right, sounds very right," Steve said, looking at me, smiling. Then he grinned. "But I don't think that's the whole story in the dream. I think there's more to it."

"That may be, but that's about all I can do tonight," I said, yawning.

Everyone started getting up from the table, stretching, saying goodnight, and I quietly breathed a deep sigh of relief. It's not easy being the focus of such probing by several people at the same time. It's harder to hide. But I did. For then.

In my next-to-the-last week in New Jersey, another close call occurred. Bob and Ed and I were sitting around trying some Cointreau when Bob asked Ed how things were going with Marilyn and Ed gave some non-committal answer.

"You're pretty vague, there, Ed," I said.

Ed said, "Why are you on my case about my girlfriend? We never hear anything about yours- or whether you even ever have one. You just sit back pushing everybody else's buttons. What's up, Bobby G?—you got a girlfriend or boyfriend or what? 'fess up!"

I was stunned. There it was: the direct challenge.

"You wanna know something all you have to do is ask. You don't have to attack me. Besides, you're still not answering Bob K's question," I replied.

"Yeah, Ed—answer my question then Bobby G can answer yours."

I gulped down the rest of my Cointreau, fastened my eyes on Ed, but heard nothing he said because my mind was scrambling for a satisfying but evasive answer.

"...so that's about all there is to tell," I heard Ed say. "All right, Bobby G, your turn."

"Not much to tell on my side either," I said. "Susan and I dated all last year while I was at Colby—never really met anyone else. We've exchanged letters this summer where she pretty much put the ball in my court, but I haven't written back since her last letter. I'm on the fence, not sure what way I'll fall. I'm as uncertain with her as I am with my future."

Bob lifted his shot glass, "Here, here!" he said. "Here's to uncertainty, and to the women of our dreams!"

Although I still had not replied to Susan's last letter, Rich and I had maintained an active correspondence all summer long, exchanging letters two or three times a week. I looked forward to his letters like a man looking for water in a scorching desert. They were the high point of my week. In a group dedicated to psychoanalytic interpretation, the guys were remarkably unquestioning about my letters from this former student, and I certainly never said anything about how I felt about Rich. I was once again in love with "the love that dares not speak its name."

Perhaps the other real clues to my state of mind were my daily dose of *Laphroaig*, a single malt scotch John had introduced me to, and my occasional forays into New York City on a weekend night, when I would go to a movie and restlessly walk the streets of the city.

Sadly, John was out of the country that summer, and so I was unable to see him on my trips into the city, and I missed horribly talking with him. As I walked through Greenwich Village alone on some nights, near his apartment, I realized there was no one other than John with whom I could speak so freely, with whom there were no secrets, with whom my simultaneous interest (albeit different) in both Rich and Susan was not viewed as bizarre.

After camp ended, Frederic invited me to come up and spend a few days with him and his family before Labor Day. He particularly remarked on the near completion of their cabin on Little North Pond, outside of Waterville, and said I was free to use it if I wanted, and that in any case, there was a tent I could sleep in "with anyone you might want to join you" (I heard "Susan" as the unspoken "anyone").

After a brief phone call, Susan agreed to join me at the Hudsons' place and we met there, with me still never having answered her letter, and hugged and kissed as if my silence since that last letter had never transpired. I helped the Hudsons in finishing their cabin in the woods, putting on wooden shingles and the roof. Meantime, what struck me most was how well she engaged the Hudson children in play, making up games and creating things out of bark and leaves in the sand. My deep desire to have children of my own was further activated by watching her with them, and the big "what if," which John had so clearly encouraged, stirred up an interest in seeing further whether anything could happen with a woman, and with Susan in particular.

It was the end of August and we all worked in shorts, the guys without shirts. We were working among tall pines and white birches on the shore of a small lake with no motor boats. The sun sparkled through the pines and the birch leaves and on the water. And I noticed what great legs Susan had and how much she looked and moved like Mary Martin in Peter Pan.

So I asked if she wanted to spend the night in the tent and she said yes. I told her we should have no expectations about anything, that we were just getting better acquainted, and she said fine. We cuddled a bit and my terror subsided somewhat. Then we slowly began to explore each others' bodies. I was happy to find that I got excited. With the full moon peeking through the canvas tent, I entered her, and she responded, and I exploded inside her and stars sparkled and comets shot across the sky of my mind and every nerve in my body felt fully alive and we kissed more deeply than ever before and then, after a couple of hours, we did it again and I don't know how we finally got to sleep.

I remember waking up with the sun glistening around us, giving the entire woods and water a supernatural glow. I felt saved at last, saved at last! and inwardly I thanked the God who died, who nevertheless lived again, which had just been revealed to me, and Susan glowed and everything shone with a transcendent glory, and I felt I loved the entire world, and that Susan was the channel of this electric vitality now surging all around and within us. I felt I had finally discovered the secret to the universe and I understood the mysteries of life and love, not with my intellect, but as a standing under, entering into, being a part of the fantastic glorious enterprise called life.

I did not want to call it God, for that would reduce the experience to something we think we know; but I did not want to say it was not God, for there was a groundedness in this vision that was the very stuff of poets and mystics. This was that of which Blake spoke, and Whitman, and D.H. Lawrence, and the Song of Solomon and Wordsworth. My heart beat with the pulse of the universe, and I felt sure that if only I could listen quietly enough, I would hear not only whale songs, but the earth turning and mountains walking.

In my journal, I wrote:

> What would it have taken for Michelangelo's fingers of God and Adam to have touched? I think I know! Beyond all dreams or expectation—this time here with Sue! Redemption, forgiveness and overcoming are real: though not completed either forward to marriage nor backward to understanding the past, I have every confidence that this process will continue. Though I can't do it with the strength that comes from practice, I want to affirm life now as good and fulfilling—and I can only do this because I have finally begun to be able to respond to the affirmation of another—Susan.
>
> August 30, 1968

I was, in sum, in ecstasy, out of my (ordinary) mind. And though I had felt such deep steeping in the Mystery of What Is before, it had never been connected to another person before. It had been God alone, or the power of nature. This happened in, with and through Susan. Susan McFerren. The profoundly holy had invaded human flesh once again. Incarnation.

And whereas previous experiences, such as my conversion at the age of nine, had their luster diminish over time, this feeling of walking on water remained with me as if it would or could never be diminished. I wanted to live in and from the place of this deep ecstasy. I wanted to enter fully into this mystery which had happened with and through Susan.

A week later, Rich showed up at Little North Pond to join the Hudsons, Susan and me in finishing the cabin. My heart raced as we hugged.

"I've missed you!" he said with his big white teeth smiling and brown eyes twinkling.

His words hit the pit of my stomach as if he'd just declared his love for me, and my mind reeled with the realization that he didn't mean it on the same level I felt it—wanted to feel it. And at the same time, I was still high from the ecstatic union with Susan, and my brain could not calibrate the tensions and excitements I was feeling. What does it mean that I truly felt love—both erotic, though different—for both a man and a woman?

"Missed you, too," I replied, thinking, "if you only knew!"

After Rich left the camp and headed back to Colby, I realized nothing in my life was different: I still didn't know what to do; I knew I still found certain men attractive; I still believed in the death of God. And yet everything was different: I could enjoy sex with a woman; perhaps I could enjoy marriage, have children, raise a family, be normal. Whether God was dead or not, I knew that what I had just experienced with Susan was vitality at the heart of the universe and, by whatever name, it was the source of all of life, all beauty, goodness, joy and grace. And I wanted to live from the core place of this connectedness to everything. How to do that? Where to do that?

Suddenly I had a new reason to go back to Union, finish my degree and continue my spiritual quest. I would focus wholeheartedly on exploring the theological implications of this experience. I would continue to see what else might open in my relationship with Susan. And I resolved to seek help by going for professional psychotherapy. I might not have known where I was going in any ultimate sense, but I suddenly knew what the next step was.

I returned to Union in September of 1968 with a purpose: to resolve my sexuality and to decide whether to get married or not. For that, I felt I needed two things: intense steeping in theology and a good psychotherapist. For theology, I took another course with Paul Lehmann, my favorite teacher because he embodied the ethics he taught. He supported our protests against the war in Vietnam and against apartheid in South Africa.. He paraphrased John Calvin, "theology is a stick of which one end is man and the other is God; it doesn't matter which end you start with, ultimately either end will lead to the other." His view of the Holy Spirit seemed especially apt: "the office of the Holy Spirit is humor, without which even God would go mad when dealing with man." Lehmann himself had humor. He delivered his eloquent lectures always in a three piece suit with a real watch fob strung across the pockets of his vest. Sometimes he wore a bow tie. I asked him to be my advisor on my senior thesis and he accepted, even though I had no topic.

Union was much the same as before I left for Colby, but a bit more intense on every front. The Tet Offensive in Vietnam had prompted a further escalation of US troops, and with that, an intensification of opposition to the war, which was reflected at Union in more protests and organizing; seminarians were more outspoken against the war in the churches they served. The Civil Rights work continued, fueled by King's assassination. What was new to me was the number of my classmates doing drugs. In the name of spiritual quest, some were doing LSD, some mescalin, some peyote, and many using pot.

As someone who had now had two major experiences of the transcendent— one in childhood, the other with Susan—I was very interested in the potentially positive value of these experiences, all the more for those who seemed to have a genuine spiritual motivation. Timothy O'Leary led the way and Ram Dass gave the "tune in, turn on and drop out" generation a psychological and spiritual rationale from Eastern religions for dallying with the transcendent through drugs.

Ed Fitzgerald was my roommate on the 6th floor of Hastings Hall that year. Fitz, as I called him, had long brown hair and a huge, handle-bar moustache. In our room, the Beatles' "Revolution," the Stones' "Street Fighting Man," or Janis Joplin and the Jefferson Airplane singing "White Rabbit" were constantly blaring. Our entire suite was on the floor: our beds were just mattresses, everywhere else was just pillows and cushions. Fitz put me in touch with various people from the seminary who were experimenting with various drugs, as was he. Even though I had a separate bedroom, there was a constant flow of music and people and smoke (grass) and I felt I was living at Union's center of all that was "cool."

One time Fitz had a huge brick of grass he was dividing up to sell. I'd never seen so much in one chunk.

"This is the path to the cross," he said as he was separating the stock from the seeds. Then he sniffed the stock, held it up high like a priest lifts the Host, and said, "Here is where you begin to let ego die and allow yourself to be carried out of hell into transcendence." As he pulled the stock apart with a small knife, he continued: "Marcuse believes we can use social wealth for shaping man's world in accordance with his Life Instincts, in the concerted struggle against the purveyors of Death. It was the genius of Freud to discover the secret power of repression and its corollary, violence"—he cut into the brick again with a thud!—"and the role of both in building civilization." He lifted up the knife and waved it at me like a teacher who had made his point.

"So let me guess," I interjected, "you're saying that, as Marcuse put it, in the modern age with technological advances, industrial production no longer requires physical labor and therefore, no longer requires suppression of our basic instincts?"

He paused as he placed the good seeds to the side. "Yes, that's exactly it, and, since the artistic, creative spirit of the human requires release from arbitrary suppression along with political repression, the human mind can be led by the experiences of ecstasy." He smiled as he cleared enough clean grass to put into a flat cigarette paper, then rolling it. "Rather than the pain and fear of internalized authoritarian, punitive constraints, our generation will be the first to understand liberation through pleasure...."

He finished rolling the first joint, licked it closed and passed it to me. I lit the joint, took a long drag on it, and passed it back to him.

He took a deep toke, exhaled slowly, then proclaimed, "Nirvana comes through happiness, not violence."

Fitz was the youth minister for the Scarsdale Congregational Church, and talked about the senior pastor, Avery Post, as if they were bosom buddies. Every Friday night, he went to lead the youth group, often staying overnight for events on Saturday as well as Sunday. One evening Avery came over and hung out for awhile, so I had a chance to get acquainted with him. There was an aliveness to Avery that made him open to what Fitz had to offer to the Scarsdale teenagers, though Fitz was careful to keep the drug stuff to himself.

With one exception at least: one evening I came in and there was this young fellow with long black hair, a couple of pimples on his face, sitting down chatting with Fitzgerald. His name was Tom Alexander. He claimed to be eighteen, but he hadn't graduated from high school yet.

"He's a member of my youth group in Scarsdale... more of a fringie than most," Fitz said with a wink at Tom, introducing him to me.

Tom giggled, said "Yeah, man!" and gave Fitz a high five. The smell of pot permeated the room.

Tom, I would soon realize, was a charmer every bit as much as Fitz, with even more knowledge of both drugs and music than Fitz. Tom was just…well, young…which made him all the more charming…and sexy. I immediately wondered if he might be gay, but when his conversation turned to show a clear delight in women, as did Fitz's, I put away thoughts that had started racing through my mind.

Tom became a frequent guest of uncertain purpose. He seemed to enjoy our slightly-older company, perhaps because we accepted him as an adult, but also because we were dealing intellectually and academically with issues that were important to him: the messed-upness of society, the search for meaning, the need for companionship based on authenticity.

When Gil told me he'd met Tom and introduced him to John, I had a huge twinge of jealousy, wondering if I had been replaced by someone younger. But since Tom made it clear he was not gay, I knew that's not what was going on. Besides, I was seeing John way less than before, since I returned to Union. It was as if his advice to me about marrying Susan ended the romantic and sexual aspect of our relationship, as if he wanted to be really clear that I was free to make that decision without any conflict regarding him.

And there was no conflict with John; however, this didn't mean there was no conflict with myself. Despite that, every other weekend either I'd go up to

Maine or Susan would come down to new York so we could be together. And our time spent together was good, better than good. Indeed, when we were intimate at night, each experience was as transcendent as our first time together in the tent in Maine.

It seemed to me that, in those days, we were all seeking transcendence in one way or another. Me as a boy in my conversion experience, Susan and me when we were making love, and even Fitz and his friends as they experimented with different ways of getting high.

I was intrigued by the comparison of my experience of transcendence with the current trend of pursuing transcendence exemplified by Fitz and his friends, and decided to write my senior thesis on "Testing the Spirits," a careful and critical look at contemporary modes of transcendent experiences, especially from drug use. The title was taken from I John 4:1:

Beloved, do not believe every spirit, but test the spirits to see whether they are from God; for many false prophets have gone out into the world.

Members of the early church were dealing with people who experienced ecstasies, including speaking in tongues. The ultimate "test" of those ecstatic experiences was whether or not they bore "fruits," specifically whether they helped build up the community or not. How would people's experiences on drugs compare to the classical religious experiences of adepts in the Christian tradition? Lehmann liked the idea and accepted the proposal.

I was curious about the drugs because I wanted to try them, but was afraid. I tried pot and really liked the incredible slow-down of time, and the feeling of having very profound insights and giggling from the euphoria. But I was afraid to try LSD or mescaline. I feared losing mental control and blurting out in a moment of ecstasy that I was attracted to guys—and that would be the end of my life. I could not envision life as a homosexual—I wouldn't be me; why I thought this way even after knowing John and having such deep respect as well as attraction to him, I didn't stop to think.

After being back at Union awhile, I became the youth minister for the Community Church of the Circle in Mt. Vernon. Every Sunday I taught Sunday School for the youth, made calls on parishioners in the afternoon, and met again in the evening with the teenage group. I always enjoyed working with teenagers. The kids at the Church of the Circle were all white, middle class, not very ambitious, but full of energy. One student, who I will call Charles, stood out as smarter and more intellectual than the others, and his mother invited me to join them for dinner after church. Charles had a ten year-old younger brother, Steven, who kept trying to enter the conversation, which obviously annoyed Charles. They lived in a modest apartment, neat and clean. Their father had died several years before. Their mother was a somewhat plain woman in the way she dressed, but quickly displayed the same intelligence I had noted in Charles.

"What do you think of our war in Vietnam?" she asked.

Two weeks before, the pastor of the church, Rev. Pelon, had preached a typical "support the establishment," "my country right or wrong" point of view. I hesitated, wondering where she was coming from. "I don't think we belong there," I said.

"Well, I don't either," she said.

Charles shuffled in his chair. "Ma, I thought we weren't supposed to talk politics at the table."

"I'm just trying to find out what Mr. Gunn thinks, Charles," she replied, moving her green beans around her mashed potatos. "I was reading an article last week about ethics by someone named Fowler, I think. He called it 'situational ethics'?

"Fletcher, I think you mean. Joseph Fletcher."

"Yes. That's it. That made a lot of sense to me," she said. "What do you think about it?"

I experienced something which was becoming common for me: women who seemed very hungry for a conversation with a man who would talk with them as a peer, respecting their intelligence without condescension.

"I think it's very common-sensical. Situational ethics describes how we really operate. We look at an entire situation, not just apply a rule from 3000 years ago." Between Steven intruding and his mother wanting to engage me, Charles was sinking back into his chair and looking at his plate. "What do you think, Charles?"

He looked up at me with his doe-like eyes—so gentle and timid and so seeing. "I think it's hard to tell anyone what to do. I think everyone has a right to their own opinion." He glanced at his mother, his eyes now fiery, as if to say "I'm talking to you, Mom!" then back to me. "I don't know about the book she read...."

"It was an article, Charles."

"Article, book, whatever....but I do believe in human freedom, freedom to think, freedom to act. We just have to be ready to take the consequences...."

I felt Charles and I understood the world in a similar way—through our minds, and that we also had trouble "fitting in." I wondered if he might be gay, but we never got close enough to the topic to talk about it, and I had no idea what I would say if it did come up. The whole conversation at the table was so revealing: a bereaved and lonely mother, an older son restless and impatient to leave his mother's house as a horse at the starting gate, a younger son who just wanted to be seen and included. What could a minister do to help people with such yearnings? Merely witnessing their struggles was frustrating to me. What could anyone do? Was "ministry" relevant at all?

Despite my fears and uncertainties about my vocation, I was still determined to move forward with trying to make sense of my sexuality and my feelings for Susan. She and I agreed to meet every other weekend either in Maine or New York, but she wound up coming to New York more than I went to Maine largely because she had a car and money while I had neither. When she was in New York, we slept on my single mattress on the floor at night and explored New York during the day. She had gone to Sarah Lawrence and had some familiarity with the city already, but together we saw things new to her, and seeing them through her eyes, new to me. We went to movies, sometimes a play, and sometimes just ate out at restaurants, most of which John had introduced me to.

Over these visits, I began to get comfortable with Susan in bed. I read books on how to make love, and the most important thing I learned probably was simply to go slow and take time. I had read of gay men who had sex with their wives by thinking of men, but I thought that was a serious betrayal of a holy intimacy and so I focused all the more intently on the physical sensations of love-making, and it seemed to work well. I experienced huge amorphous fears in having sex with her, what Freud would probably have labeled "castration anxiety," fears of being swallowed up, losing my penis, losing all sense of "me" or "I." My assumption since the ecstasy in the woods after our first time was that God was leading me to Susan and through Susan, and therefore I could trust God to lead me beyond these fears. I always seemed to have some hymn or another running through my mind back then, and when having sex with Susan, the words from *Amazing Grace* were clear: "'twas grace has led me safe thus far, and grace will lead me home."

On one point, however, I thought it might be pushing things to rely on grace rather than human responsibility. "We should think about protection," I said one night. "The rhythm method is really not reliable."

"I've already talked to my ob/gyn doctor," Susan said with a smile. "She says the pill doesn't work for everyone and recommended a diaphragm. So I'm getting fitted this week."

When Susan wasn't visiting, I was struggling with my issues in my class with Lehmann. The essential paradigm of salvation in the Hebrew Bible, Lehmann said, was the Exodus, in which God called the Israelites out of slavery and constantly stood by them, teaching, remonstrating and leading them through the wilderness to the Promised Land. In our day, the salvation event is our deliverance from narcissism, living solely focused on Freud's pleasure/pain principle as slaves to our own self-absorption.

The people of Israel at times wanted to return to "the fleshpots of Egypt," where at least they never suffered from hunger or thirst. Slavery had its benefits, and their resistance ultimately culminated in idolatry, the creation of the golden calf. Was my continuing homosexual interest my resistance to liberation from my own narcissism? Were my homosexual desires my own golden calf? It is our narcissism, according to Lehmann, that prompts our drive for power and security, and leads to addictions and false consciousness (the *mauvaise foi* of Sartre).

From everything I had read, homosexuality was a case *par excellent* of narcissism. Rather than loving someone different, homosexuals love someone like themselves, just as Narcissus fell in love with himself reflected in a pond. I therefore saw my experience with Susan as God's call to leave the slavery of my homosexual preoccupation and enter the promised land of being-in-relation to the ultimate Other—a person of the opposite sex, out of which all blessings would flow as befits the land of milk and honey.

In late October, I took my struggle to the resident psychotherapist at Union at the time, Jack Biersdorf. He was a sandy-haired, clean-shaven young man, maybe ten years my senior. His office was fairly dark with the exception of a fish tank that had a light illuminating the bubbles of the aerator and the beautiful gold and white fish swimming gracefully and peacefully inside. I brought in a dream of diving underwater and having to choose between two alternatives. After I talked on awhile about my sexual struggle and my family history, he said, "it looks like you tend to see things in terms of either/or, black or white."

"Of course," I replied. "Either I'm straight or I'm homosexual. What else is there?"

"Maybe that's what we should explore," he said. And I talked on with his barely commenting until he said, "I'm afraid our time is up."

"Well, thanks for your help," I said, and rose to walk out the door.

"Mr. Gunn, I didn't mean this was the end of our work, but only that we will have to pick it up at another session. I strongly suggest we meet once a week for a few times to see better how to help you."

I was taken aback. Even though I had read many books on homosexuality and psychoanalysis and knew of the "fifty-minute hour," I hadn't thought that applied to me or to him, since he didn't have a couch and was not Jewish (and he didn't have a beard!).

"Oh, okay," I answered, and we made another appointment. In the third session he explained that the seminary policy was that he could see a student for six times and if they needed on-going therapy, he had to refer them to a low-fee clinic. In our remaining sessions together we continued to look at the ways I set up either/or situations in my life and I was amazed to see the recurrent pattern. I was either homosexual or heterosexual; somebody special or a nobody; a spiritual person or a Bowery bum. After the six sessions were up, he recommended that I continue my therapy on a once a week basis at the American Foundation of Religion and Mental Health on

West 29h Street. It was in the offices of Marble Collegiate Church, where Norman Vincent Peale was still pastor and preacher. I had devoured avidly Dr. Peale's books on the "Power of Positive Thinking" when I was eleven years old. That link to my childhood strengthened my hope.

I began therapy with a new therapist at the American Foundation. Richard was of slight build, round-faced with glasses that were large enough and thick enough to render the rest of his face indistinguishable. That's how I felt about him—he was bland, indistinguishable from the masses, and just not very interesting. Biersdorf had class and style, mild-mannered though he was. On some level, I was attracted to him. This guy's clothes looked like they came from Penny's. Richard never said much. To me he was a limp dish rag. He looked like he had been to seminary, though he never made any personal comment about his own life. He was a *nebbish*. But perhaps a *nebbish* was what I needed.

As he asked me questions about my childhood and family, I saw with new clarity how enraged I was at my father because of the divorce, and how deeply disappointed I was in him, and how afraid I was that I would be like him, which I'd resolved never to be. And I never told Richard about my involvement with the Death of God movement because I was afraid he'd reduce it all to my father issues.

I didn't really want to talk about my feelings about my mother either, because I loved her and however ambivalent I was about our relationship, I didn't want anyone else telling me what to do with it. So I never told him about the dream of several years before where I was stabbing her in the chest.

And I realized how resistant I was to talking about my brother Bill. I was trying desperately not to cry. I did not want Richard or anyone else to make any comments about Bill or about my relationship to him. It was sacred and I was afraid that if Richard didn't handle the issue just right, I would just stop the therapy. Which is also why I never told Fred about Bill when we were roommates at Columbia. I couldn't be friends with anyone who was not completely empathic.

As for my sister, I loved her and thought the world of her and had no problems with her, so I didn't see any reason to talk about her.

I was desperately looking, though, for some insight that would help me decide something about my sexuality: I <u>wanted</u> to reduce it to an either/or proposition, despite Biersdorf's warning that a premature forced resolution doesn't really solve anything. The constant tension was hard to bear.

What I remember most of our few short months of work was his bringing up a Zen koan in response to my conflict around sexuality and whether to marry Susan. The koan is short: there is a goose in a bottle. How does the goose get out of the bottle? I had absolutely no clue, and he gave me no helpful hints to understand it. I did, however, go back to my books and discovered the small volume edited by Paul Reps in which the koan appeared. I felt that my therapy was as little help as the koan.

Although I continued with him, consciously I looked more to books for help than to therapy. However, I liked the experience of talking about what bothered me to someone who was not only not critical, but who pointed out how severely harsh I was on myself. And I liked that he encouraged me to express my feelings and thoughts more clearly and deeply than I usually did. What began slowly to emerge was the realization that my feelings of self-hate about my homosexual attraction had their origin in my upbringing in family and religion and were not rooted in objectivity. However little I thought of this therapist, I was, without realizing it, engaged positively in a process of self-reflection that I did not want to stop.

Meanwhile, the news of the ever-escalating war in Vietnam and my involvement with friends in protests and resistance (some burned their draft cards, one student refused to be drafted and was sentenced to jail) created a growing mental, moral and spiritual tension between my newly-developing awareness of my internal psychological self-involvement and the need I felt to be more externally involved with others in protest. Like other students at Union and other seminaries, I was classified 4D, which exempted me from military service. We had long discussions about the guilt we felt for protesting a war that was manned by a lottery system that had exempted us.

I began to question how valuable our protests and demonstrations were. I thought they served a purpose in forcing public scrutiny of the huge human cost and moral bankruptcy on which the war was based. But so much of our protests were not as non-violent as they purported to be. So many of us were filled with anger and disdain for those who disagreed with us. Although many in the opposition shared an equal disdain toward us, it was hardly the basis for healing and making real peace.

My thoughts regarding the relationship between the internal and the external, as I began to explore my own psyche in a systematic way, led me to the writings of Thomas Merton. A Trappist monk in Gethsemane, Kentucky, Merton wrote extensively and powerfully regarding the roots of violence and war, especially in two books, *Faith and Violence* and *Conjectures of a Guilty Bystander*. One image from his writing stayed with me: those who are so anxious to end the war tend to make a lot of noise and create a lot of commotion that is like the stirring up of a large cloud of dust, he said. From within that cloud of dust, you can no longer see yourself nor anyone else; all your efforts merely create commotion and blindness. For peace, clarity is required, and a calm spirit. This is the point of contemplation. With this in mind, I began to feel some connection between my internal struggles and the chaos of the external world.

After finding a bridge in the work of Thomas Merton between my internal struggles and the external struggles I observed around me, I delved into the writings of Carl G. Jung. Indeed, I began reading Carl Jung again as if my life was at stake—which I felt it was. On at least three levels, Jung spoke to me in a way that Freud did not: first of all, his appreciation for the feminine as an aspect of everyone's personality, not just women's, resonated with something that Susan had triggered, in terms of an awareness of the feminine that I felt when she danced, for example. His theory of the *anima* spoke to me on a level for which I had no words. That society might pigeonhole an individual based on the gender he or she was born to, fascinated me and yet I still had no idea how to put that together with my issues of sexual orientation. Secondly, his view of the unconscious and archetypal forces intrigued me: if God as father was an archetype that monitored cohesion and destructive impulses, the death of God might be seen as the prelude to an amoral politics that I associated with the war in Vietnam and the lost credibility of authority from governments to universities. Thirdly, Jung offered a deep appreciation for the spiritual and the constructive as well as demonic potential of religion, whereas Freud seemed to dismiss it with no appreciation for what I considered to be a human longing for transcendence.

I was also taking a course with Christopher Morse in Systematic Theology that focused on the writings of Swiss theologian Karl Barth. Barth's insistence on God as the Wholly Other placed God too far away from direct human experience and knowing for me, plus, his language was based on the theistic assumption of God as an object apart from the human, which I felt was precisely the god who had died. Nevertheless, I found in Barth's writing a resonance with the evangelical experience of my childhood, and thus found my core Christian faith revived and reviving. My head and heart felt opposing tugs and resonances: Tillich appealed to my mind, and Barth, appealed to my little boy's heart, but Barth's God crowded out the multiplicity of the world and the complexity of my inner struggle.

It all came to a head for me over Barth's assertion that the distinction between male and female represented the epitome of Otherness, such that men would overcome their narcissism by engaging the Otherness of a female, and women would overcome their narcissism by engaging the Otherness of a male. I challenged this point of view in a paper for the class, arguing that Barth was reifying heterosexuality without an in-depth understanding of the complexities of human sexuality, which had already been shown in the work of Alfred Kinsey to be manifested as a spectrum of both sexual activity and sexual desire, not a simple dichotomy. I suggested that in an actual relationship, the Otherness of the other was manifested in a full appreciation for the specific nuances and complexities of the individual person, and could never be reduced to a gender generalization. Furthermore, following my most recent readings in Jung, I noted that every person has elements of masculinity and femininity, which, if not appreciated and made space for, leads to a distorted view of the partner; thus, to reduce otherness to genitalia would be to betray the complexity with which we are all endowed.

I turned in the paper feeling very anxious for challenging the theological giant. I fretted over Christopher's reaction, knowing how strongly he seemed attached to Barth's point of view. When he returned the paper with an A and supportive comments, I felt not only confirmed in my argument, but encouraged to bring my own personal complexity into the realm of the intellect.

When, therefore, on December 11, 1968, I woke to see the front page of the *New York Times* with photos of both Thomas Merton and Karl Barth, announcing that each had died the previous day, I felt like two more giants in the Christian faith had fallen, and I took it personally. Carl Jung had died in 1961 as I was reading his *Modern Man in Search of a Soul* in my freshman year of college. John F. Kennedy was killed in 1963. Paul Tililch died in 1965. Martin Luther King was assassinated in April of 1968. Robert F Kennedy was assassinated in June of 1968. And now at the end of the year, Thomas Merton and Karl Barth died. All my intellectual and spiritual heroes had died, and I felt empty inside. Although they lived on in their writings, the cumulative effect of their deaths signaled a shift of responsibility to oneself akin to the death of a father. Was this, too, I wondered, one of the meanings of the death of God?

Later that morning, as I returned from class, the phone was ringing.

"Bob?" Susan said when I answered. She had never called in the middle of the day before.

"Yes, hi, are you okay?"

"Well, yeah. I was actually calling about you, wondering if you're okay."

"Yeah, sure. Why not?"

"Rich brought in a copy of the *Times* with the obituaries of Karl Barth and Thomas Merton, and I wondered how you're feeling. From what you've said before, I know they were both important to you."

"Oh, wow! How thoughtful of you! Yeah, I don't quite know what to make of it. Dying the same day, half way around the world from each other. They were so-- so different from each other. One Protestant, one Catholic, but both giants in thought in the Christian world."

"Well, I just wanted you to know I was thinking of you."

"Oh, yeah, I'm so amazed that you would, and that you'd call." Susan's genuine care for me, and for her to recognize how important these two Christian thinkers were to me enough to give me a call: I suddenly felt loved. We'd never yet used the word. But in that moment, I knew it and felt it, and I felt warmed all over. Suddenly I had a thought.

"Listen, I know it's kind of sudden and you don't have to answer right now, but—how would you feel about going down to Florida with me for Christmas and meet the family?"

"Oh!" she exclaimed, "I'd love to!!"

I immediately asked myself what I'd done and got all nervous. Was I more nervous because I'd asked her or because she'd answered so quickly without thinking about it, which meant I couldn't think about it any more either?

"Oh, great! Cool!" And suddenly neither of us said anything.

"Well, I guess we can figure out the details later. I'm so glad you called."

"So am I," she said quickly. "But I do have a class waiting for me, so…"

"Yeah, talk to you later. And thanks again."

My therapist said it was a bold move. I wasn't sure what he meant by that, whether he was saying "bravo for your courage" or "you poor impulsive thing, now you've really set yourself up for a problem." I felt both.

I had actually had the thought of her meeting my family earlier, but hadn't really made a decision. It wasn't like it meant we had to get married, I reminded myself. One thing I did know: if there were any possibility of a future together, she would have to pass "the Bill test." How would she respond to Bill? Would she be overly solicitous and treat him like a child? Would she be subtly, perhaps unconsciously, turned off or disgusted by his condition? How would she get along with my mother, and how would my mother get along with Susan? My sister Jeanne I had no qualms about; Jeanne naturally liked everyone and everyone liked her. Perhaps I was simply setting things up for my family to decide: how they would react to her, and how she would react to them. If either didn't get along with the other, I would quietly fade away and feel relieved of the responsibility for a decision. "Not exactly a bold move, Richard," I mentally said to my shrink.

When Susan was introduced to Bill, he shook her hand and held it.

"I'm very glad to meet you, Susan," Bill said. "You know I live in Ft. Lauderdale at Wood House."

"Yes, Bob told me," she said, sitting down in the chair next to him while letting him continue to hold her hand. "What's it like there, Bill?"

"Well, I tell you, Susan, most people are pretty nice, but sometimes, they can be very difficult." He let go of her hand, patted it, then raised his forefinger to make a point. "I have a friend named Peter. He and I have been friends ever since we were in Sunland. You know in Orlando?"

"I know where Orlando is."

"Well, I used to be there; but now I'm in Ft. Lauderdale. Anyway, Peter's my best friend at Wood House. He's very nice."

"I see," Susan replied.

Bill moved his hand back to where Susan's was on the chair. She let him take her hand in his again.

Susan passed the "Bill test." She related to him with ease and was not condescending or solicitous. She followed his cues without hesitation.

But I could feel my mother's discomfort with Susan. Susan's speech was different from ours: no pauses, each word enunciated, no drawl, no umms or ahhs. Although Susan grew up in Ohio and Michigan, her speech pattern seemed to have been shaped at Sarah Lawrence. It wasn't pretentious, but it did seem learned, just short of affected. I had not really noticed it until I experienced her talking to Mom. It carried a tinge of aloofness, of standing apart and perhaps somewhat above. I knew Susan certainly didn't mean anything by it; but I also knew that for most of her life, she was raised in an affluent family. Her father worked for one of the largest construction firms in the Midwest as an engineer. They lived in Bloomfield Hills, Michigan. There was a class difference between the McFerrens and the Gunns, and though I realized it before, I felt it more keenly in the exchange between my mother and Susan than I had previously. My mother struggled to do the right thing, to please Susan.

"Susan, what would you like to have for dinner tonight?" Mom asked. "Any preferences or something you can't eat?"

"I'm good with anything, Viv," Susan replied. "Do we need to get some groceries?"

I did not realize it at the time, but my mother saw me as entering a world beyond her imagination. Not the world of her dreams, but a world that was closed to her because of her background, her family, her near-edge-of-poverty experiences growing up. It was a world to which she did not feel entitled, a world where she felt very unworthy, unequal. It was like inviting Dr. Andre to our home in Jensen Beach. Susan doubtless felt it, but she and I didn't talk about it. The issue was my mother's, and was not a reflection on my mother's opinion or affection for Susan. By the end of the week, Mom, Jeanne and Susan were all cooking and going shopping together, and that was just fine.

With Susan having passed the family approval test, I felt an inner pressure that countered my wish for clarity about my own sexuality. For reasons I myself could not understand at the time, I felt a pressure to make a decision about marrying Susan in spite of, or perhaps because of my fears, doubts and questions. Oddly, given my direct knowledge of John, whom I held in the highest esteem on every level, I could not imagine a life for myself of respectability as a homosexual. The few sordid experiences I had had in Times Square represented to me the fate of homosexual men: consigned and condemned to furtive searching for sex with strangers—no names, no love, a bottomless vortex that would suck all life, all truth, beauty and love out of your body until you were a ghost, a vampire or a zombie.

These were my subconscious fears and assumptions. It seemed clear, however beautiful the love depicted in the books John had given me, the ultimate outcome of James Barr's *Quatrefoil*, Mary Renault's *Last of the Wine* and *The Charioteer* was unanimous: queer love always ended in suicide, stoic resignation or public scandal and humiliation, as in the case of Oscar Wilde. There was no such thing as a happy ending. In my mind, this fate, which could be worse than death, was precisely what John was trying to save me from by recommending I get married if I could. In this sense, my urge to marry Susan was the desperate act of a man trying to escape a descent into hell; not the hell of the Bible, but the hell of social depravity and ignominy.

With depravity on one side, and Susan dancing on the other, I thought of the future. I could marry a socially upwardly mobile and professional woman, enjoy her company and have a family with her, and if she could get along with my family--wouldn't that be a happy-ending-kind of story? <u>If</u> I could do it—be sexually gratified and gratifying to her also, and could meld my lower middle class background with her upper middle class family—the positives and the negatives were clear. Q.E.D.

Topping it all off, of course, was the God issue- not just the God of my great grandmother, but the God —by whatever name—of the experience I had

had with Susan on Little North Pond. Where did that ecstasy come from and how could it be seen other than as a divinely-inspired opening of a new life possibility which offered so much more hope than the "fleshpots of Egypt" which I automatically felt were equivalent to homosexuality (here, it was not hatred of homosexuality so much as the church's hatred of sexuality in general I was dealing with)?

Amid the turmoil of all these thoughts and feelings, Susan and I were having great sex. On the sheer physical level, Susan was a great sexual partner, exciting, sensitive, expressive and unafraid of trying things beyond the "missionary position." I found myself able to respond to her, to enjoy her and take risks in ways I had never done with a man.

On our return trip we stopped in Fayetteville, North Carolina, near Ft. Bragg, and stayed at the Holiday Inn, where Grant Luckhardt and I had often stayed returning to college. We went out for dinner, and I bought a bottle of Johnny Walker Red to take back to the room. By the time we were ready for bed, I had successfully calmed my fear and trembling with Johnny Red, and, as we made love, I asked her to marry me, and she said yes. I felt happy, proud and anxious.

When we reached New York, she stayed overnight with me before heading up to Maine, and that evening, we called her parents, whom I had never met nor spoken to, and told them of our engagement. They responded with great enthusiasm and wondered whether we had set a date. We told them June 21, which would give both Susan and me time to finish our semesters at Union and Colby. Then we invited them to come to New York for a weekend visit.

The day after Susan left, I woke up with red spots all over my body, small, pin prick-sized spots that looked like measles to me. I went to St. Luke's Hospital emergency room and the doctor agreed that that was what they looked like, but none of the tests confirmed measles. In fact, all my blood work returned normal. Without telling me that it was a psychosomatic reaction to my most recent stress-filled event, he said wait and see if it goes away within the week. It cleared up after three days. I suffered the fears of the damned, but not sure whether I was damned for having betrayed myself or for having betrayed God by not trusting in my decision. In any case, my anxiety and apprehension remained as a *basso continuo* amid the many other voices of happiness and hopes.

My therapist's interpretation of the pseudo-measles was probably the simplest and best explanation: "you have a lot of feelings around your decision."

Prompted by one of Lehmann's references to D.H. Lawrence, I got a book of his poetry. In stanza II of Lawrence's "New Heaven and New Earth" he says, "I was so weary of the world/I was so sick of it/ everything was tainted with myself…" Then in VI,

> I put out my hand in the night, one night, and my hand
> touched that which was verily not me
> verily it was not me…
> So I put my hand out further, a little further
> and I felt that which was not I
> it verily was not I
> it was the unknown…
> Cortes, Pisarro, Columbus, Cabot, they are nothing, nothing!
> I am the first comer!
> I am the discoverer!
> I have found the other world!....
> VII
> It was the flank of my wife
> I touched with my hand, I clutched with my hand
> Rising, new-awakened from the tomb!

My own heart was pierced by these words! To me, they thoroughly described my experience when Susan and I first made love on Little North Pond. The ecstasy—meaning, out of the ordinary state of self—was a perfect expression of my experience and linked it completely together with Lehmann's emphasis on deliverance from narcissism. Lawrence here confirmed not only what I experienced, but the meaning of it, psychologically and spiritually and physically: transcendence, a new world, the world of the Other. This poem confirmed for me that I was on the right track, that there was an inner revolution I was undergoing and it was all part of God's plan to deliver me from the prison of myself. I did feel that making love to Susan was transcending the projections of my own ego, The poem thus confirmed the spiritual value and truth of our relationship. 1969 was indeed going to be a new beginning.

This powerful deepening experience with Susan served to maintain my own equanimity when Rich called in late January to tell me he and Cathy Pagano were engaged. Cathy was pregnant and she and Rich were both finishing their last year at Colby. In February, Rich and Cathy drove down with Susan, and the four of us went out on the town, taking in a foreign movie and getting cheap eats in the Village. I managed not to focus on Rich; I felt a certain pang at the inner loss of what I had dreamed of and imagined with him, though we continued to resonate in our perceptions and feelings during conversations, often with one of us ending the sentence of the other. There was nevertheless something new and satisfying about being a couple with another couple that I liked. It seemed to me that this must be what ordinary people experienced. It seemed so normal. And yet I still felt a certain emptiness inside.

A few weeks after Rich and Cathy had visited Susan and me in New York, I went to see John and told him about my engagement. He offered his congratulations and asked that Susan and I meet him for dinner when she came to the city again. In early March, Susan came down and we met at John's apartment for drinks and then went around the corner to the small Czech restaurant, the first one John had taken me to. I was very anxious about the meeting. I desperately wanted Susan to like John and for him to like her. John could not have been more charming: ever the quintessential gentleman and consummate host, he engaged Susan in conversation about her own field of dance, as well as theater.

John knew enough about the history of ballet and modern dance to elicit more about Susan's knowledge and experience than I had ever heard her speak of. I felt a bit like the third wheel, except I was deeply gratified—even jealous at John's spirit of generosity, and impressed all the more with Susan's response.

When, however, we returned to John's after dinner for a nightcap, and Susan started talking about the escalation of the war under Nixon, John chuckled.

"So you joined the Christian idealists to change the world...." It was not so much a question as a statement of bemusement.

"Oh, God, Susan, don't go there," I thought to myself.

"Oh, yes," she answered with the excitement of one who expects to be agreed with. "I think this war just has to stop, don't you?"

"I think it's a human tragedy, the loss of our troops, but I think it has a purpose," John replied, setting his scotch down. The line of his mouth was suddenly straight, not smiling, and he looked at her, as he had at me many times, challenging her to argue for her position.

Susan sat up straight like the dancer she was and suddenly I thought of John's mother, whose spine always seemed so straight, and wondered at this conjunction of images and whether John noticed.

"What is the US death toll, now?" she asked, looking at me. "44,000?"

"44,650, according to today's *Wall Street Journal*," John answered.

Susan's face, tense with its furrowed brow, expressed her utter seriousness and care. John's face, on the other hand, remained relaxed and attentive. As they talked on, in spite of myself, I found myself thinking of what it was like to make love to each of them—so different! John's body so much bigger than mine, with a man's smell and muscle. Susan's so light, soft and lithe, so responsive to my every touch. Paradoxically, watching them in such close proximity, thinking of them each specifically, made it easier to accept my own feelings for each of them than when I thought about them in the abstract. In the abstract, it was an either/or again; but here, bodies in front of me, there was no conflict, just difference.

"I don't think any purpose could justify that many deaths—not to mention how many Vietnamese we have killed," Susan said.

"We lost 400,000 men in World War Two. Hitler had already killed 6,000,000 Jews. What's the price of freedom?"

Susan and John eye-balled each other for a moment. John clearly thought he had checkmate.

"I just don't consider them analogous," Susan said. "Vietnam has not invaded a foreign country, not even a country that is a friend of ours, much less our own."

"Well, Susan, Robert and I have been over this issue many times and have simply agreed to disagree. Meanwhile, though I disagree with you both, I admire you both for standing up for what you believe, and for doing the grunt work of trying to convince others." He stood and reached for her glass and mine. "More scotch or Armagnac?"

With the growing approval of Susan from friends and my own family, all that remained for me was to meet her parents. Susan's parents, Don and Flo, came to meet me in New York and Susan came down again from Colby at the end of March. We got along very well. Don was a very outgoing man with a lot of enthusiasm for new things. He was balding on top, with only a wisp of hair. His right eyelid was often half shut, but he was a very personable man, easy to talk to.

Don didn't like the hustle and bustle and noise of New York, but he did enjoy seeing "The Man of La Mancha" which had just opened at the Martin Beck Theater. (I totally identified with Quixote and saw Susan as my veritable Dulcinea, in terms of the way Dulcinea kept hope and dreams alive for Quixote.) Flo was more reserved, but striking with her full, bright, white head of hair. Flo tended to be talkative, but she was always upbeat and considerate.

They seemed to like me (and most of all, like the fact that their daughter was getting married! After all, Susan was almost 29!), and I liked them. What we had in common was Detroit and cars: her father built General Motors office buildings, my father sold their cars, and I loved cars. I suggested we go to Luchow's on 14th Street, and they loved the violins wandering among the tables. Flo, coming from German heritage, especially appreciated the experience. Then, of course, we had to honor Don's Irish side, and so we went to O'Rourke's, an Irish pub on the upper east side.

We began to make detailed plans for the wedding. We chose our crystal and china, a pattern from Genori's on Fifth Avenue. We chose wedding rings that reflected our mutual agreement that our relationship should have open spaces as well as connecting points. We shared a similar aesthetic sensibility.

We liked the poem, *On Marriage* of Kahlil Gibran:

> Then Almitra spoke again and said, 'And what of Marriage, master?'
> And he answered saying:
> You were born together, and together you shall be forevermore.....
> But let there be spaces in your togetherness...

Yet, even as Susan agreed to this metaphor to be expressed by spaces in the wedding bands, I knew that what she meant by it and what I meant by it were different things, and I felt guilty. I had accepted John's advice to get married, but had dismissed out of hand the correlative piece of advice, that I tell her about my attraction to men. Certainly I wished and hoped that, as a pointing by God toward a new path, that my conflict would be resolved and I would be happy as a heterosexually-married man. It was like inwardly, I was placing a bet on something I really didn't believe in, though I hoped for it. And so to speak to her of my alter-sexuality would be to make more real something I hoped would disappear.

By April, Susan and I had sent out engraved invitations to the rehearsal dinner and the wedding. Although I finished all my coursework in early May, it became clear that I was not going to finish my thesis on "Testing the Spirits" in time for graduation. So I took a one-year extension, said goodbye to my therapist, packed up, and left for Maine. Frederic had offered his place on Little North Pond for both the rehearsal dinner and the wedding, and we instantly accepted.

The plan was to have a traditional Maine lobster and clam bake on Friday night at Little North Pond, return to the house for more socializing into the evening, then return to the Pond for the wedding at 11 a.m.

Susan's parents, her Aunt Marge and Uncle Warren, and their children drove in from Michigan in a motor home. My mother, my Aunt Billy, my father's mother, Maw Maw, and my sister Jeanne drove up from Florida in the '64 Impala which had been paid for by a loan to me from John.

In the end, my father said he simply could not afford to come. The truth was, the divorce being only three years old, his presence would have cast a troubling pall over a celebration that needed to burst forth full throttle with joy and hope for our own marriage.

The entire Colby faculty had also been invited, and most of them came, including most of the students Susan or I had taught. John Elliott came up, along with Gil Winter and Tom Alexander. Steve, Dan and Ed came up from the New Jersey house. Fred Collignon came up from Cambridge. Phil and Linda Merrill brought Franklin, their short-haired, brown and white St. Bernard whom they named after FDR. He lumbered amiably about, sneaking snacks from those who failed to notice him.

With ample *Pouilly-Fuissé* to go with the lobster and clams, the Friday evening gathering gave everyone a chance to get informally acquainted before the actual wedding. The sound of the loons on the pond as the sun went down gave a natural musical background to the conversations and laughter.

By 11 p.m., we had all reconvened back at our house in Oakland. All seemed to be going well, Then, about 2 a.m., when the crowd was thinning out and I heard Phil speaking in strident tones face to face with John, with three others clustered around the two of them. I had no idea what they had been talking about, but as I approached I heard John, who stood about four inches taller than Phil, say, "Young man, you have many strong opinions, but--have you ever suffered?" It was more an accusation than a question.

Phil, who had led Colby's debate team, responded quick and strong, "You're damned right I have! What, you want my credentials? You want to see my scars?—you can't—they're inside!"

John shot back, "I don't think so. Oh, I'm sure you've been hurt. Everyone has. But have you suffered?"

"I don't know what you're talking about."

"That's what I thought."

"What are you talking about? Why are you on my case?"

"Because," John said, lowering his voice, "you're so damned arrogant. You think you know everything, you have an answer for everything, but you really don't understand the first thing about people, yourself included."

"Oh!" shouted Phil. "I'm the arrogant one! Here you are pontificating about me when you met me just five minutes ago, and exactly what qualifies you to make that call?"

Distressed by the volume of his master's rising voice, Franklin, the St. Bernard, pushed his way into the circle that had gathered and started licking

Phil's hand with such unexpected force that Phil dropped his glass, splashing scotch over both John and himself.

"Shit, Frank! Go lie down!" Phil hollered.

Linda suddenly rushed over with napkins and gave some to Phil and started dabbing John's wet shirt and saying, "I'm sorry. I'm sorry."

"A little more on the outside won't hurt," John said, suddenly smiling.

Phil's pants were more thoroughly wet, and he said, "Excuse me, I need to...." And strode toward the bathroom.

The little group scattered.

"What was that all about?" I asked John.

"He thinks he knows more than he does," he replied, still wiping his shirt and pants with a napkin. "Anyway, Big Shot, it's late and you have a big day ahead of you tomorrow, so I think it's time to call it a night."

In bed, I turned to Susan, "Except for that tète-a-tete between Phil and John it was a great evening. I still don't know what that was about."

"Yes, you do," Susan said. "John's right. We all know Phil is arrogant and a blowhard. It's just that John had enough to drink and enough chutzpah to say so. Nobody ever talks to Phil that way, unless it's Linda!"

"And Franklin! St. Bernard to the rescue! I still wonder, though, why John chose to ask whether Phil had suffered. If he only wanted to point out Phil's arrogance, he didn't need to bring up the issue of suffering."

Suddenly I turned on my side and looked at Susan. "Did I ever tell you about John's work with the Friends?"

"You mean the Quakers?"

"Yes. John started college at Harvard but then, for some reason dropped out and went to Europe and worked for two years with the Friends in France and Germany."

"When was that?"

"He graduated from Phillips Exeter in 1945 so it was after a semester at Harvard, in 1946. He went there to help with the recovery from World War II."

"So he saw a lot of suffering...."

"Yeah. Quite a guy." I gave her a kiss. "Good night."

"Good night."

Thus, our last words to each other in bed, the night before our wedding, were not of our impending nuptials or our future life together as husband and wife, but words reflecting on a man I had been intimate with and who had played such a strong role in steering my course, even the very marriage I was about to start the next day.

June 21, 1969. The sky was resplendently sunny. Off to the side of the Hudson's cabin was a large gray, shoulder-high granite rock that served as the center stage of the wedding. We had rolled logs in on three sides for people to sit on, facing the rock, and beyond it, through the pines and white birches, the lake, glistening in the sun.

As people gathered for the ceremony, a Colby string quartet, at one side of the rock, played Baroque music.

Susan's father, Don, had asked to walk with Susan alone and pick daisies with her before the ceremony. Then, later, Don walked Susan to the pond as she held the cluster of white daisies for her bouquet that they had picked together. As he escorted her down to the rock where Frederic and I stood watching, the quartet played and Fred Collignon sang a Handel baritone aria called "Where e're you walk."

Frederic, as officiating minister, stood in front of the rock; I was on his left. He wore white pants and a pale blue and white striped T shirt. I wore a blue blazer with a solid aqua shirt, a white tie filled with splotches of brown and navy blue, and white bell bottoms that hung over my brown ankle boots. My hair was long enough to cover my ears.

Susan came down the path on her father's arm, in a beautiful, pure white embroidered dress that went slightly below her knees, but had no train. She carried the white daisies in her clasped hands and beamed as she walked toward me. Don gave her a kiss and released her to me, and sat down on a log with Flo. I took her hand and we both turned to face Frederic.

Frederic gave a short homily on the meaning of marriage at that particular point in history. "In a time when the dominant forces lead us into war by deception and no authority or institution can be trusted, including the authority of church, state and the academy…in such a time of unreliability, to make a marriage vow is an assertion of faith and hope, and a commitment to a future that is uncertain. As Bob and Susan now make their vows to each other in this idyllic setting, the authenticity and simplicity of their style stand out as a protest against all that is fake and deceptive, and in these days, style is everything!"

Susan and I had agreed to make up our own vows, but not to let each other know what we were going to say. We turned to each other and held hands. Susan spoke of our love and her commitment to be with me through all the uncertainties of our times. "I promise to stand beside you, but to leave spaces for you to be you and me to be me. I look forward to our growing old together," she said.

I spoke of our love as a beacon of hope in very dark times, and the beauty of this setting as an ever-present reminder of how life was intended to be. "Marriage is a journey in love of two people, both of whom are seeking to be rooted in the ground of love itself. I look forward to our journey together."

Frederic declared us to be husband and wife, we kissed, the quartet burst into a Bach chaconne, and everyone broke into applause.

Frederic then asked people to offer whatever words they felt like sharing with us. For nearly an hour, people talked about the meaning of our individual relationship to them and the meaning of our marriage. The theme of social and cultural turmoil, uncertainty—indeed, fear—was pervasive. Everett MacKinnon, who we knew by the grapevine was having marital problems of his own, inscribed in a book of Daniel Berrigan's latest poems to us: "Here on Little North Pond, love and beauty; and elsewhere----?" We were all struggling for hope and love to overcome the specter of Vietnam and the unpredictability of a government that was more responsive to market forces than to human beings.

Susan and I walked up to the table, cut the cake and smooshed it into each other's mouths, to great laughter and applause. Champagne was passed around and Fred Collignon initiated the toasts. When everyone had had their say, Susan and I started milling around, greeting our guests. After awhile, I walked over to Steve, Dan and Ed and suddenly burst into tears. "I don't know why I'm crying," I said as Steve hugged me. "This is supposed to be the happiest day of my life."

We said goodbye to our families, packed Susan's 1966 beige Mustang with some clothes, and headed down to Georgetown and Reid State Park, where Bob and Dorothy Reumann had invited us to use their camp for two weeks. As John's gift to us, he offered us two weeks at a farmhouse he had recently acquired on Mt. Desert. His other gift was a bottle of Chivas Regal. This was our honeymoon: two weeks on the coast of Maine at Georgetown, and two weeks at a farmhouse from the 1800's on a tidal saltwater marsh on Mt. Desert. Susan had nothing to do at Colby until August when she would have to begin preparing for the fall. I intended to seek a pastorate either with the Methodists or the United Church of Christ. I wrote to the Bishop of the Maine Conference of the Methodist Church and to the Maine Conference Minister of the United Church of Christ, and waited to hear back from them.

The Reumanns' rustic cottage sat on a large rock that was about twenty feet high above the beach, with walls of barnboard, red-checkered plastic tablecloth on an old kitchen table, two windows looking out to the sea—one from the kitchen, the other from the small living area. Surrounded on three sides by tall pines, inside, the cottage felt dank and dark; only the windows' view of the ocean offered an opening to the sun. In the living room, the Franklin stove's sole purpose was emitting heat, not light, so there was no fire to be seen.

We spent our days combing the beaches, reading, sunning on the beach, eating, shopping for eats and drinks, making dinner (Susan assumed the full role of cook, which was just fine with me), reading, drinking and making love. Before dinner, we said grace, holding hands. When it rained, we walked the beach in the rain or watched from the porch as it came down on the sea. There was no television, only a radio fixed on NPR.

We didn't talk a lot. Sometimes the silence was comfortable, but as the days wore on, it increasingly wasn't. After a week of this natural beauty with growing gaps of silence, I began to wish we had more to say. "Shall I wear my trousers rolled up?—"Do I dare to eat a peach?" I thought to myself.

Our sex could not have been better. We made love on the couch, on the kitchen table, on the beach at night, we even tried in the water, but it was too cold. Each time we had sex, my anxiety lowered, and I felt it was another point for my heterosexuality. I had feared impotence, but that was not a problem. I feared not being able to please Susan, but that seemed no problem either.

And yet....And yet, each time we made love, as physically exhilarating as it was, and as real as it was as an expression of my love for her and hers for me, after the climax I felt an emptiness inside that I could not understand, and that made me very anxious.

My anxiety grew. Making love and drinking gave temporary respite from the growing sense that there was a space between us—a space where we were not connected at all. Something about it was very scary. Like, what if this whole marriage was a mistake? What if Steve's observation about Susan's idly fondling the rubber tree leaf, when he'd visited me at Colby, was a true pointer to this huge emptiness and disconnection? What if my assumption that this marriage was God's will was a mistake? I began to drink more to suppress the lurking anxiety and made love to reassure myself.

On the twelfth day I took a stroll by myself up the beach, longer than usual. Around a bend in the shoreline there was a stretch of sand about a half mile or so where the peninsula was too narrow for building cottages, and because there was no place to park, few people ever went there. On this day, however, I could see an isolated figure sunning on a blanket in the distance. As I approached, he came more clearly into view. He was lying on his back, had one arm over his eyes, had a deep bronze tan and wore very low-cut denim shorts. Probably in his early twenties, he reminded me of Rich with his brown beard and long hair. My heart raced as I got closer. I thought about turning around and just going back but my feet kept moving forward.

That moment on the beach, as I kept walking forward towards the handsome young man lying there as if waiting for me to appear, as if God had set him in my path, something took over me. There was no thought of the pretty new wife waiting for me in the cottage. There was no thought really at all beyond letting my legs keep moving, propelling me forward, closer to the young man, the complete stranger who seemed to be drawing me to him like a super-powered magnet.

When I was steps away from him, I felt my heart racing and wondered, what would I say? 'Nice day?' 'Pretty isolated here, isn't it?' 'Want to get it on?' Then I thought, 'What makes you think he would be interested in you, stupid!'

It was then that I suddenly became conscious of my new wedding ring on my left hand, which he would be able to see. I tucked my fingers closer to my palm. As I drew even with him, he raised his arm and looked at me. Our eyes met in the split-second long enough to signal interest. I kept walking. Why are you still walking in this direction, I said to myself. Everything you want is behind you....him....or Susan. How can you even think of such a thing? You just got married! But a quick roll on the blanket...no one visible....Isn't that what you want? And then what? Is this what my married life is going to be...sex with Susan interspersed with sex with strangers?

I turned back and sprinted past him and didn't stop until I passed the bend and was out of his sight. Then I began tormenting myself: Fool! Opportunity knocks and you run away from it! Good for you, you passed your first temptation. Coward! Good man! I ran into the freezing water to wash his image from my mind, but I held onto it even as I dunked my head into the brine. I dashed out of the water into the house. Susan was reading in a chair. I grabbed her hand and pulled her into the bedroom.

"What's this?" she said grinning.

I undressed her and led her into the shower where we made love standing up, fast and hard.

"Oh! Oh! Whatever got into you...I like it!" she said.

After we left the Reumanns' cottage, before finishing our honeymoon at John's new place on Mt. Desert, we stopped by our new home. In a twist of irony known only to me, Susan and I had heard by the Colby grapevine that Don, the bookstore assistant manager who had invited me for dinner and failed to seduce me, was leaving his duplex in Oakland. We had taken it as soon as we saw it. It was a grand old Victorian with four bedrooms, a kitchen, dining room, living room, a parlor with a Franklin stove, and, best of all, a piano. The piano was a 100 year-old Henry Miller upright that had a very sweet tone.

I sat down to play it a bit before we finished unpacking. However much I enjoyed being other places, after being away for a few days without a piano, my fingers longed for the feel of the ivories. I began playing Beethoven's "Moonlight" Sonata, which seemed fitting honeymoon music, but I was hardly into the opening broken chords of the Adagio when my reverie went back to the beach and the young man, and I suddenly stopped playing, jumped over to the Presto Agitato, which conjured up the shift I'd made that afternoon from fascination with the young man to making reckless, passionate love to Susan. I put my whole self into the piece and brought the movement to its own superb, breathless climax.

"Bravo!" Susan hollered from the kitchen. "It's very exciting!"

"Isn't it!," I replied. Then, "Time to get down to business and look for a job."

I had been raised a Methodist, and had answered "Methodist" whenever I confronted the religion blank in college registration forms. But I was having doubts about it ever since I learned that you had to sign an oath that you would abstain from alcohol. Dick Monkman said no one took it seriously, and I should not worry about it. But it bothered me that I would have to start out my ministry with a lie. Also, the more I was involved in anti-war activities, the clearer it was that the United Church of Christ was way ahead of the Methodists and most other Protestant denominations in terms of social conscience, particularly on the Vietnam war and the civil rights movement. On a very personal level, I was very deeply impressed with Avery Post; if I were going to be a minister, I wanted to be like him: sophisticated, eloquent and yet able to relate to diverse populations and interests.

In the letter from the Methodist Bishop, he thanked me for my interest and said although he had nothing for me at present, he would keep me in mind. The tone was "official business" which I read as disinterest. I tossed it into the wastebasket.

The UCC Conference Minister, William Thompson, welcomed me to Maine and the UCC. He said I should be in touch with the Area Conference Minister, Bill Booth, whose office was in Augusta, regarding opportunities nearby. Encouraged, I called Bill Booth immediately. He said he had received a fax from the conference office with my resume and would like to see me. Was I available in the afternoon? Of course I said yes.

Bill Booth's office was behind the First Congregational Church of Augusta. He was tall, lanky and wore a black patch over one eye. His handshake was firm and strong. After chatting a bit about my being a newly-wed and the move to

Maine, he told me about two different openings. One was a full-time position in Madison; the other was very part-time in Jackman. I told him I needed time to finish my B.D. thesis, so I was only looking for a part-time situation. He stood up and pointed to spot on a large map of Maine. When you see the whole state of Maine, Jackman was on a latitude slightly above Bangor, but Bangor was still only half-way up the state.

"Jackman is a frontier town," Bill said. "Everybody has a pick-up with a 30-30 hanging in the rear window. It's also a border town, the last stop on the way to Quebec. Most of the town is French Canadian and Catholic; they speak Franglais....you know what that is?" he asked, winking his one eye.

"A combination of French and English?"

"That's right. Everyone works either for International Paper or Great Northern, logging, or for the Immigration Service. The nearest shopping mall is 60 miles south..." His finger traced Route 201 south. "...to Skowhegan. The winters up there can be pretty nippy." From his accent, I could tell he was a true Mainer, and this understatement clinched it. "Now, on your way up from Oakland, after Skowhegan, the territory gets interesting....you begin climbing the mountains." His finger moved back up the map. "You don't see grass from October to June—it's all snow. The people are just ordinary folk. They don't mind telling you what they think and they don't like B.S., unless it has a twist of humor in it," he said with a broad grin.

"Sounds like my kind of place!"

"There's a small ski lift...doesn't amount to much, but if you ski, there it is."

"All the better."

"Well, then, I'll call Bill Andrews, he's the local sheriff up there and chair of their search committee, and tell him to call you."

"I'm going to be away for two weeks, we're headed over to Mt. Desert. Our last bit of honeymoon."

"Oh, God's country! No better place! I used to be pastor at the church there in Bar Harbor. Okay, so why don't I give you his number and you can call him when you get back."

"Sounds good." I started to get up to leave.

"How about if we have a word of prayer before you leave?"

I was taken aback. It seemed so intimate I felt embarrassed. I had memories of prayers with Allen Stuart, which always turned me off because he seemed to be listening to himself more than God was. But it all came so natural to this strange, warm, welcoming one-eyed man, that I was deeply moved before he even began.

"Heavenly father, we give you thanks for Bob's coming to Maine. We pray that you bless his ministry wherever it unfolds. Bless him and his wife Susan, and may all they do prosper, according to your will. Amen."

"Amen."

And we shook hands and I somehow felt at home in Maine in a new way.

The serious prospect of a job gave me a sense of being grounded. I would still have to interview and be hired by the church, so it was not a done deal. But Bill Booth's description of it excited me.

As Susan and I did the laundry and packed for the second two weeks further "downeast," my anxiety shifted and grew. At the beginning of the honeymoon, I had been worried that I could not perform sexually. No matter how many times we had already had sex, there remained for me a tinge of anxiety which I usually handled by nightcaps. But the image of the young man on the beach stayed with me the way the color red does when you tell someone, "Don't think red."

It was not that I expected to find another Adonis on Mt. Desert, but that I feared the memory and the image would dominate my thoughts and I would not be able to concentrate on Susan when we made love. So I resolved to let my mind soften around the image and to practice letting it go without turning it into a mental fight. Without realizing what I was doing, I was finding my way to live with a constant separation in my mind between what I was thinking and what I was letting others know about myself. Of course, all of us do this to some degree. But my marriage signified a commitment to someone else's reality other than my own—Susan's. So my task, as I saw it, was to do whatever was necessary to make our marriage work; things that did not fit in, had to be put aside. I was mentally constructing a room in the corner of my mind, called "Big Secret Shed- Do Not Enter," into which I could put all the pieces of my life that didn't fit inside the house of marriage.

The farmhouse John gave us for the second half of our honeymoon was just below Seal Cove on Route 102 on Mt. Desert, fifteen miles from his place in Southwest Harbor. The white clapboard house sat back from the water about a hundred yards. The land sloped down from the lawn to a patch of wheat, past the dark mud to Blue Hill Bay.

"Oh, it's lovely!" Susan exclaimed as we drove in. As soon as I stopped the car, she jumped out and started running and dancing on the lawn. I loved her spritely spirit and her great legs moving through the air, seemingly unrestrained by gravity. I followed her into the wheat field to the mud flats. She kicked off her sandals and walked into the sucking mud.

"This has to be filled with clams," she said with the enthusiasm of a veteran clamdigger. I kicked off my moccasins and followed, feeling the oozing black stuff and the shells of clams or what was left of them, sometimes sharp-edged.

"Does the mud ever stop?" I shouted.

"Of course, silly!" she said, and forged on.

While glad to be moving out of the muck, when the water was above my knees my feet began to find rocks that were slippery and then I lost my balance and fell in.

"See? Isn't this better?" Susan shouted, turning back to splash water at me.

"Yeah, well, why don't you try it?" I pushed her backwards into the water.

"Oh my God, it's so cold!"

Then I helped her up, pulled her to me and we kissed and held each other until she started trembling and I saw goose bumps on her arms.

"Back?" I asked.

"Y-y-yes!"

As fast as we could, we stepped our way back over the rocks and the mud, picked up our shoes and ran back to the house. The back door was unlocked and we ran upstairs to what had to be the master bedroom. I turned the water on in the shower to get hot as we undressed, then wrapped her in a towel because she was shivering. After a couple of minutes the water was still cold.

"The water heater must not have been turned on yet," I said. "So we gotta do a quickie!" I pulled her into the shower, soaped her all over and rinsed her quick. She got out, I soaped and rinsed, grabbed a towel and dried myself fast, then followed her into a high double bed with large soft pillows and a huge down comforter.

"Welcome to the fa-mhouse, m'lady" I said, trying to make the flat "r" typical of the Maine accent.

"Welcome to me!" she said as we snuggled, warming each other up until we stopped shivering, then fell asleep.

Sometime later, Susan woke me from our nap, asking, "What time is it?"

I picked up my watch from the side table. "Almost five."

"Time to start dinner."

"Mmhm."

"Time to get up!"

"Mmhm."

She started beating me with the pillows. "Wake up! Wake up!"

"Ow! Ow! Ow!" I feigned, defending myself against her blows. Then I grabbed her around the waist and pulled her down to the side and got on top of her. I looked down into her blue eyes. She let go of the pillow.

"Don't you want dinner?" she looked up at me with a smile.

"Dinner can wait." This time we were very slow and I left no part of her untouched, unkissed. And I was able to lose myself in her, totally absorbed in her contours and shadows. After we made love, we were both so exhausted, we skipped dinner and fell asleep again.

The next morning Susan made blueberry pancakes. "Fresh maple syrup," she said, as she placed it on the table.

"So are you going to be okay if I spend most of the time reading for my thesis?"

"Of course. I have plenty to read myself and I can work in the garden. And I can begin planning for classes and performances.

Thus began our routine: wake up around 8, breakfast and coffee until 10. Read and write 'til 1 or 2. Lunch. Nap. Read and write until 6. Cocktails and dinner. Read and write. Nightcap. To bed. Make love. Sleep. Start all over again.

After a few days, I realized there was a very different feel to this farmhouse than the camp at Reid State Park. From the mudroom where boots were left, through the kitchen with its wood stove large enough for cooking, one walked through the small dining room with an old crystal chandelier, into a living area with a huge picture window, obviously of more recent vintage. The whole house seemed to telescope down and out toward the sea. It beckoned us to stay.

"It's hard to imagine what kind of farming was ever done here," I commented one evening as Susan was preparing supper. "The center roofline looks like a swayback horse. The wide plank floors and low ceilings make it seem like it was built in the early 1800's. What do you think?"

"I love it," Susan said as she dropped corn on the cob into boiling water.

"Yeah, me, too....What do you think it'd be like to live here....? You could commute to Colby....only about 3 ½ hours each way." I grinned.

"Yeah, right! And you? How much are they going to pay you at Jackman, which is another 2 hours beyond Waterville?"

I pulled a Liebfraumilch out of one of the bags, put it in the freezer to chill. "I don't know....Maybe $50—75 a week?"

"Great. And how much does John want for this?" In a separate large pot, she lifted the lid and steam shot up into the air. She reached over and picked up one lobster, its claws moving in the air, dropped it in, then the other, and covered the lid. The crackling of their claws against the pot slowly stopped. She turned and looked at me.

"I know. I know. More than we can afford," I said. "Just a fantasy...."

"Well, it's a good one!" She gave me a peck and stirred the melting butter in a small pan.

During cocktails, which at the end of the week turned out to be Rob Roys, I lifted my glass to hers and said, "How many children do you want?"

"We said we were going to wait for my sabbatical next year, right? Why are you asking right now?"

"I know. I just want to know how many times to make love!" I said, grinning.

"Oh, so it's only going to be once per child, eh?"

"Too late for that!"

She smiled and her eyes twinkled. "Definitely more than one. I wouldn't want anyone to have to be the only child like I was....you?"

"Definitely not more than three. Three wasn't bad in our family, but our ages were so far apart, four years, five years. It added to my feeling of being the real parent. Children should be about two years apart. Mother has a little time to recover, but the siblings can feel more like peers. I always felt like I was alone."

"Funny," she said, "I really was alone, and you felt it even though you weren't."

"Yep. So let's make it two." These words popped out of me, spontaneously, before I even thought about it.

"Mmm...maybe we should just wait and see?"

"Sure," I said. Something about the question made me anxious. The house had gotten to me, in a way. The urge to have a family was very strong. This place said to me, 'This is how it can be, your children can play on the lawn, the two of you can have cocktails after work, Susan can work in the garden, and you can not just work for peace, you can be at peace.' Such was the house's beck and call. Perhaps it also suggested to me that having children would fill the emptiness inside, divert my mind's wandering off to other possibilities.

Toward the end of our honeymoon at John's place, one night a question popped out of me as I was lying in bed with Susan. "We don't have to make love every night, right?"

"Bob, we don't have to make love for me to feel noticed. I'm not that narcissistic!" she said, running her fingers lightly over my chest, twirling the hairs. The gesture reminded me of Steve's comment about her fondling the rubber plant—some piece of unconscious showing. Now her words were contradicted by her seductive gesture.

"Okay. Good. So, I don't feel like sleeping just yet. I think I'll go back down and read for awhile, okay?" I was growing restless with our idyllic routine. I thought of John a lot—we were, after all, in his house. Not that he'd ever lived here, but it was his. I tried to imagine him on the lawn and immediately knew he would never stay in this place. This is an investment property for him; not a place to live. Compared to Grand Pré, the house was not only too small, but the vista too limited. There was no mountain behind or in front. Across Blue Hill Bay from here was not the open ocean, but the Blue Hill peninsula, an enclosed horizon. Many people would be grateful for this vista, precisely because it was contained. But not John. And me? I wondered. What was the true vista my heart longed for the most?

After an hour of failing to read a single page downstairs, but only wrestling with racing thoughts and drinking, I returned to the bedroom, grateful to find Susan fast asleep.

The next night was Sunday, July 20, the last night of our honeymoon and we heard that Neil Armstrong was landing on the moon, and that it would be televised. A neighbor loaned us her 13 inch black and white portable television and we put it at the foot of the bed. It was nearly midnight when the broadcasting began, and though the reception was somewhat snowy, we were able to see Armstrong step off the Eagle and speak his now famous words, "That's one small step for a man, one giant leap for mankind."

Susan looked up at me and said, "It's kind of like us, isn't it?"

"What do you mean?"

"It's a perfect ending to our honeymoon...honey-moon, get it?"

"Pssh! What a bad joke!" I rustled her hair.

"No, but really...this is our big step forward into a new world."

"Mm. Yes." I turned off the TV and turned toward her. "I know exactly what you mean. You are my new world."

"And you are mine."

We loved. Not made love. Loved. And whatever the future held for us in this new world, and whatever elements of the old world still lingered, we were stepping forward, leaping with less gravity over dangerous craters, onto unknown ground.

www.ingramcontent.com/pod-product-compliance
Lightning Source LLC
Chambersburg PA
CBHW061429040426
42450CB00007B/967